PRASE F

for *Hell On High Seas*

'Eclectic collection of disaster at sea stories –
brilliantly written – gripping and entertaining'
Lindsay Eaton, *goodreads.com*

for *Fatal Storm*

'The famous killer 1998 Sydney–Hobart Race has
found its chronicler in Rob Mundle. An Australian
journalist who was on the scene, he tells a gripping
story of battles between small boats and a dreadful
storm – battles often bloodily won by waves one sailor
called 'white-capped mountains'. Mundle's portrayals
of courageous sailors and heroic rescuers fighting for
their lives are as vivid as any I have read'
John Rousmaniere, author of *Fastnet, Force 10*

'You don't need to be an offshore racer to enjoy this
book. Without question – thousands of people who
have never been on a sailboat will buy it and enjoy it
immensely. But those of you who have sailed offshore
should run – not walk – to your nearest bookstore and
pick up a copy, right now!' Tom Leweck, *Scuttlebutt*

Hell on
High Seas

ALSO BY ROB MUNDLE

Hell on High Seas

Amazing true stories of survival against the odds

ROB MUNDLE

HarperCollins_Publishers_

Attempts have been made to contact and credit copyright holders. If there are errors or omissions, copyright holders are asked to contact HarperCollins*Publishers* so that acknowledgements can be updated.

HarperCollins*Publishers*

First published in Australia in 2009
This edition published in 2016
by HarperCollins*Publishers* Australia Pty Limited
ABN 36 009 913 517
harpercollins.com.au

Copyright © Rob Mundle Promotions Pty Ltd 2009, 2016

The right of Rob Mundle to be identified as the author of this work has been asserted by him in accordance with the *Copyright Amendment (Moral Rights) Act 2000*.

HarperCollins*Publishers*
Level 13, 201 Elizabeth Street, Sydney NSW 2000, Australia
Unit D1, 63 Apollo Drive, Rosedale, Auckland 0632, New Zealand
A 53, Sector 57, Noida, UP, India
1 London Bridge Street, London, SE1 9GF, United Kingdom
2 Bloor Street East, 20th floor, Toronto, Ontario M4W 1A8, Canada
195 Broadway, New York NY 10007, USA

National Library of Australia Cataloguing-in-Publication data:
Mundle, Rob.
  Hell on high seas/Rob Mundle.
  ISBN: 978 1 4607 5100 8 (paperback)
  ISBN: 978 0 7304 4997 3 (epub)
  Voyages and travels – Anecdotes. Adventure and adventurers – Anecdotes.
  Survival after airplane accidents, shipwrecks, etc. – Anecdotes.
910.45

Cover design by HarperCollins Design Studio
Cover images: supply vessel by Rosi Stefano; wave © Pixland/Corbis
Illustration on page 369 by Nives Porcellato and Andrew Craig
Typeset in Bembo Std by HarperCollins Design Studio
Printed and bound in Australia by Griffin Press
The papers used by HarperCollins in the manufacture of this book are a natural, recyclable product made from wood grown in sustainable plantation forests. The fibre source and manufacturing processes meet recognised international environmental standards, and carry certification.

To those who run with the spirit of adventure,
and those who wish they could.

CONTENTS

INTRODUCTION

It struck with the speed of a viper: the heavy wire locked instantly onto my legs with horrendous tension and the whiplash effect that came from above was so violent that my head didn't hit the deck; I went from being upright to upside down in a blur.

Suddenly my body was hurtling unimpeded through the bitumen-black night sky, and right then just one thought went spearing through my mind: 'This is how you are going to die … you're dead!' I was a human rocket that had been launched across a rough and despicably uninviting sea, and I was certain there was no coming back.

The only ineffaceable memory from the ensuing 30-plus seconds is the brief glimpse I caught of the deck of the yacht which was illuminated by lights mounted on the mast. I was then in mid-air and upside down, and the yacht was a terrifying distance below me. I was being flung around like a stuffed toy in the mouth of an over-zealous dog – a dog that was actually an enormous 460 square metre (5000 sq ft) wildly flogging spinnaker that was set from the top of a mast 30 metres high. It was during one of those flogs that the wire ripped free from my legs, but I was still attached to the sail by what was my one chance for survival – a death grip: my lifeline. My fists were locked vice-like onto a rope, the sheet, which was attached to the corner of the sail, and I wasn't letting go.

The scene came at 10 pm on a wildly windy night when we were 20 miles off Cabo Maisi, the easternmost point of Cuba in the region known as the Windward Passage. The year was 1971 and I was aboard one of the great racing maxi-yachts of the era, American Huey Long's *Ondine II*. We were destined for Montego Bay, Jamaica, and the finish of the 811 mile race that had started in Miami some 48 hours earlier.

Ondine II boasted an impressive list of successes in many of the world's great ocean races, including line honours in the 1968 Sydney to Hobart classic and twice in the Newport to Bermuda race, but great as she was, this 79 foot aluminium-hulled ketch that weighed in at 50 tonnes was actually a pig of a boat when racing under spinnaker in strong winds, and that's what we'd been doing most of the time since we left Florida. She had a mind of her own when she surfed the big waves that had been generated by the 25 knot tropical tradewind. Each time she bullocked her way down the face of a wave even the most seasoned helmsmen struggled to retain control — there was no way of guessing which way she would veer off course, port or starboard, when she buried her bow into the back of the wave ahead. It was during one of those unpredictable veers when the entire rig went under massive load that the heavy wire restraining the spinnaker pole couldn't cope. It literally exploded. BANG! And with that the sail became a raging bull.

I was a fit 25-year-old back then, and for this race I'd been drafted as one of the foredeck crew; a member of the young team that did the hard yards, setting the huge, heavy and cumbersome 150kg headsails and the spinnakers.

The call for 'all hands' when the wire broke had those of us on the off-watch scurrying up the companionway stairs and onto the deck to discover what was causing the yacht to shudder so violently, and what needed to be done to stop it. The spinnaker pole was smashing against the forestay at the bow each time the gyrating sail thrashed around in the powerful wind, and it needed to be restrained.

The deck lights had been switched on and I could see a cluster of crew on the leeward side of the mast hauling on a rope and wire. They were trying to bring the corner of the sail down to the deck so they could unclip the spare wire attached to it. The obvious plan was to take that wire to the windward side of the yacht, attach it to the spinnaker pole and then winch the pole and sail back into position so we could resume racing mode.

I scampered forward in bare feet to lend a hand,

and as I neared the scrum I realised that if I hoisted myself high on one guy's shoulders I could reach the elusive clip, snap it open and free the wire from the corner of the sail.

Great idea – bad timing!

I leapt up towards my target with all the right intentions, but as I did the yacht rolled to windward and the spinnaker filled with wind as if it had been hit by a jet blast. There was no stopping the spinnaker – it burst open as if someone had pulled the ripcord on a parachute – and there was no stopping me going with it!

The power then in the sail was grossly greater than the strength of the manpower trying to haul it to the deck, so my crewmates, quite sensibly, let go. I'd assumed someone had been taking up the slack on the loose wire so the sail could be contained should a situation like this eventuate. I was horribly wrong.

As the sail exploded skywards the spaghetti-like coil of slack wire that was on the deck somehow snapped around my legs like a giant bear trap: this was bungy jumping with no bungy. I was convinced I was on a one-way trip through the air and into the water, and once I hit the water ... well, I may as well have been going through the trapdoor of the gallows. It would have taken a saint-making miracle for the crew to get the yacht back under full control, turn her around then retrace a course of around five miles through the darkness to where I had become 'man overboard'. There was no chance they'd find me alive.

It's because of another miracle that I sit here today writing *Hell on High Seas*: the death grip! It was something I'd heard about but never believed possible.

Somehow during those first few seconds of my eviction from *Ondine II*'s foredeck I managed to get both my hands on the spinnaker sheet — the rope attached to the corner of the sail that is used to control its shape when set. The split second I realised that I was in life-threatening trouble my mind sent an urgent message to my hands: 'If you let go of that rope then we are off to meet our maker.'

That certainly wasn't my preferred option, so this man on a rope locked on for dear life.

There was one other thing in my favour — the calibre of the crew, especially an offshore yachting legend, the late Cy Gillette from Hawaii, who was on the helm at the time, and Sam Field, who had been with me on the foredeck. On realising that I was still hanging on to the sail, Cy knew the only thing to do was to immediately, and dramatically, change the yacht's course to leeward so that the spinnaker would collapse in the wind shadow created by the mainsail. If the move was successful then I would crash to the deck like a bird without wings – safe, but a bit knocked around. That was the only hope, and Cy's execution of the manoeuvre was near perfect. However, instead of crash-landing on the deck, my downward trajectory had me missing by a metre or so – just outside the yacht and heading for the water – and my chances of hanging on to the rope once I was being dragged along in the water at around 15 knots were three-eighths of stuff-all.

Incredibly, Sam saw me descending from the heavens and had the foresight to run to the side of the yacht, grab hold of the mast sidestay, lean out over the water and somehow, miraculously, get a hand on me. His actions were enough to slow my descent and allow other crewmates to grab hold of various parts of me – arms, legs and clothing – and hang on to me. I was conscious of them screaming at me to let go of the spinnaker sheet, that they had hold of me, and I was aware that they were trying to force my fingers to unlock my grip on the sheet, but my mind wasn't sending the 'release' message to my hands; the adrenalin pump that had brought about the death grip still wasn't convinced I was safe. The crew feared that the sail would fill with wind and again take me with it, and that's where their enthusiasm to get me onto the deck solved the problem. They dragged me aboard feet first with one leg either side of the 10cm diameter steel roller fitted around the sidestay. The crushing impact on my credentials brought an immediate result – my eyes watered, I felt excruciating pain, I got lumps under my ears and I let go of the rope!

Adrenalin is a remarkable thing when it comes to survival. Once I realised I was on deck and in safe hands I stood up, walked back to the cockpit and went below as though nothing had happened. But the moment I lay down on the settee in the main cabin the adrenalin was gone – instantly – and shock kicked in. I remember Jim Pugh – now a highly successful international yacht designer – standing there staring at me while I was fed a fistful of drugs from the emergency medical kit, saying with a look of disbelief, 'You're not here. You are dead.'

That was my miracle in a lifetime of offshore sailing, but it's nothing compared to the wide spectrum of the great survival stories that the world's oceans have divulged. Some are simply amazing and almost beyond comprehension while others are nothing short of miraculous, and all have the sea as their foundation.

Hell on High Seas is a compilation of some of the best of those stories.

Rob Mundle

CHAPTER 1

KAY COTTEE

This story starts in the middle of a horrid storm, deep in the Southern Ocean, some 300 nautical miles southeast of the Cape of Good Hope, on the southern tip of the African continent.

The wind was hammering in at hurricane force – more than 75 knots from the southwest – while gigantic breaking waves, some around 50 feet (15 metres) high, roared out of the pitch-dark night and exploded into towering and frighteningly powerful liquid landslides.

It was 12 April 1988, and locked in the jaws of this dreadful maelstrom was *Blackmores First Lady*, a small, 37 foot (11.3 metre) long fibreglass yacht, with just one person aboard: an extraordinary 34-year-old woman named Kay Cottee.

She was there through design, not misadventure: Kay was trying to become the first woman ever to sail solo, unassisted and non-stop around the world.

To achieve that lofty goal she had to survive everything nature decided to put in the path of her yacht, including this dreadful storm. By this time, she was more than four months and some 15,000 nautical miles into her planned 22,000 nautical mile circumnavigation, which had started in her home town, Sydney, on 29 November 1987.

When she was planning the trip she knew she had to be prepared for the worst weather Mother Nature could muster and hurl in her path, and that it was likely to be at its most vicious in the vicinity of that legendary graveyard of ships and men, Cape Horn. But that would not be the case: much to her delight, she had rounded that southern-most point of South America in near-benign conditions. Since then, though, the weather had brought her every emotional high and low imaginable, and this latest storm in the waters off the Cape of Good Hope was – among the many storms that had confronted her – the worst she had to survive.

She had taken a hammering just 10 days earlier, which she recorded in graphic detail in her bestselling book *First Lady: A history-making solo voyage around the world*: 'I had not had a decent sleep for the past 72 hours. After yet another rough and restless night, the sky lightened to expose an ocean foaming and frothing with fury. The wind was up again to 35 knots and the waves were bigger still; I estimated them to be 14 metres high. It would have been bearable if we were riding with the seas instead of heading into them. I was now in a daze, so tired, every movement seemed to be mechanical and in slow motion.'

But that storm was surpassed by this latest tempest. To keep her yacht as safe as possible while making slow progress, Kay lowered the mainsail to the deck and kept only a minuscule headsail set. During the afternoon, however, even this amount of sail was putting the yacht, and Kay, under considerable duress – and it became even more threatening. By early evening the wind had increased in strength and the seas were becoming larger, but, even so, Kay was not expecting what followed: 'I was sitting on the seat at the aft end of the dinette contemplating the dismal situation when I heard a tremendous roar. It grew steadily louder. I shuddered as the bow rose higher and higher until the boat was almost vertical, then we levelled out. I knew the boat was completely out of the water and in mid-air. The seconds ticked away, then, spurred on by a massive dose of adrenalin, I moved the fastest I've ever moved in my entire life. I sprang to my feet, reached up to brace my hands on the cabin roof and spread my feet apart to wedge them against the seat on the port side [of the cabin] and the bunk on the starboard side so that when we landed I was not thrown up, to break my neck on the cabin roof. It seemed an age before we plummeted to the bottom of the trough and finally landed with an ear-splitting crash.'

Kay's first thought was that the mast could not have survived such a brutal impact. She climbed through the companionway and into the yacht's cockpit, with her usual two safety harness lines attached to strong points, expecting to see carnage – a tangled mess of mast, rigging and sails. But, incredibly, the mast was still in place.

What she did realise in an instant, though, was that *Blackmores First Lady* was out of control: the force of the impact when it fell off the wave had caused the automatic pilot to disengage. Kay grabbed the wheel, turned the boat more downwind and reset the automatic steering so that some semblance of normality would return to the scene.

Her next priority was to go below, into the cabin, and look for signs of damage to the hull, her fear being that it could have split open in any of three places: close to the bow, where the deck joins the hull, or where the keel was attached to the yacht's bilge. Much to her relief, the damage was minimal. The yacht was still watertight – fair tribute to Kay's ability as the builder of the boat.

The storm continued to rage through the night, hurling the yacht around as if it was an enraged steer, which in turn deprived the already exhausted sailor of any decent sleep.

By morning, the most brutal part of the storm had passed, so Kay went back on deck and set the mainsail with three reefs in – making it about twenty-five per cent of its full size.

At 4.20 pm on that day, 4 April 1988, Kay had cause for celebration. *Blackmores First Lady*, then 360 nautical miles offshore, was crossing the longitude of the Cape of Good Hope – one of the five Southern Hemisphere capes Kay was required to round as part of this historic circumnavigation. There were only two more to go before she returned to Sydney: Cape Leeuwin in Western Australia, and the southern tip of Tasmania.

It was relatively easy going for the next six days, but then the barometer once again went into free fall – confirmation that the next storm, as forecast by meteorologist Roger Badham, was marching Kay's way. Before long, the south-west wind was peaking at above 55 knots – a Force 10 storm/whole gale under the Beaufort Scale – while the swells were becoming so full-bodied and so far apart that they had clearly definable seas on top of them. *Blackmores First Lady* was then surfing down those waves at up to 16 knots, but surprisingly Kay would note that she 'was not perturbed at all and had in fact settled down easily to life in the Southern Ocean with its continuous depression systems and cold fronts'.

The conditions deteriorated even further over the next 48 hours until they developed into that heinous tempest of 12 April. Lead-coloured clouds charged across the sky and the swells became even more threatening: it was a weather system that would soon take the yachtswoman and her yacht to the brink on two occasions.

Kay noted in her log that she was 'flying at 16 knots under the storm jib alone. The boat is humming like a tuning fork and almost out of control'. As reckless as this approach may sound, Kay knew it was the safest way for her then well-proven yacht to proceed east in those conditions.

The first drama came when the yacht was overwhelmed by a huge, breaking wave, and was capsized and driven sideways with the mast in the water. It was a situation that did not cause Kay any great alarm, though: she was mentally prepared for such an eventuality. Suddenly, what seconds earlier had been the side of the yacht had turned 90 degrees and become the 'floor'. All she could do then was stand on what would otherwise be the vertical side of a bulkhead and wait for the yacht to turn upright.

When that happened, Kay heard a mighty 'whoosh' as *Blackmores First Lady* righted herself, seemingly spring-loaded. The interior of the yacht looked as though it had been blown apart by a bomb.

'It was a total mess with clothes and gear everywhere and water sloshing across the floor,' Kay recalled in her book.

Her immediate concern was the welfare of her mascot 'Teddy', a small bear that had been given to her before she left Sydney: 'Teddy looked pathetic standing on his head in a pool of water where he had landed after being catapulted from his favourite seat beside the mast.' Such was her affection for her mascot that saving him was her priority, even before grabbing a bucket and bailing water out of the cabin – water that had found its way in through a small gap in the companionway leading to the cockpit.

The weather worsened during the day and into the night, but the yacht seemed to be coping with it okay – until it suddenly surfed at an alarming speed down what Kay sensed to be an extremely large wave, amid a roar that was almost deafening below deck. She knew it was time to set a sea anchor, a safety device that would ensure the stern remained pointing towards the waves and considerably reduce the speed.

Kay clambered up the companionway stairs, out of the cabin and into the cockpit, where she began preparing to set the sea anchor on a long line so it could be deployed over the side. It was pitch black outside. Suddenly, for some unknown reason, she looked into the night sky behind the yacht. A pall of dread overwhelmed her: 'I saw the loom of light in the clouds. I stopped work and watched in fascinated horror as it grew brighter and brighter. Frantically, I started taking compass bearings. The bearings didn't alter – we were on a collision course with whatever it was. Truly, I now understood the old expression "my heart was in my mouth!"'

Being so far south of the Cape of Good Hope at this time was part of a plan Kay had devised to ensure she would be well clear of the busy shipping lanes around the cape – or at least she thought that would be the case. But it turned out that the 'loom of light' was a ship bearing down on *Blackmores First Lady*.

'I started to panic, realising that if I could see even reflected lights in those conditions, they must be pretty close. I dived into the cabin and turned on every light above and below decks, tuned both radios to the emergency frequencies and started shouting into both microphones at the same time. No answer. I rushed back on deck again with the powerful spotlight and shone it on the white mast. By now, I could see the actual lights on the ship and they were getting clearer by the second. Nothing for it, it's life or death now, I thought, I have to let off a flare. I grabbed one of the white flares I had for such an emergency, crawled aft, stood up clinging to the radar tower and ignited the flare …

'I was sobbing and shuddering with fear as a great steel structure lurched closer into view on the top of the waves then totally disappeared in the troughs. How on earth would they see us, a tiny white speck in the foaming froth of such a furious ocean? The waves must have been 18 metres high by now and breaking like the mighty surf does in Hawaii. It seemed like hours but must have only been minutes before I noticed a slight alteration in their course.'

Still shaking, Kay stayed in the cockpit and watched in awe as the huge ship lumbered past, only metres away, and disappeared into the night. She was safe once more, but even so, this part of the world was planning one last, life-threatening hurdle for her before allowing *Blackmores First Lady* to continue on towards Australia.

For the second time in one hour Kay's life 'flashed before her eyes'.

Without warning, *Blackmores First Lady* was knocked flat by the force of both the wind and a gigantic wave, and again the mast went into the water and below horizontal. Kay, with her two personal safety harnesses still attached, clung on for dear life, but she was no match for the surge of a big wave that washed into the cockpit. Within a split second, she was overboard.

'I was washed just over the top of the leeward safety railing before my [safety] harness lines pulled me up short. I held my breath under the water until my lungs felt they would burst, willing my lovely *Lady* to right herself and praying that the two harness lines did not give way. She took her time, but true to form, gracefully rose once again, this time with me dangling over the side.'

Kay would later reveal that while the yacht continued surfing down the huge waves at more than 10 knots only one thought flashed across her mind: 'I thought to myself, "This is going to be a stupid way to die," knowing that with the yacht being on auto-pilot, and me having no way to stop her, it was highly likely that I would not be able to drag myself back aboard.'

Maybe it was Poseidon or Neptune caring for her or perhaps it was Teddy thanking Kay for 'saving' him earlier; whatever it was, Kay survived in miraculous circumstances. In less than a minute, *Blackmores First Lady* was again knocked down onto her beams' end but then, amazingly, the yacht came upright just as the surge of another wave washed Kay back over the side rail and into the cockpit.

'I landed on my back, sloshing around in the water-filled cockpit. I was exhausted and bruised from head to foot. I realised I could take no more that night so dragged myself below to the disaster that used to be my lovely cosy haven. With shaking hands, I poured myself a very stiff gin and downed it in one gulp. Sopping wet and still wearing my oilskins, I fell into my bunk. I lay there, my body prostrate but my mind working overtime, thinking of what might have been and how fragile and vulnerable life is. But the thought of giving in never crossed my mind – I was more determined than ever not to let the experience get the better of me.'

For Kay, being aboard *Blackmores First Lady* and spearing across the all-too-often callous Southern Ocean towards Australia meant one thing: every mile sailed saw her one mile closer to the fulfilment of her dream.

No doubt, at some time, her mind would have revisited the first time she was alone on the water: when aged only four she was seen to clamber onto an old mattress and begin punting it across a shallow swamp near the family home in Sans Souci, 15 kilometres southwest of the heart of Sydney.

Having been born into a yachting family, Kay was under sail for the first time when she was only two weeks old. This was with her parents, Joy and Jim McLaren, aboard the family yacht her father had built. By the time she was 11, Kay realised that school represented the period between her morning and afternoon sails aboard her small dinghy – either alone, with girlfriends, or with the boy next door and his Labrador dog. Kay's reflection on that part of her life says everything about her then: 'School was so trying [for me] that I missed a lot of my final year. I spent a lot of time gazing out to sea from my classroom window, or sitting on the headland at Botany Bay, dreaming I was setting off across the ocean. I studied for the Intermediate Certificate making model boats and listening to an audio cassette I had made of my school work. Mum thought I was reading aloud every night.'

Somehow she scraped through her final exams and went on to study at a secretarial college, but by the time she was 17 things changed: she became engaged to Neville Cottee, the son of family friends who owned a plumbing business in Sydney's eastern suburbs. They were married the following year, their common bond being sailing. The union lasted a decade, but in that time their passion for being under sail led to them setting off on a 1700 nautical mile cruise from Sydney to the Great Barrier Reef in a yacht that was just 22 feet (6.7 metres) long. It was a voyage full of exhilaration and anticipation, until the rudder snapped off when they were some distance off the Queensland coast. Grave fears were held for their safety after their dinghy was washed onto a beach on the coast when the yacht was already overdue at their next port of call. A search ensued and eventually their yacht was spotted by a plane hired by Kay's parents. A giant bulk carrier was diverted to the wallowing little yacht, and the couple were rescued.

By the time Kay was 30 she was describing her role in life as that of an artist, writer, boatbuilder and charter-boat business manager. However, she had one additional and overriding aspiration: she knew that no woman had ever sailed around the world single-handed and non-stop — and she wanted to be the woman who did it.

Her thoughts had progressed into a passionate pursuit towards that world first, an attitude further fuelled by the thought that, later in life, she did not want to be sitting on the veranda of her home telling her grandchildren about her dream of a solo circumnavigation of the world, and then having to add, 'I wish I had done it.'

In the mid–1980s, after working long and hard, Kay was in a position to purchase the hull and deck of a Cavalier 37, a design she believed was capable of carrying her safely around the world. The two large fibreglass pieces of the yacht arrived at her home on the back of a truck, and were then duly craned onto the front lawn. From that moment, being a boatbuilder was the most important thing in her life: she was about to convert a bare shell of a boat into an ocean-going yacht. Every available moment of her time was filled with shaping timber, fibreglassing pieces into place, being a mechanic, and creating creature comforts for one. It was a remarkable effort on her part, and the end result would have done a shipwright proud.

Kay's budget was tight, but good fortune came her way when Marcus Blackmore, the principal of Australia's pre-eminent healthcare products manufacturer, Blackmores Laboratories Ltd, agreed to support her financially for the first two stages of the lead-up to the voyage around the world: a two-handed race across the Tasman Sea from Sydney to New Zealand, and then a single-handed race from

New Zealand back across the Tasman to Mooloolaba in Queensland. Kay completed both challenges successfully and came away confident she could sail her yacht, then named *Cinnamon Scrub* after a Blackmores product, around the world. But there was one thing missing – the money needed to prepare the yacht for such a long and arduous undertaking.

Here, again, Marcus Blackmore came to the rescue. He developed a concept with Kay whereby the voyage would be used to promote his business and raise funds for Life Education Australia, the country's largest independent health and drug education provider for school children aged 5–13 years. *Cinnamon Scrub* was then re-named *Blackmores First Lady*.

A frenetic program aimed at preparing every part of the yacht for the voyage began almost immediately. The rig was strengthened, the interior was modified and special sails were made. Simultaneously, a list of all the provisions that would be needed to support Kay for more than six months at sea had to be prepared in meticulous fashion. This included food and fuel, along with clothing for the widest imaginable climatic conditions: from the stifling, sauna-like weather of the tropics, to violent snow- and ice-laden storms in the Southern Ocean. Medical supplies and replacement parts for the yacht were equally important. Kay also sought special training in weather forecasting, communications, mechanical repairs and the operation of a telex, which, as well as the radio, would be a key form of communication with family, friends and the media.

Finally, with the assistance of her many supporters, everything was ready for her mammoth undertaking on the eve of the Southern Hemisphere summer – the best possible time to set sail.

A small fleet of boats carrying well-wishers, spectators and the media was out on Sydney Harbour on Sunday, 29 November 1987 to farewell her. Emotions ran high as Kay hugged and kissed her family and friends before leaving the dock and setting sail towards the harbour entrance.

Once she was clear of the coast, the last of the spectator boats and media helicopters turned back for home. It was then she had her first realisation of solitude – and she was ready for it.

Kay's initial course was towards the South Cape on Stewart Island, off the southern tip of New Zealand's South Island: the first of the landmarks she was required to round as part of her circumnavigation. *Blackmores First Lady* left New Zealand in her wake just 12 days after departing Sydney. The next 'corner' was Cape Horn, over 4200 nautical miles east from New Zealand, on the southern-most island of South America's Tierra del Fuego group.

On this leg, there were three memorable moments for Kay: she reached a position where she was as far as a person could be from civilisation; by rounding the cape she sailed to a latitude of more than 56 degrees south – her highest latitude for the entire voyage; and she was confronted by her first major issue on the voyage, when the boom fractured. This last event, which occurred when *Blackmores First Lady* was 1400 nautical miles west of Cape Horn, was a considerable setback. At the time, the yacht was sailing downwind in a breeze gusting to 40 knots. A 'very tired' Kay later noted, 'Bummer of bummers! Just found a big crack in the boom. Must have happened when the boat did a radical gybe just before we got knocked flat.'

It was too rough at the time to make repairs, so Kay set about devising a way to strengthen the fractured spar so she could set full sail when the weather permitted. Her engineering skills came to the fore:

'It was a slow process as all cutting, shaping and drilling had to be done by hand. I didn't have a spare boom (impossible to stow on board), or even a spare section of boom aluminium, so I had to improvise by cutting up spare sections of spinnaker pole aluminium. These had to be opened out and bashed with the hammer to the shape of the boom for a neat fit. It was very hard work, trying to open out these sections using only blocks of wood, a crowbar and a mash hammer. Quite dangerous too, as sometimes the jamming pieces of wood would fly out and ricochet around the cabin, making me dive for cover.'

It would be more than three weeks before the weather would be calm enough for the repair to be completed. As well as using the aluminium tubing she had fabricated, Kay ensured the damaged boom was as strong as possible by unbolting a piece of aluminium track that was in the cockpit, cutting it in half, and bolting one half on each side of the initial repair job.

The reason for this additional strengthening was simple: if the boom broke completely then Kay would have to complete the rest of the voyage using a tiny trysail instead of the full-size mainsail, reducing her speed dramatically.

But that repair was weeks away – after *Blackmores First Lady* had rounded the Horn. In the meantime, as the yacht approached the Cape, there were two significant threats emerging: a wicked westerly storm, with winds gusting to well over 60 knots, and icebergs. In consultation with her meteorologist, Roger Badham, back in Sydney, Kay had to plan her course very carefully. Their joint decision was that she should hold the yacht on a course towards a rugged, remote and inhospitable part of the coast of Chile, 450 nautical miles northwest of the Horn. By sailing this extra distance relatively slowly, Kay hoped to avoid the worst of the huge storm they expected to blast through to the south. This course would also minimise the chance of being confronted by icebergs, a fact of life in this part of the world as the coast of Antarctica was less than 500 nautical miles south of the Horn. Kay recalled: 'Continually looking out for icebergs, keeping up the daily running of the boat and working persistently on the boom repairs, I was becoming more and more exhausted. Day after day I was averaging only two or three hours' sleep in 24. When the weather was really bad and the seas really high, the radar didn't work as the screen was full of clutter from the mountainous waves and I couldn't sleep at all. I spent most of my time on deck, in the freezing conditions, scanning the horizon for treacherous 'bergs.'

Despite this effort, the final week of the approach to Cape Horn was laden with drama and real danger. Kay noted that even the sea anchor, with a chain and 70 metres of line attached, barely slowed the boat. The waves were approximately 20 metres high and 'breaking with a nice curl', and despite Kay's fear of the boat being pitch-poled stern over bow, she was in awe of 'the beauty of the aquamarine colours of the sun shining through the peak of the next approaching wave'.

The following day, 15 January 1988, she finally admitted to being scared: 'Wind up to Force 11 [between 55 and 63 knots]. First time I've ever felt real fear since leaving home and that comes from huge waves, and thoughts of capsizing. I cannot relax or sleep at all in these conditions; just try to take my mind off it for short moments by reading. *The Lady* handles it all beautifully; no matter what sails are up she keeps moving fast and the motion is not too bad. It's actually very comfortable below.'

The morning of 19 January heralded another momentous occasion. When Kay came on deck she saw in the distance magnificent snow-capped mountains and a spectacular coastline – a sign that Cape Horn wasn't far away.

A few hours later, on a sunny day and in relatively calm seas, Kay Cottee and *Blackmores First Lady* were at Cape Horn. Kay celebrated with her first good wash in two weeks, followed by a meal of baked beans and toast on deck, where the temperature was just two degrees. She then guided the yacht as close as she possibly could to the legendary landmark and took 'selfies' with it in the background. That afternoon, when due south of the cape, she opened a bottle of one of Australia's most famous red wines, Grange Hermitage, which she had been given for when she achieved this milestone, and noted in her log, 'What a big day for a girl!'.

She would later write in her book: 'After all the stories I had read about this ocean graveyard, here we were, only a few miles from it. I had thought it would give me a spooky feeling, considering the number of sailors who had been dashed to death on the treacherous black cliffs, or drowned in the mountainous seas. But my prime emotion was excitement and I had a great sense of accomplishment that I had reached what I then perceived to be the major obstacle in the voyage.'

Her great achievement did not go unnoticed back in Australia: it made headlines, and 24 hours later Kay received a special message from the then Prime Minister, Bob Hawke. It read in part: 'Personally, and on behalf of all Australians, I should like to congratulate you as you pass one of the world's great maritime landmarks: Cape Horn. That you have undertaken such a great adventure in Australia's Bicentennial Year is a reflection of the spirit and character that has helped shape our nation. Our thoughts are with you as you continue your epic voyage.'

While adrenalin, excitement and fear were never far away, frustration was another constant companion for Kay on the voyage, as on the night she finally got the time to cook a 'decent' meal, instead of dining out of a can. She decided to cook some fettuccine using a combination of canned food, fresh onions and pasta. It was everything she had dreamed of over recent weeks ... but, wouldn't you know it, just when the meal was ready to be served, the yacht lurched dramatically and the saucepan full of food set off on its own course: it skidded off the stovetop, hit the side of the yacht and emptied its entire contents down the back of the stove and onto the floor. 'I sat on the cabin floor and cried my eyes out,' Kay said. 'I scraped the disastrous mess into a bowl and ate it!'

Reaching the Falkland Islands in the South Atlantic was her next goal, and there she would be able to make contact with humans for the first time in 53 days. In a pre-arranged rendezvous, she transferred letters to four men from the island who came out to meet her. This had to be a perfectly executed manoeuvre where Kay had to throw the package to the boat, because if she made physical contact with the men, or they touched her yacht in any way, it would be deemed to be 'outside assistance', which would render her voyage invalid in official record books.

Additionally, for Kay's voyage to qualify as a world-first circumnavigation, she was required to cross the Equator and enter the Northern Hemisphere. She did this by using the remote St Peter and St Paul Archipelago as her turning point in the Atlantic and the halfway point of her voyage. This tiny archipelago – 55 nautical miles north of the Equator and 1250 nautical miles east of the mouth of the Amazon River on the coast of Brazil – was a target that could be easily missed: 15 small and rocky islets in close proximity, the highest point of which is just 18 metres. The islets are waterless and barren, as Charles Darwin noted when he visited them aboard HMS *Beagle* in February 1832. Darwin wrote that there was no flora whatsoever on the islets, and the only fauna of any interest were two birds and a large crab.

On approach, Kay was in regular radio contact with her family and friends and the media back in Australia, as well as the radio officers on a large cargo ship, who had become enthralled by her endeavour.

On 23 February, just four days before she rounded the archipelago, she revealed how relaxed and content she was in her isolated world: 'Everybody seems so surprised to hear me sounding so cheerful and happy. Guess they can't understand how much I love it out here by myself – no phones, no pressure, just the challenge to live with the elements every day. Peace. I suppose in another three months I'll have had enough of my own company and run out of things to amuse myself with, but for now I wouldn't swap places with anyone in the world.'

However, rounding this sprinkle of islands was not easy. A severe thunderstorm struck when *Blackmores First Lady* was just 10 miles to the southwest of this turning point, and it began driving the yacht towards what was an extremely dangerous lee shore. Kay then had to change course dramatically and 'hightail' it out of there.

After rounding the islets with a wide berth, Kay set her yacht on a southeasterly course towards the Cape of Good Hope, about 3500 nautical miles away.

To fill in some of the time she had to spare, Kay had taken to writing poetry – so it wasn't surprising that on reaching the halfway point she penned a special piece of verse, titled *Halfway*:

Haven't chafed one thread, nor torn a sail
Dodger still up through gales and hail
Rigging pins still sit well, intact
Boom good and strong, repaired over crack
Jib furler still goes round and round
Winches and blocks don't make a sound
Still using original rope on vane
Climbed up the mast – felt like Tarzan's Jane
All seems to be OK up there
Now sittin' in sun without a care
(… and rollin' on deck laughing at own wit!)

In the six weeks it would take to cover the distance to the Cape of Good Hope, she experienced an extremely wide range of weather conditions – from calms in the steamy equatorial regions to bitterly cold gales in the south, which held the potential to end her voyage at any time. It was vitally important that she routinely check every piece of equipment on the yacht for wear or fatigue, a task which, as she mentioned in her poem, included her climbing to the top of the 51 foot (15.5 metre) mast to check for deterioration of the halyard sheaves and other equipment.

There was one other round-the-clock task she could not avoid: looking out for ships and ensuring *Blackmores First Lady* was not on a collision course. This meant that when in a shipping lane she had to be on deck scanning the horizon every two hours, as it was possible for a ship to come from beyond the horizon and into her zone in that short space of time.

Even after surviving the tempest on the Cape of Good Hope and planning her course towards Cape Leeuwin, Kay expected no respite from the storms. She would be sailing along the southern border of the Indian Ocean, a stretch which legendary French solo sailor Bernard Moitessier had described as the most vicious of the world's three great oceans. The storms, many of which were conceived in the high latitudes of the bleak Southern Ocean, came towards *Blackmores First Lady* in wave after wave.

On 9 May, Kay felt a tinge of excitement as she crossed the longitude of Cape Leeuwin, the fourth of the five great capes she was required to pass. *Blackmores First Lady* was then 400 nautical miles to the south of the coast, but being back in Australian waters didn't mean Mother Nature would lay out the welcome mat. The five-day forecast Kay received in mid-May read:

Friday: Northerly 45–55 knots

Saturday: North to north-westerly 45–50 knots

Sunday: North-westerly to westerly 45 knots

Monday: Westerly 40–45 knots

Tuesday: South-westerly 35–40 knots

The widely varying conditions over the next stretch to Tasmania's South Cape, 1500 nautical miles away, saw *Blackmores First Lady* average less than 4 knots over 17 days. The yacht was then closing on the coast, presenting the earliest opportunity for the media to catch up with Kay – and this author, who was a television and newspaper journalist at the time, was the first to reach her. We initially flew over her in a helicopter, then took a small high-speed boat out to intercept her, 30 nautical miles off the coast.

It was like a reunion for the two of us, as my friendship with Kay and her family stretched back to when she was a child. When it came to interviewing Kay for that night's television news, I asked if she was looking forward to getting back to Sydney. She said: 'I don't really know. I am so at peace with the world out here and in my element. I think I could keep going.'

But there was a huge reception being planned for her arrival in Sydney, 750 nautical miles to the north. However, these final miles would prove to be frustrating for the sailor and her yacht, as the wind came from every conceivable direction. Through sheer guts and determination, she arrived in Sydney Harbour on cue – 'at 12.32 hours on Sunday, 5 June 1988'. A spectacular armada of pleasure craft, ferries and a naval support boat was on the water to welcome a new national heroine, but there was an even greater surprise awaiting Kay when *Blackmores First Lady* approached its dock in Darling Harbour, on the city's waterfront.

As the yacht passed under Pyrmont Bridge, there was a huge crowd lining the bay.

'What's going on here?' Kay asked, when confronted by the sight of 100,000 cheering people.

'They're here for you, you idiot!' a friend replied.

With that, she turned to me with a look of disbelief and said most genuinely, 'I only went for a sail!'

As well as being the first woman to complete a single-handed non-stop circumnavigation, Kay achieved many other records as part of her history-making voyage, including becoming the first Australian woman to sail around Cape Horn single-handed.

Other accolades followed: she was named the 1988 Australian of the Year, and awarded the prestigious Order of Australia Medal. However, more importantly for her, she was able to combine her energy with that of her sponsor, Marcus Blackmore, and go on to raise more than $1,000,000 for the Life Education Program.

www.kaycottee.com

CHAPTER 2

ROSE-NOËLLE – 119 DAYS UPSIDE DOWN

Horror makes a noise: a roar, like a deep rumble of thunder rolling across the heavens. It was just before sunrise when John Glennie heard it coming – a phenomenal freak wave more than 16 metres high was bearing down on his small yacht like a dam-burst of water. It was horrifying.

Within seconds the wave had exploded onto the scene, and it dealt with the yacht like a huge tsunami smashing its way across a low-lying island: anything in its path was destined to be bulldozed out of the way. Suddenly, after three days of battling this ferocious storm off New Zealand's east coast, the worst fears held by Glennie and his three crew were about to be realised. The 12.65 metre long trimaran *Rose-Noëlle*, which had been lying beam-on to the seas, was engulfed by an avalanche of white water, pitched to 90 degrees then flipped upside down.

Inside the yacht it was as if a house had been inverted in an earthquake. There were shouts and screams amid the darkness as the crew struggled to free themselves from the debris that had crashed down on them. It was a vice-versa world to what they had known a few minutes earlier: their ceiling was now their floor. Everything that had been below them was now above their heads, and there was a cold ocean swirling into their habitat. Where would it stop? Were they going to sink?

When this calamitous situation stabilised there was just darkness and near silence. Being upside down meant they had been soundproofed from the howl of the storm that raged outside. Before long the water level settled. They were still afloat, and destined to stay that way until ... whenever!

For 19 years, Glennie had dreamed of this voyage from his native New Zealand to Tonga and onwards to other enchanting islands in the South Pacific. He was a highly experienced offshore yachtsman with more than 40,000 cruising miles to his credit, and that included sailing in the Roaring Forties. He had designed and built *Rose-Noëlle* in Sydney a few years earlier based on this experience. The yacht took its name from Rose-Noëlle Coguiec, a French–Polynesian woman from Tonga who died tragically in 1973, aged 19. For Glennie, who had met her on a previous cruise to the island, she was the personification of a South Pacific princess.

It was 1989 and his plan was to escape the clutches of the worst of the New Zealand winter, but as the departure date of 1 June drew closer, his frustrations associated with crew selection and the general preparation of the yacht were rising proportionately. His initial desire was to have friends join him for the cruise, but when those friends, who were all good sailors, advised at the last minute they couldn't make the trip he opted for three people he barely knew, and they had little or no sailing experience. His first recruit was 41-year-old Phil Hofman, who was keen to try bluewater sailing. Surprisingly, he had never ventured in any way outside New Zealand even though he lived aboard his yacht in Picton. Next came another New Zealander, Rick Hellreigel, 31, who had heard that Glennie was looking for crew. He wanted to erase the memories of a disastrous cruise to Fiji some years earlier by giving offshore sailing another chance. Jim Nalepka, 38, was an American cook and the third crewmember to sign on. Even though he had never been sailing, he jumped at this opportunity after Rick, who was a close friend, told him that he was going to make the voyage and suggested they go together.

This happened just a few days before the planned departure, and it was so unsettling for Glennie that, even on the day he was due to cast off, he was wondering if he should put to sea. The thought was also influenced by an unfavourable and stationary weather pattern to the east of New Zealand. However, a last-minute analysis of the conditions convinced him that while the first stage of the passage would be uncomfortable it was safe to set sail.

With crew and stores aboard and everything in readiness, he triggered the outboard motor mounted on the stern, brought it to life and moved his bright yellow yacht away from the dock while family and friends waved farewell, all the time harbouring envious thoughts of the tropical adventure that lay ahead of the four adventurers.

When relating his story in the book *The Spirit of Rose-Noëlle – 119 Days Adrift: A Survival Story* (which he co-wrote with Jane Phare), and subsequently in an interview, Glennie stressed that reaching the islands was, for him, far more important than the actual voyage: 'Leaving on a journey and arriving at a new port or island is for me the best part about the cruising life. In fact, if I am honest, I dislike sailing; it bores me to tears. I suspect that if pressed, many bluewater sailors would admit that at times they, too, feel the same way.

'Sailing across an ocean out of sight of land for a month is fun – at first. But I found the novelty soon wore off. So did the prospect of hour upon hour at the wheel, getting seasick in bad weather, changing sails and being soaked by unkind waves, and keeping watch through the night.

'Cruising is a life of extremes. You cannot appreciate those highs if you don't go through the lows. At times you are putting your life on the line, pitting yourself against the elements. For me, it was the only way of seeing the world and taking my home with me. And those hours alone on the helm gave me time to think, time to dream up new dreams. While I did not build the trimaran in response to a nautical yearning, I did enjoy being at the wheel of *Rose-Noëlle*, for she handled beautifully under sail.'

By late afternoon *Rose-Noëlle* was cruising down Marlborough Sound with the crew absorbing the overwhelming beauty of the region while they made last-minute preparations before entering Cook Strait – the passage between New Zealand's north and south islands – and then sailing out to the east. Glennie was also excited by thoughts of the exotic tropical lifestyle that would come when they reached Tonga about 10 days later.

At 4.15 pm Glennie made radio contact with a friend to advise they were proceeding well. Incredibly, this would be the last contact he had with the outside world for 119 days.

Cook Strait provided a favourable wind and soon *Rose-Noëlle* was scooting along at up to 16 knots, a speed that impressed all on board. As darkness settled the wind increased in strength and the seas grew accordingly. It quickly became apparent that it would be a long night ahead: Glennie would have to be alert at all times simply because of the inexperience of his crew. There would be no 'breaking-in' period in relatively dormant weather conditions. Even so, he established a watch system where everyone had a two-hour stint on deck and four hours below.

The wind remained strong from the northern sector overnight so Glennie continued on a course away from the coast, a course which he maintained for the next 24 hours. He noted that the barometer was dropping – a sign of deteriorating weather.

'As the day wore on, the wind strength grew and so did the alarm of the crew. I reefed down again and finally dropped the mainsail altogether. *Rose-Noëlle* was running with the waves under a partly furled headsail, but she wasn't yet surfing. The conditions were no different to those I had sailed through many times before.

'Phil was on the wheel but was having trouble steering. He seemed really frightened by the strength of the wind and the speed we were doing, yet of the three crew he had the most experience as a sailor. I took the wheel, and the steering felt fine to me, but Phil's alarm had unsettled the others.'

Rick and Phil called on Glennie to launch a small sea anchor off the stern to help reduce speed, even though he didn't feel there was any reason for concern: 'It was the beginning of a series of events over which I should have taken more control. It was my boat, and I was by far the most experienced person on board.'

While Glennie was convinced they were safe, the anxiety coming from what was by then an increasingly vocal crew saw him acquiesce to their demands. When the sea anchor was set they were 140 miles offshore and still south of the 40th parallel. This was the Roaring Forties – the breeding ground for some of the worst storms imaginable.

From this moment the problems compounded. The gale-force winds strengthened and the breaking seas increased to alarming proportions. Enough, thought Glennie: it was time to lower all sail and set the large parachute sea anchor he had bought for such a situation. It would hold the yacht's bow into the seas while they rode out the storm.

When this was done, the crew were able to retire to the cabin below, climb into their bunks and wait. For them, there was nothing else they could do.

During the early part of the evening Glennie sensed that the motion of the yacht had changed, and it concerned him. He donned a safety harness, clambered on deck and quickly realised that the parachute anchor had failed. *Rose-Noëlle* was lying beam-on to the seas – the most vulnerable attitude she could take – but Glennie remained confident that even in such extreme conditions, *Rose-Noëlle* would never turn over. In fact, he was so confident about the stability of the design that he hadn't fitted escape hatches in the main hull when he'd built the yacht – hatches that would allow the crew to get out in the event of a capsize.

The crew lay in their bunks listening to the fury of the storm that raged outside. The wind was gusting at between 50 and 60 knots and the yacht was being rocked violently from side to side each time the three hulls crested a wave. The atmosphere in the cabin was full of tension and dread, so Glennie tried to calm the situation by turning on the radio and tuning into some soothing music. However, Phil remained at the opposite end of the relaxed scale: 'He had steadily worked himself into a panic. Nothing Rick, Jim or I could say or do would calm him down. He was absolutely convinced the boat was going to capsize. He was terrified and at times close to hysteria. He would lie for a few minutes in his bunk, leap up, peer out of the window, and call out, "We're going to flip over. We're going to flip over."'

Between 4 am and 6 am on 4 June, the wind began to abate and while the crew were convinced they were seeing the end of the storm, Glennie knew otherwise. A rapid reduction in wind strength was no guarantee that the waves would also abate. A short time later he knew he was right. He heard the roar of what would be their final wave …

'The death of *Rose-Noëlle* came quickly. The wave hit her like a freight train roaring out of the darkness towards us, the terrified passengers stalled in its path and trapped inside. There was nowhere to go, nothing we could do. We had only two or three seconds to be frightened, for our guts to clench in that final knot of fear. The giant wall of water came out of the darkness without warning, drowning out all other sound. Its roar overpowered the scream of the wind generator outside, the howl of the wind, the crashing of sea against the trimaran's hull and decks. It drowned out the sound of the radio playing in the cabin. It drowned out the heartbeat thudding inside our heads.

'The wave hit *Rose-Noëlle* side-on, and she did not hesitate. Six and a half tons of boat flipped over sideways as if it were a toy plucked from a bath by a child's hand and dumped unceremoniously on its head. It was 6 am, 4 June 1989, mid-winter in New Zealand and still dark.

'The capsize toppled me onto the roof of the cabin above the dinette seat where I had been curled up under a rug, listening to the storm. Rick and Jim were lying in their sleeping bags on the opposite starboard double bunk. When the wave hit they hurtled up in the air and crashed down onto the dinette table below. They landed in a bruised heap on the skylight hatch in the ceiling. I crawled across the roof – now the floor – to join them, water swirling up around our legs.'

Panic-stricken shouts that pierced the darkness revealed Phil was in strife. He was trapped inside his sleeping bag in a coffin-like single bunk that was now upside down. Water was pouring over him and debris prevented his escape, but within seconds a surge of adrenalin that came from the terror associated with his predicament saw him break free and crawl to the middle of the boat where his crewmates were standing on the cabin ceiling. While water was pouring rapidly into the upturned yacht, Glennie was confident it would soon reach a state of equilibrium and rise no further – the buoyancy of the outer hulls and the buoyant nature of the actual structure of the yacht would combine and stop it from sinking. However, Phil's panic accelerated: he was convinced that an escape route was their only way to survival, so he rushed at the companionway doors at the rear of the cabin and smashed them open. This action would prove to be an incredibly expensive mistake, even then. The waist-deep surge of water that immediately came into the boat saw many things that would be vital to their survival, including emergency flares and food, washed out of the cabin and lost forever.

Realising that everything that had been dislodged inside the boat could go the same way, Glennie ordered the crew to grab anything within reach and store it. At the same time all four men had to accept that they were trapped in what could be a watery grave, and if it wasn't to become that, it would be their survival raft for an unknown period of time – days, weeks, months. Because there had been no radio communication with the outside world prior to the capsize, searchers, should they ever eventuate, would not know where to start looking. It could be anywhere between Cook Strait and Tonga.

Within hours all four had accepted their predicament, including the only two outcomes: life or death. However, while from the outset Glennie was absolutely certain that they would somehow survive the situation, no matter how long it took, the three sailing novices for the most part believed otherwise. According to Glennie, Phil became increasingly convinced they were doomed and showed little desire to assist the others and work on their survival. (Jim, who would later publish his own account, *Capsized: the True Story of Four Men Adrift for 119 Days*, had a different and more positive view of Phil's contribution.)

With the yacht inverted, its attitude on the sea surface meant that the aft cabin, small as it was, would have to become their principal place of residence as it was the one place where they could build a platform above water level and create a bed. It would be an oppressive, kennel-like environment but in that situation it was their only option.

The natural forces that came with the capsize and the incessant surge of water within the hull created a hellish environment for them in every sense: 'The water inside the main cabin had quickly turned to a murky soup after we capsized. A large container of muesli had spilled everywhere and a five-kilo bag of wholemeal flour had split open when it toppled out of a locker beneath the dinette seat. At one stage Phil watched his camera float past in its case and out through the companionway. Much later he cursed himself for not scooping it up because tucked inside the case was $400 in cash and his new passport.'

Ingenuity was the call of the day as the four inverted sailors struggled to build their new abode.

They used blankets, wet weather gear, boots, clothes, cupboard doors and even two dozen toilet rolls to create their version of an island bed above water level. Then, with it complete, they crawled one by one through the 600cm x 600cm tunnel into the tiny cavity to lie down: 'Everything, including our clothes, was soaking wet. We huddled like sardines in a tin in a space as small as a queen-size bed. We had to lie facing the same way, nestled against each other like spoons, wet spoons in a cutlery set. Above us we had just 20cm of headroom. It was like being trapped in a dark wet cave. Suddenly I remembered the words of a clairvoyant I had visited shortly before leaving on this trip: "You will have an adventure in an underground cave." Was this it? I wondered.'

Their next two priorities were to search for and secure all the food that could be found in the boat and activate their EPIRB distress beacon. Before long their cache included some tinned food, a three-litre cask of orange juice and soft drink. Rick revealed he had diving skills when he found his way to the submerged fridge and claimed a block of cheese, some butter, two litres of milk and two legs of smoked ham.

'It was a bizarre picnic,' said Glennie of their first meal in 24 hours, 'lying soaking wet in the dark with a sickly smell of battery acid still in the air, listening to the fury of the storm. We sliced off pieces of ham with my fishing knife and ate it with cheese and English mustard.'

Incredibly the thought of rationing their supplies did not go remotely close to entering their minds as they were completely convinced they would soon be rescued. To ensure this would happen, Phil and Glennie moved into the flooded forward cabin where, using what tools they could find, they hacked a hole through the side of the hull leading to the underside of the wing deck that extended between the main hull and outer float: 'The toilet was in the way and, as we couldn't think of a use for an upside-down porcelain pan, we smashed it out with a hammer.'

The EPIRB, which was attached to the side of the hull with the aerial poking outside, was activated and much to their delight the blinking red light confirmed an SOS message was being transmitted to the outside world. It would only be a matter of time before a commercial airliner flew overhead and received that signal – or at least they thought that's what would happen.

Before long Glennie was wishing he had postponed his departure so that his original crew, all friends, could have joined him: 'I found it difficult to talk to three virtual strangers about private and personal matters of my life, so I tended to hold back. As time went on we would gradually discover more and more about each other. Rick and Jim, already friends, were to become particularly close, effectively shutting Phil and me out.'

The storm that caused the capsize of *Rose-Noëlle* persisted for four days before abating, and the stress of four anxious humans being in such a life-threatening predicament over that period was generating considerable tension. Fortunately, by day six – 9 June – the weather had calmed to the degree where the wingdeck was no longer awash, so the entombed sailors could escape their claustrophobic and very wet environment for the first time by venturing outside and breathing fresh air. After their eyes had scanned the horizon they realised just how isolated they were and how small their world had become.

This was also the first time they could shed their wet clothes, and when they did they realised the extent of the salt water sores that had already started to fester on their bodies. The good news was that Glennie had managed to salvage the medical kit from the forward cabin before it was washed out of the boat and this meant they had the antiseptic cream needed for their lesions.

With the sea so calm, the decision was made that they would establish a watch system so a lookout for would-be rescuers could be maintained around the clock. But this system lasted only until the next storm, when it was realised that there was no real benefit in being exposed to the elements for so long and sapping their energy unnecessarily.

By day, they kept themselves busy trying to make good their surroundings. Their bed was rebuilt and they carried out a wider search for anything that might be of use during their drift towards the unknown. At one stage Glennie found a mask and snorkel, so he stripped off and did a thorough underwater search in the main cabin. One of these searches provided a much-needed 20-litre container of water. This would prove to be extremely valuable as the yacht's three main water tanks had drained to empty through their breather hoses when they capsized. This had been a shattering blow to their morale.

Their spirits sank even further on the eighth day when the EPIRB stopped transmitting due to a flat battery. They were now very much on their own and at the mercy of whatever nature wanted to throw at them. There was great uncertainty about what the future would bring so, for the first time, it was decided that they should begin to ration food. Immediately, a psychological battle emerged between the four sailors when it came to food. While Phil continued to be resigned to the fact that they were destined to perish, food was the one thing which always held his interest: 'If rationing had been left to him, our supplies would have dwindled rapidly. We seemed to be always arguing about what and how much to eat. The only solution was to vote. Gradually we developed a workable and fair democratic system where each of us spoke before we voted. If the subject was to do with food and whether or not we should eat something, Phil would say, "Well, it's no good asking me. You know my opinion." These discussions would become quite intense and sometimes argumentative; if nothing else, they helped pass the time. Jim was a careful thinker. He would speak slowly and deliberately and often was the most conservative voter of any of us. Rick and I were somewhere in the middle, although Rick used to fluctuate, voting against eating a food item one day then voting in favour of eating something else the next. Somehow we rarely had a tied vote, and if this did occur, we opted for the conservative decision.'

Up until the EPIRB failed they shared a single can of food among them, but after that a single can represented four meals, just two or three spoonfuls each.

At this stage the only positive information Glennie could glean was that they were drifting aimlessly to the east, away from New Zealand at between 12 and 15 miles a day, and they could do nothing to stop it.

As time went on, the four crew continued to salvage food from lockers that were underwater, and what was worth keeping was stored in a small compartment which had been a storage area in the bilge of the boat when the yacht was right-way up. It was now located above their heads in the cave, which had become their bedroom, living room, galley and, in rough weather, their bathroom. While their supplies remained somewhat meagre, they continued to retrieve cans of corned beef, mackerel, baked beans, beetroot, sweet corn, fruit, condensed milk, reduced cream, and coconut milk. However, one of their best finds was five trays of kiwifruit which Glennie located. They stored them in a dark locker and shared one each day over the next 100 days: this provided them with a much-needed source of vitamin C.

With no sign of salvation coming their way after 14 days, Glennie decided to erect a mast on the upturned main hull and drape a large array of bunting from it in the hope that they might be easier to spot from the sea and air should a search ever be initiated. In doing this, they realised that when they were active their minds were concentrating on more positive things than their plight.

Still, after two more weeks of drifting, both food and water supplies were becoming seriously depleted:

'We began to ration our food supplies even more. For the first time in our lives we knew real hunger: the empty cramps in the stomach, the feeling of lethargy and endless dreams about food – lots of it. The nights were the worst, particularly when we couldn't sleep.

'More urgent than the hunger was the overwhelming desire to gulp fresh, cold water. Once we realised our water supply had disappeared, we began to ration our [other] liquids until we were down to just three ounces – measured out carefully in a little spice jar – a day. We usually drank it at night, and sometimes we would vote on whether or not we could do without it. Down in the stuffiness of the aft cabin, our mouths became unbearably dry in the middle of the night. Fortunately, I discovered the packets of sweets I had on board ready to help pass the long, dreary hours on watch during the voyage. We would suck on a fruit jube or a jellybean to get us through the night. Occasionally we treated ourselves to sharing a juicy kiwifruit, a slice of apple, or took a spoonful of powdered orange juice to dissolve in our parched mouths.

'Breakfast became quite a ritual. Each morning we mixed up a bowl of bran, oats, wheat germ, sultanas, nuts, and perhaps a spoonful of jam or honey. Then we cubed an apple and mixed that in. The bowl was passed around and we each ate a dessertspoonful. The idea was to ladle as much as possible onto the spoon and cram it into our mouth before any of the muesli dropped off. Rick used to complain about this method, claiming that his mouth wasn't as big as ours, and he was therefore not getting his fair share.

'As the days passed, we began to cut down the amount of muesli we made up and ration the apple, using only one-quarter each morning. Eventually I dived down to the galley cupboards and found a set of dessert plates so that we could serve equal portions onto individual dishes. Using teaspoons to convince ourselves we were eating more than we actually were, we could proceed at our own pace and savour each mouthful rather than gulping it down like wolves.'

The deterioration of their world was exacerbated with both time and tide, especially during storms. The surge of water through the interior of the yacht would wash anything that wasn't secured out through the smashed companionway doors. With it becoming very apparent that they were likely to spend an exceptional amount of time drifting towards destinations unknown, they decided to resume a watch system in fine weather just in case a vessel might come their way. Each watch was of one hour duration, a period that was measured accurately using their only remaining timepiece, Glennie's wristwatch, until that too was lost in a surge of water.

After 40 days of living their nightmare, the four were still managing to survive on food and equipment they were regularly able to scrounge from the submerged lockers within the yacht. For the most part their emotional stability was retained due to a firm belief that they would be rescued at any moment, although Phil maintained his doubts.

However, despite this belief, the three crewmen told Glennie that they wanted to erect a jury rig atop the main hull of the upturned yacht and try to sail back to land: 'We had several arguments on this subject because I was convinced our priority was to remain safe and well, and to concentrate on survival, using the resources aboard the boat until we were spotted by a ship or found land. That meant building a reliable water-catchment system and establishing a regular supply of fish, something at which we had been unsuccessful so far.

'To me, the water-catchment system was our top priority as our precious supply of soft drink dwindled and we struggled to survive on three ounces of fluid a day.'

The first heavy rainfall had come three weeks into their ordeal, and they were able to catch some water using a plastic sheet and guiding the water into a pot, it then being transferred into empty plastic soft drink bottles. This was to be the only time they would experience such heavy rain during their entire drift.

Glennie now realised he needed to devise an alternative way of collecting every possible drop of fresh water each time it rained: 'I started to lie awake thinking about the problem, trying to remember what materials I had on board and how I could design a system that would catch water without our having to leap up on deck every time it rained. I remembered noticing lengths of plastic conduit pipe while diving to get something out of one of the floats.'

However, the clever concept he had conceived was dealt a severe blow when he went to retrieve the conduit pipe needed to realise it. The majority of it had been washed away and there were only a few lengths left. He and Phil split in half those which they were able to retrieve from the float and created a vertical catchment system which would direct water into a sheet suspended below it. At the same time Rick and Jim attached timber strips fore and aft on the hull using epoxy glue and nails they had found inside the boat. Their intention was to trap the water running down the sides of the upturned hull, which was like the gable of a roof, and channel it into a catchment area from where it would run through pipes directed into the main cabin. This system meant that each time it rained the person nearest the front of the 'cave' could reach out and put a bottle under the pipes to collect the rainwater. There would then no longer be the need to go on deck every time it rained so they could replenish their water supply.

Glennie's strongly held belief that at least he would survive this ordeal gained some strength when it rained the day after the water-catchment system was completed: 'I began to believe in our ability to manifest miracles. When we desperately needed a sign that someone was watching over us, we got it. Jim came to believe that, too, in time.

'From that day on life was just that little bit more bearable. We were able to make cold drinks of Milo and coffee and mix water with orange powder to make juice. It was a luxury after our 40 days of strictly rationed liquid.'

It was still winter and the violent storms that were legendary in that part of the world occurred on a somewhat regular basis. One such storm brought a stark realisation to Glennie about the magnitude of their plight and how careful they must be if they were to survive. It came when he elected to crawl outside and onto the upturned main hull to collect additional rainwater from the other catchment system.

'The reality of what had happened to us then hit me for the first time. Here I was crawling across the keel of my beautiful, perfect boat, which was upside down in a howling gale heading to nowhere. And here I was, risking my life – feeling miserable and scared – to fill up two water bottles. A wave nearly took me with it, and a feeling of anger replaced the sorrowful regrets of a moment before.'

This experience also led to Glennie becoming concerned that the toxic antifouling paint on the hull was contaminating the water they were collecting, so on the next fine day he and Phil spent all their time on deck chiselling off the paint that they had put there only weeks earlier.

Glennie had wanted to keep a log and record daily events soon after they capsized but Rick had talked him out of this as he considered it to be bad karma: he did not want to accept that they would be adrift for a long while. One day, some six weeks into their drift, he was able to retrieve books and stationery from within the hull and set about keeping a record: 'I began to write down what we did each day, what we ate and how much, how we organised ourselves, and descriptions of our various inventions. To keep myself occupied during the long hours spent in the aft cabin, I began to write articles on capsize intended for multihull magazines. I wrote about how we tipped up, what I would do differently next time, survival hints, the mistakes we made and the lessons we learned, which equipment we found useful, and ways in which we improvised. I also began writing letters to family and friends; it was such a comfort to absorb myself in communicating silently with those close to me.'

Ironically, Rick soon decided that keeping a journal wasn't such a bad idea after all. He used an exercise book that Glennie had recovered to write letters to his wife, Heather; it gave him comfort letting her know that they were still alive.

In time, as there were no guarantees that the food they had retrieved would last them for the duration of their odyssey, they began to turn their attention to alternative food sources, primarily fish. 'From my years of sailing I knew not to expect to see fish unless we were near the coast, a reef or an island – in the South Pacific at least. However, two days after we capsized, a big groper swam lazily through the companionway into the main cabin. We watched it poke curiously into open cupboards before it slowly swam away.'

Four weeks later Jim set about catching another obviously inquisitive fish that had found its way into the cabin. A few days earlier they had recovered a fishing line, so he baited the hook with some pieces of tinned sweet corn: 'We lay quietly and watched. Suddenly Jim jerked the line and the fish was hooked.

He lifted it straight out of the water and landed it on our bed while we whooped with delight. Jim's face lit up; I had never before seen him so delighted. We were so excited and eager for the taste of fresh fish that we attacked it on the spot. Jim cleaned it and I took over, filleting it in the cabin. Blood, fish scales and bones went everywhere, and we stopped just short of eating the flesh raw. Fortunately I had 10 litres of vinegar stored up forward, and I marinated the fish for 20 minutes before we stuffed the delicious morsels in our mouths.'

Immediately, fishing for anything that might come by the interior of the boat was as much a sport as a necessity for survival; however, the nosy groper, which they named Harry after it continued to pay visits regularly, managed to avoid capture despite their best efforts. If there was an upside to them having been upside down for so long it was that the yacht's external deck and cabin superstructure, which were then underwater, were becoming home to tiny molluscs and goose barnacles, and the more this marine growth proliferated the more fish this artificial reef would attract.

'They came to feed on us, and we planned to feed on them,' said Glennie.

Whenever the weather permitted, their fishing expeditions moved to the outside of the yacht: 'We spent hours with baited hooks and lures, but the fish refused to be tempted. Occasionally we would fluke a catch but our fish meals were frustratingly sporadic, and we grew thinner and more hungry. We needed to rethink how we fished. Phil helped to speed up the process by losing the fishing rod one day. By now we were careful to tie every item on a line, both inside the hull and out on deck. All except Phil. Either he was naturally clumsy or he didn't care. He seemed to be always losing things, and the three of us were constantly admonishing him about his carelessness.

'One day I was up on deck when I heard Phil curse. He had decided to read a book and left the fishing rod wedged in the cockpit without tying it on. Something tugged at the line, and it had disappeared over the side. Even though we weren't having much success fishing, that rod represented a food source and was therefore one of the most precious items on the boat.'

Rick and Jim then set about creating another fishing weapon, a gaff comprising a strip of timber which had a 10cm hook lashed to one end. They increased their chances of being successful fishermen by also making a net using a timber frame and some prawn netting. This would allow them to scoop the fish out of the water.

'One of the first times Rick used the net the fish were boiling in a frenzy on the surface of the water off the wingdeck. He lunged and scooped and caught four kingfish in one go, a record that was never beaten.'

Harry the Groper also remained in their sights as he had become increasingly complacent. One morning, Jim spotted him swimming idly into the main cabin and before Harry knew what had happened, Jim had swooped on him with the net and 'Harry was history'.

'He thrashed and flopped all over our bed, but I soon had him cut into large fillets. Harry fed us like kings for several meals.'

While their fishing activities were invaluable when it came to staying alive, Phil, for much of the time, continued to be an emotional burden on the others.

'We began to rely more and more on the gaff as a method of catching fish. It served a double purpose: not only did it eventually become the main fish-catching tool, it changed Phil's pessimistic attitude towards our chances of survival. Jim, Rick and I fluctuated between feeling sorry and concerned for Phil and being annoyed and at times enraged by him. Right from that first day, when he kicked open the companionway doors and caused the loss of valuable gear, he had been a liability. He was continually losing irreplaceable items, and he just did not seem to care. His mind was elsewhere.

'We couldn't convince Phil that we had a fighting chance. He would sit for hours looking out at the sea, thinking about his family, thinking about dying. At one stage he considered tying his wedding ring round his neck and writing a final letter to his wife, Karen, in case he was just a skeleton when he was found.'

This reminded Glennie of a conclusion reached by Dr Alain Bombard in his book *The Bombard Story*. In a remarkable feat, Bombard, aged 27, successfully crossed the Atlantic Ocean in 1952 in a small inflatable boat. Bombard wrote:

'If drink is more important than food, instilling confidence is more important than drink. Thirst kills more quickly than hunger, but despair is a greater danger than thirst. The survivor of a shipwreck, deprived of everything, must never lose hope. The simple and brutal problem confronting him is that of death or survival. He will need to bolster his courage with all his resources and all his faith in life to fight off despair.'

After three months on the drift there was growing concern that Phil might take his own life by diving from the boat and swimming away, so Rick, Jim and Glennie confronted him, telling him he must change his attitude and become a team player. It didn't work. There was no change in his demeanour until his ego was boosted by the realisation that he was becoming extremely adept at catching fish using the gaff.

'Suddenly he had a purpose on the boat: he was the provider. The more fish he caught the more fuss we made. He used to put more hours into fishing than any of us; he became obsessed with catching fish.'

A major setback came about this same time when, during a storm, the box containing all their fishing tackle was washed away. Most importantly the box contained spare hooks for the gaff.

They continued to use lures in a bid to catch the large number of kingfish that were gathering under the boat. But while the fish showed an interest in the colourful devices, they refused to bite each time the lure was pulled towards the surface.

'Gradually, as we improved our skill, the four of us developed into an efficient team. Jim would deftly dangle a lure from a line and entice the kingfish to the surface. Phil would be poised ready with the gaff, his eyes wide and intent on the task. When he struck, Rick was ready with the landing net. If our prey somehow wriggled off the gaff before it was in Rick's net, we would have no show of catching the slithering, flapping kingfish. We would desperately lunge at our vanishing prey, grabbing at it, kicking it, anything to stop it from disappearing over the side.

'In the final month we began to get a lot of good weather, and the fishing got better and better. On good fishing days we forgot to look for ships, we didn't argue, we stopped dwelling on our loved ones and wondering if we would ever see them again; all we thought about was catching fish … and more fish.'

Whenever a storm arrived, the fishing gear was stowed and the four sailors retreated to their claustrophobic cave within the boat. They were like bears going into hibernation as on many occasions the storms would see them confined for up to five days. The only benefit to come from this was that they were able to catch up on lost sleep, because when the weather was good they spent their days trying to catch fish and their nights watching for ships.

To emerge into the outside world after days below was like coming out of solitary confinement. The lack of exercise and the stifling atmosphere left them with aching bodies while emotionally they felt weak and depressed: 'Lying so close to one another, unable to get up and walk away when things got too much, our moods plunged. We prayed for fine weather … and for more fish.'

While the fish remained prolific and their haul continued, they saw little else in the form of animal life. Occasionally they spotted a seabird but only once during their entire drift did they see a shark.

Even though they were catching fish they continued to ration their food, but there was one plus-side in that Jim was able to exhibit his talents as a chef: 'We all admired his skill; with a few ingredients he could make us think we had just eaten a sumptuous meal. We were restricted to just a few spoonfuls of food a day, but Jim prepared and served it as though it were a work of art. He soaked rice in cold water for 24 hours to add a teaspoon or two of carbohydrate to our rations, working hard to make sure whatever went with the rice was varied and interesting. We lay for ages at mealtimes savouring every mouthful.'

Jim's talents extended to him grating seawater-saturated apples then pickling the pulp with vinegar and sugar which had been salvaged after the capsize. When the supply of rice began to go mouldy they were rationed to about three teaspoons a day, so to make this more satisfying to the palate, Jim would add a dab of Marmite, jam or homemade pickle to enhance the flavour.

'I consider it was Jim's culinary expertise that contributed more than anything to keeping up morale during those 119 days. But no matter how hard you tried to dress it up, cold food is cold food. And in the middle of winter in a soaking wet cabin that can be very depressing. Every so often Jim would mutter, "If only we had some heat."'

Suddenly this ignited Glennie's mind. He remembered that a stainless steel barbecue was stowed in the port float, and in no time at all the four sodden sailors were on their way to a change of diet: hot food! They already had timber, kerosene and matches, and now they had the barbecue. They needed nothing else. Their decision was to try to fry some bread as they had the ingredients necessary to create raw dough. It was too rough outside to light the fire, so instead their excitement led to them setting up the barbecue inside the cabin.

'As the rest of us crouched in the cabin and watched Jim pour oil into a big frypan, our saliva glands were drooling in anticipation of what was to come.

'The oil spat as it heated and the smell sent more signals to four sets of nostrils starved of that welcome odour. When Jim dropped the first of the dough lumps into the pan, the loud sizzling was one of the most delicious sounds I have ever heard. As fast as Jim could cook them, the four of us tore the hot bread into pieces with our fingers and wolfed it down. The dough filled our mouths and burned our throats. We concentrated on nothing but the taste and when the next piece of fried dough was coming out of the pan.'

Their enthusiasm for eating this delicacy so engrossed them that they failed to realise that as the oil in the pan was getting hotter the cabin was filling with black acrid smoke, and within moments they were choking and coughing and their eyes were stinging. For nearly 50 days since the capsize they had survived everything that had confronted them, including a pounding from storms, and now their insatiable desire for hot food saw them facing the prospect of dying from smoke inhalation or serious burns from an out-of-control barbecue. After that they only ever lit the barbecue up on deck when the weather was calm.

About halfway through their ordeal their diet took another interesting tangent when Jim hooked a big seabird on his fishing line. It was quickly skinned and boned. This time Jim marinated the meat in soy sauce, vinegar, water and Chinese barbecue sauce before cooking it on the barbecue.

All along, Glennie knew there were two large gas bottles located in the yacht's submerged and then difficult to reach cockpit, but it wasn't until their 90th day at sea that their worsening situation had him consider how he might concoct some form of gas burner which would operate off the gas hose line attached to the stove in the cabin. Through ingenuity and determination it was a successful effort and the four were soon able to realise what incredible joy came with being able to boil water and make a cup of tea. It also gave them a far more effective method of cooking: 'Once we were able to cook regularly, the four of us discovered that the tastiest parts of the fish were those that we would normally throw away – the head and the guts. Jim would lightly sauté the guts in a little oil, sometimes adding Chinese barbecue sauce or some shelled molluscs for extra flavour. We would eat sautéed fish guts for breakfast or as a special entrée before a fish dinner. They have a strong, rich flavour like nothing I had ever tasted … out there they were like caviar.

'We boiled the fish heads for just a few minutes and ate everything – the eyes, bones, even the gills, which we discovered were one of the tastiest parts. Seafood chowder made from the heads and tails was another delicacy.'

They continued to create a wide range of other culinary delights: 'One day I remembered our container of burley – saturated cocoa and biscuits. It smelled well and truly off when we inspected the contents, but we refused to throw it out. We drained off the seawater and added fresh water but it did nothing to improve the sight or smell of the mixture. In the end Jim mixed it with flour and made burley biscuits glazed with jam in the frypan. Cautiously we bit into the first piping-hot sample … they tasted wonderful! "Exquisite," as Rick used to say.'

Back in Picton it wasn't until about three weeks after the *Rose-Noëlle* set sail on 1 June that the first glimmer of concern about the safety of the yacht and its occupants began to emerge. Jim Bramwell, who had a loose arrangement with Glennie to maintain some form of radio communications, had not heard anything. One night he did receive a garbled message which he thought might be from *Rose-Noëlle*. The latitude and longitude he noted from that message would later throw the search and rescue effort onto a false trail. It put the yacht 360 nautical miles north of where *Rose-Noëlle* capsized.

Before departing Glennie had filled out official documentation and gave 15 June as his expected date of arrival in Tonga. But he had not been this specific with family and friends: 'Giving an optimistic arrival date causes those back home to start worrying prematurely if the yacht is becalmed or delayed for some reason.'

Calls to Tonga on 18 June confirmed there had been no sighting of the yacht there, so by 20 June a growing belief that the yacht might be missing led to search and rescue authorities in New Zealand being contacted. Even so, it wasn't for another 10 days that an Air Force Orion aircraft took off to search a total of 20,000 square miles of ocean south from the Kermadec Islands, that area being based on the corrupted radio message that was only 'thought' to be from Glennie. In fact, their position at that time was around 600 nautical miles south of the search area.

The search was fruitless and on 1 July *Rose-Noëlle* was officially listed as missing.

Close friends who knew Glennie refused to believe he and his crew had perished, so on 6 July a large group gathered in Picton to decide a course of action. Their aim was to convince authorities that the search should continue, something that would have annoyed Glennie no end as he was firm in the belief that if you get yourself into trouble at sea it's up to you to get yourself out of trouble.

However, with no accurate information which would pin-point a search area, authorities declared that a new effort to find them would be highly unlikely to succeed and therefore a waste of money. Glennie would later agree that the decision was correct.

Consideration was then given to the holding of a memorial service, something that became more likely in August when the New Zealand Water Safety Council decided to give them up for dead. They were listed as having drowned somewhere near the Kermadec Islands.

But hundreds of miles away from those islands, somewhere to the south and well to the east of New Zealand, the inverted *Rose-Noëlle* continued on a meandering course, drifting at the capricious will of wind, wave and current. The four sailors marooned on this tiny man-made island could only continue their fight to stay alive and wonder when the end, whatever that may be, would come.

Glennie's ongoing positive attitude that they would at some stage be either rescued or safely reach shore never sat well with the others: 'I had accepted our situation more or less straight away. There was nothing any of us could do about our predicament. There was no point in laying blame or regretting ever having set foot on *Rose-Noëlle* – although I am sure all three of them did.

'To my way of thinking, the whole experience would be a total tragedy if we did not learn from it, and I don't mean safety procedures or survival techniques. I mean learn personally from our enforced time adrift, all those hours to think and reflect. No one was about to help us; our hope, our belief, had to come from within. We had to create our own good luck, our own future, drawing on faith that we generated ourselves.

'In a strange sort of way I didn't really want to be

rescued too soon. "If a thing is worth doing, it is worth doing well," my mother always used to say. If we had just capsized and then been picked up after a week, I really would have lost everything. *Rose-Noëlle* would be gone, we would have spent one uncomfortable week huddled together, and none of us would have learned a thing. As each day passed, we developed a new skill or invented something to make survival a little easier. We were undergoing an experience that no one could ever take away from us.'

Glennie felt that Rick and Jim were convinced that the time they were spending drifting across the ocean was time wasted: their lives were passing them by. Rick spent a considerable amount of time writing to his wife in an effort to contain the emotional stress he was experiencing. On the other hand, Phil rarely displayed his emotions although he held no doubt that they were doomed. The other three were continually working to assure him otherwise: that they must operate as a team if they were to see their loved ones again.

Inevitably time took its toll. Tolerance was eroded between all four; even Rick and Jim, who were close friends, were prone to intense arguments.

'The worst arguments happened at night. We always seemed to strike bad storms at night, when the hours of darkness dragged on and on. Most of the complaints were over the single blanket, which never seemed to quite cover the four of us, or over not having enough room.

'We had to piece ourselves together like a jigsaw puzzle, and in the early weeks that was how we kept warm. We would move up or down until we fitted, so that our hips weren't banging together and our shoulders weren't jammed. One of us would only need to move a fraction and it would upset the whole cabin and someone would yell, "Hey, give me some space. I don't have any room over here!"

'It would take us ages to get settled again. In the cold weather I often mused about how lucky we were to have four on board. If there had been five of us, we could not have all sheltered in the aft cabin at the same time; if there had been three, we would have been considerably colder.

'Little habits and mannerisms began to irritate. Sometimes I would clean the bowls with my finger, and that irritated Rick. I know that my cheerful attitude towards our predicament irritated everybody. In the early days Phil used to have a variety of habits that grated, from belching to sighing loudly after he had drunk his ration of liquid. Phil was bald, but he grew long, wispy hair down the back of his head. When we were nestled together at night, he could never keep still. He had a habit of jerking his head up and the long hairs would tickle the face of whoever was lying directly behind him, usually me. Eventually I got so impatient I used to pull his hair to make him lie still.'

It was Rick's birthday, 19 August, and Glennie was on deck to watch yet another stunning sunrise when suddenly his eyes locked onto a white triangular shape on the horizon. It was a sail! He shouted to the crew and they scurried from the inside of the yacht like rabbits running from a burrow, and once outside they confirmed the sighting. Immediately there was a panicked rush to fire up the barbecue in the hope that the smoke it would send skywards would be seen. The initial smoke content was improved when it turned black due to the addition of a rubber flipper and some epoxy resin to the flames. But what little hope they held for salvation on that day was quickly snuffed out when a breeze sprang up and the smoke dispersed sideways. They then watched with a feeling of deepening depression as the white sail disappeared over the horizon.

There was a hint that they might be drifting into warmer climes when the air temperature showed signs of improving and the storms that had punished them so severely for so long became less frequent. Even so, the times they did have to spend below during foul weather became even more testing emotionally as their physical condition continued to deteriorate. Further aggravation came when Phil in particular left the others in no doubt that he felt he was being cheated out of his fair share of what little food remained. His suggestion that they divide all remaining food into four equal portions was quickly dismissed by the others as they felt this would only mean that he would rapidly consume the food he had available to him then expect the others to share theirs. Soon this already tense situation worsened when it was realised that there was a 'rat' on board: someone was raiding the food cupboard. As a consequence, it was agreed that at no stage would anyone be allowed to go alone into the cabin where the food was stored.

They kept a record of the number of days they had spent drifting by etching marks onto the side of the aft cabin. September 11 was a red-letter day: 100 days since the capsize. They agreed that the time had passed faster than they would have expected.

'All four of us had lost a lot of weight, and Rick and I were particularly thin.

'Phil had lost his big paunch, and in its place were handfuls of skin hanging down from his stomach. When he stripped off to dry out his clothes, he was quite a sight, with his long hair and beard, his sagging skin, and a tattoo of his wife's name, Karen, on his shoulder.

'Overall we had been blessed with good health during our time adrift. Although we were cold and wet for much of the time during those early days, none of us caught colds. Rick had not suffered from asthma nor been even the slightest bit wheezy. He was dismayed to find that within a week of returning to land he once again needed his inhaler. In the early days Phil used to need medication for his heart condition, but he eventually stopped taking that. Perhaps he'd taken it more from habit than anything else.'

Despite the length of their ordeal and the stifling environment they were living in, the only medical condition that really troubled them was the occasional bout of constipation. Surprisingly, it wasn't until after the 100th day had passed that they recognised their energy was on a more rapid decline. They were losing muscle tone and looking terribly bedraggled thanks to their gaunt physiques, long and unkempt hair and straggly beards. Glennie was the only one to suffer any real problem, and that was self-inflicted. It came when he was cleaning his ear with a cotton bud and the bud became lodged in his ear canal. For three days he and the others tried in vain to dislodge it, and by then an infection was setting in. There was nothing on board to treat the inflammation so in desperation Glennie took a piece of copper wire, formed the end into a tiny hook and then had Rick dig around inside his ear until the offending cotton bud was retrieved.

Initially, Phil was the only one to suffer from claustrophobia when inside the hull, but towards the end it was Glennie who had the problem. 'I think it was the spicy food. Jim had become so adventurous with his spices and seasonings that he used to load everything in together – tandoori, chilli, pepper, curry, the works. I would wake up in the night, my body on fire, panic-stricken that I was being smothered. I would have to clamber over the others and escape on deck. I would tear all my clothes off until my body temperature dropped and I began to feel cold.'

Unlike the others, Glennie was preparing himself mentally for the possibility that they may well be at sea for another 100 days. Accordingly, he insisted that they did everything they could to catch and conserve rainwater for drinking.

They were also beginning to suffer as a result of their food supply dwindling, so much so that at times they were forced to eat fish that was 'on the turn' just to get some nourishment into their bodies. When possible they also tried to dry fillets of fish in the sun so they could replenish their food larder and therefore have a food supply handy when they were confined inside the hull because of bad weather. However, the meagre portions they allowed themselves, and the stress that came with being locked in their 'cell', began to affect them psychologically.

'Jim and I began to notice bizarre behaviour on the part of Rick and Phil at mealtimes. Jim called it "fish fever". It became the source of amusement to the two of us, and we began to monitor it. Jim was fascinated by the state of mind that was causing the classic symptoms of gold fever. It was strange witnessing the behaviour and being aware of the change in Rick and Phil, but remaining detached from it.

'Jim and I would just want to get on with preparing a meal, but the other two were adamant that the fish had to be divided exactly, to the last scrap. I am sure that if I had been able to weigh the fillets they would have been exactly the same, but each one had to be carefully examined for size. Rick and Phil insisted that we each take our turn choosing which piece of fish we wanted to eat. Phil would cut a dried fish stick into different lengths and we would each solemnly pick one from his clenched hand. The whole performance became quite ridiculous.'

On their 116th day adrift Glennie wrote in his log: 'It's been 116 days today. Is that enough? Can I go home now?' - an entry based on the fact that he remembered that Maurice and Maralyn Bailey, who in 1973 lost their yacht in the Pacific, had been rescued after they had survived 116 days in a liferaft and rubber dinghy. 'I considered we had done well. We had coped with the initial shock of capsize. We had surmounted the problems as they arose, and we had learned to work as a team. Each one of us had done a great deal of thinking during our time adrift, and I knew I was a better person for the experience. None of us would be the same.'

They were starting to believe that land might be close because they were seeing bluebottle jellyfish in the water, catching different species of fish, and land-based seabirds were being sighted. Glennie became more convinced of this as two ships had been spotted in the distance at night, and they had seen a yacht on the horizon a few days earlier. However, it was the planes he sighted overhead that gave him the strongest clue. One particular day they spotted two aircraft that were calculated to be flying northeast, and this meant that *Rose-Noëlle* had drifted to a point where it was directly beneath an air route, but they were unable to guess which airport the aircraft had come from.

'Then one day we saw a jetstream right overhead, and I was able to get a direction of magnetic north with the hand-held compass. That meant we were somewhere north of New Zealand. The international airports of Christchurch, Wellington and Auckland are all roughly in line and the plane was heading north.

'On the afternoon of day 116 … I looked up to see a plane flying overhead, low enough to see and hear clearly. We estimated it was about 15,000 feet up and still climbing. It flew directly overhead, and I took a bearing. It was heading magnetic north.'

The four lost souls then spent hours deliberating on how far an aircraft would travel to reach 15,000 feet and decided that it was 80 miles. They also convinced themselves that the aircraft could not have come from Wellington or Christchurch. Taking this information and the direction of their drift they then positioned themselves on a small chart they had retrieved and realised they were heading towards the Hauraki Gulf, which was an outer area of Auckland harbour.

Incredibly this 'guess-timation' was almost spot-on because on 28 September they sighted land. Rick, who was perched on the top of the upturned main hull, was transfixed by a dark cloud formation on the horizon which he was convinced was not moving or dissipating. Soon after, Jim joined him and he too noticed, without any prompting from Rick, what appeared to be land low on the horizon. When Glennie went up on deck Rick said casually, 'Can you see anything out there?' while pointing in the general direction of the object.

'I spotted the shape instantly. It was a dark image within the cloud, and I knew what Rick and Jim were thinking. "It certainly looks like land," I replied. "Let's have another look in 10 minutes and see if it's changed shape." It didn't move, and Rick and Jim told me they had been watching it for a while. When Phil climbed up on deck he stood up and looked around. "Land!" he cried out. "That's land!"'

Strangely the four dishevelled sailors didn't leap for joy, even though they had been marooned on their upturned abode for more than 100 days. Instead, their reaction was calm; almost ho-hum. The challenges they had endured since the capsize saw them far from certain that, while they could see land, they would be walking on it any time soon. Even while looking at the land coming closer ever so slowly, they still wanted to convince themselves their minds weren't playing tricks on them. As a precaution they continued to fish.

The entire situation was enough to send Glennie's mind into the world of fantasy: 'It was like a script from a B-grade movie. A sense of absurd took over, and I chuckled to myself as I imagined us floating up Auckland Harbour to step ashore before an astonished crowd of weekend shoppers. Or maybe a local fisherman would discover us and give us a tow while passing us cold drinks and taking our photographs.'

At sunrise two days later all four waded from their sleeping quarters, through the waist-deep water that still filled the inverted main saloon, and then exited to the outside world. Excitement reigned immediately: the outline of land was very clearly defined and hues of dark green were entering the image. They were definitely drifting towards shore. Later in the day Rick and Phil became increasingly convinced that the mountainous shape they were seeing was Great Barrier Island, just 53 miles northeast of Auckland. All the time Glennie clung to the hope that someone in a boat would spot them and take them in tow. He desperately wanted to be able to salvage what was left of his yacht. Those hopes would be dashed after sunset when a large ship cruised by a couple of miles away, its crew unaware they were sailing past one of the world's most remarkable stories of survival.

That night was to be their last aboard *Rose-Noëlle*: 'We slept fitfully, the atmosphere below tense, wondering what the morning would bring. Then there was the welcome sight of lush green bush, the white outline of breaking waves on Great Barrier's coastline, and a northeasterly wind that was steadily pushing us towards the island. It was obvious that we were going to hit land that day and I scanned the horizon anxiously for fishermen or pleasure cruisers who might be in the area.

'Knowing there was no longer any need to conserve food and water, we ate well that day. Jim caught a fish in the landing net and bent the handle in the process, but it no longer mattered. I made up fish soup using leftovers and we ate Jim's fresh fish, pan fried. The meal fortified us for what lay ahead.'

Torment came soon after midday when a light plane circled overhead, the pilot intrigued by what he believed to be a yellow trimaran which was right-way up and heading out for a day's fishing. The crew waved frantically on seeing the plane but unfortunately for them it was too high for the pilot to be able to recognise the situation. *Rose-Noëlle* continued on the drift that would send her and the occupants crashing onto the rocks.

'Nervously I eyed the wild and rugged coastline looming before us and constantly scanned the horizon for any sign of a rescue boat. If help was on its way, they had better be quick.

'An hour and a half after the plane circled, it became obvious that once again we were on our own and that we were going to hit Great Barrier, probably in an unfriendly spot. Further out we had seen long, white beaches, but as *Rose-Noëlle* drifted closer we could only see cliffs and rocks.

'High above on a ridge across a valley I could make out the pitched roof and television aerial of a well-built house, the first sign of life. I decided that would be a good spot to head once we got ashore.

'Ahead of us lay a tiny cove with a strip of beach, and we hoped we would be lucky enough to drift ashore there. But the wind pushed us past to a neighbouring but much wilder cove, guarded by a reef about 75 metres offshore.

'While the sea had been relatively calm offshore, the waves grew stronger and angrier as we approached land, and now they picked *Rose-Noëlle* up and pushed her towards those rocks. She hit with a sickening crunch; the waves lifted her firmly onto the reef and abandoned her, leaving the full weight of the upturned trimaran to grind itself over the remains of the mast and rigging.

'Phil looked at me and said quietly, "I'm sorry about your boat, John." In the first few weeks after we capsized, Phil had been vehemently outspoken against multihulls, but as time went on, his attitude softened. Towards the end he had, in fact, talked of the possibility of buying the remains of *Rose-Noëlle* should she be salvaged.

'I shook my head and told him it didn't matter. I had designed and built *Rose-Noëlle* to the highest standards of strength, and I had known all along she would hold together for as long as it took for us to find land or be rescued. She had carried us home safely, and that was all I expected. If we escaped with our lives, the spirit of Rose-Noëlle Coguiec would have guarded us to the end.'

The dying moments of *Rose-Noëlle* were agonisingly slow, as if it was in slow motion, and all along the crew were never certain that they would safely reach the rocky shore.

The island was tantalisingly close and the safe sanctuary it promised taunted the survivors. Glennie was adamant that they had a better chance of surviving if they stayed with the yacht until the very last moment: it was quite possible that it would eventually wash off the reef and end its drift by depositing them on the rock at the base of the cliff.

Rose-Noëlle continued to grind its way across the reef for more than an hour, each wave lifting it then dumping it down hard and causing more damage to the structure. The crew had donned life jackets but they still remained vigilant for a rogue wave that might come along and wash them into the turbulent and threatening sea. How tragic it would be should they die at the bitter end of such an intense and extraordinary fight to stay alive!

With darkness beginning to close on the scene, the crew realised they would soon have no option but to tempt fate: they would have to swim for their lives towards the island. Then that all changed: 'The wave hit without warning. It smashed into *Rose-Noëlle*, lifting her off the rocks and posing a new threat. Suddenly 6.5 tons of trimaran was moving, threatening to wash over me and trap me beneath. In that split second I wondered whether to dive off … but the decision was made for me. The wave washed underneath *Rose-Noëlle* and carried me with it in a whirl of boiling seawater. Like an out-of-control roller coaster I flew across the rocks, waiting for the painful jar I remembered so many times when I had come off my racing bike. But suddenly I was clear of the rocks and floating in the swell not far away.

'*Rose-Noëlle* had floated free … and I could hear Phil, Rick and Jim yelling at me to swim towards the boat. But I was having difficulty swimming; for a start I was fully clothed, and the life jacket was riding up over my face because Rick had cut the fastening straps off to make wicks for our kerosene lamp weeks before.'

Somehow Glennie managed to grab a light line the others had thrown towards him and he was pulled back to the yacht, which was then continuing on its way towards the rocky beach: 'Finally we hit rocks near the foot of the cliff and waited until the wreck could go no further. It was time to leave. We stumbled and clawed our way through the water until we reached dry land. We had made it.

'Behind me the gleaming yellow hull of *Rose-Noëlle* was starting to break up. She had stayed with us until the end having floated 1900 miles around the ocean looking for somewhere to rest. I never even looked back at her. I had long decided it was all meant to be for a reason, and losing the boat did not worry me. I had believed in our future. I had done what was expected of me, and *Rose-Noëlle* had done the same.'

When the yacht reached its grave the four gathered up some bundles containing food, water and other supplies they thought they might need on the shore, then they crawled and staggered their way around a rocky headland in a bid to find their way to the beach they had seen. But life wasn't meant to be easy. They were confronted by another obstacle: a deep chasm of ocean which they had to swim across. All survived and once on the beach they collapsed, absolutely exhausted.

'We discovered after four months adrift that we had lost our balance and, seemingly, the skill of walking in a straight line. Anyone observing us from the bush might have assumed we were drunken revellers making our way home from a beach party. We were all soaked through, and I wanted to take my clothes off to wring the excess water out, but Rick told me not to. He was worried about hypothermia and thought we should just get moving.

'We walked and walked up through the bush as the darkness closed in until we could no longer see where we were going; the whack of branches in our faces was the only indication we were still upright. We stumbled over rocks and fern roots, sometimes on our hands and knees, until eventually we had to stop. We had no idea where we were going and very little strength left to get there anyway. Were we going to die from exposure here in the bush after all we had been through? Where was the force, the being, the God who had watched over us so far?'

As if that wasn't enough, it then began to rain and the temperature dropped to a miserably cold level. The realisation dawned on them that while they might be on land there were still no guarantees they would survive. They could only huddle together for warmth under the partial canopy of a large fern and accept the fact that they would have to get through yet another tormenting night. They did, and at first light, after sharing a can of food, they continued on their exhausting trek towards the top of the hill where they knew they would find civilisation. They had no real idea as to where they were heading; they just knew it was up. Eventually they found a track which they followed: it led to their very own Garden of Eden – an orchard of grapefruit which they raided with great gusto, consuming the fruit until they could eat no more. By then they had climbed more than 300 metres, and soon after, as they continued moving forward, they came across a partially completed and vacant house. Peering through the windows they realised it offered everything they would need for that moment: food and shelter. They gained entry by prising open a window and once inside immediately set about bathing and dining like kings. It was a world they had not experienced for four months, and much to their delight there was a bed each for them to sleep in that night. The only problem was there was no telephone: for yet another 24 hours the outside world would remain unaware they were still alive.

Next morning Phil, who had taken a walk further along the road, came back and shouted excitedly: 'Hey, guys, I can hear a phone ringing in a house up there!'

Phil and Jim returned to that house and managed to get inside by breaking a latch. There, mounted on the wall, was a classic old black telephone complete with the turn-handle and a voicepiece. As ancient as it was, it was the link they so desperately wanted to civilisation. There was a list of Morse codes alongside the phone which could be used to reach various destinations on the island, including the police. Phil lifted the receiver and wound the handle vigorously. His call was answered.

A short time later a somewhat disbelieving Constable Shane Godinet arrived at the house where the four shipwrecked sailors were to be found: 'He was standing there smiling, dressed in police overalls, a jersey, and boots, shaking his head while Jim kept calling to Rick and me, "We're outa here guys."'

Constable Godinet looked at the gaunt and bedraggled men, and on realising they were from *Rose-Noëlle* he simply said: 'I never thought I'd see the day when I would meet four ghosts.'

Special thanks to John Glennie for his assistance with this story, and for his permission to use extracts from his book, The Spirit of Rose-Noëlle – 119 Days Adrift: A Survival Story.

CHAPTER 3

MAN OVERBOARD

It's said the joy of ocean yacht racing is one of the world's best kept secrets, and if ever there was an event to confirm this then it could well be the 627 nautical mile Sydney to Hobart race. It can be a brutal experience – a bit like riding a bucking bronco while being inside a huge barrel that's cascading over Niagara Falls. In short, the race's reputation is justified: the world's most physically and mentally demanding middle distance ocean contest.

The potential exists for drama and life-threatening challenges because the course crosses two of the world's most menacing and often unpredictable stretches of water, the Tasman Sea and Bass Strait, the shallow expanse between mainland Australia and the island state of Tasmania. Added to the mix is a rapidly flowing coastal current, and when the water it pushes south collides with a storm front sweeping north from the frigid precincts of the Southern Ocean, then hellacious conditions are the consequence – waves that stand like towering cliffs and crests that threaten to crash down on you like a massive avalanche.

Despite its fearsome reputation the annual Hobart race has stood as a pinnacle of achievement for sailors the world over since 26 December 1945 when nine yachts drew the attention of the entire nation as they set out for the inaugural edition of what is now a classic.

For the tens of thousands of people who lined Sydney Harbour to see the fleet head for Hobart that year, and those who then followed its progress via newspaper and radio reports, there was a universal struggle to understand why these seemingly insane sailors would take to the high seas and put their lives on the line in the name of sport. Incredibly though, through excellent seamanship on the part of the competing sailors, often favourable weather for most of the way, and probably the most stringent safety regulations of any of the world's major ocean racing events, the Hobart race retained a remarkable safety record over the decades.

That record could easily have exploded into horrendous proportions in 1993 when the fleet of 104 yachts was confronted by a cyclone-like storm that hammered in from the Southern Ocean. A deep and extremely large low pressure system – 986hpa – developed. Its magnitude became apparent via a rare (at the time) satellite photograph which revealed a spiralling band of cloud that covered the majority of the Tasman Sea, from the Queensland coast to New Zealand and back across to Tasmania – and the storm centre was in Bass Strait! The next time a similar storm was unleashed would be in the 1998 race – and that had fatal repercussions. Still, the 1993 race went extremely close.

Only 38 yachts reached Hobart; conditions were so tough not even the maxi-yachts were capable of going the distance. For the first time ever two race yachts sank and the waterlogged crews from each were rescued from liferafts. But it was the miraculous survival story involving the owner of one of the yachts that stunned everyone.

Just before midnight on the second night at sea a breaking wave of mesmerising proportions, more than 10 metres high, overwhelmed the 35 foot sloop *MEM*. The incredible force of broken water that descended on the yacht bulldozed it onto its side and swept the owner, John Quinn, over the side and into the wildly agitated ocean. He had been steering at the time and was wearing a safety harness that was attached to a strong-point in the yacht's cockpit, but the shock load that came on the harness when his body hit the water and stopped, while the yacht continued to charge forward, was so powerful that the webbing strap snapped like a dry twig.

Quinn surfaced and immediately faced the terrifying realisation that his safety harness had parted and he was no longer in contact with the yacht; a situation made more dramatic by the fact that in the darkness and amid the marauding seas he could see *MEM*'s white stern light disappearing into the distance. Knowing that his only escape route would be of his own making, he set about doing everything he could to remain afloat while his crew turned the yacht back and initiated a search. Fortunately, Quinn's ocean-racing experience over many years – he already had 13 Hobart races in his wake – saw him wearing oversized sea boots, so he was able to discard them with ease immediately. If he had not been able to do this he may as well have had house bricks tied to his ankles.

With *MEM* turned back and heading towards where Quinn was lost, the shocked crew had their eyes probing as deeply as possible into the darkness, desperate to see some glimpse of their skipper, but the conditions were so rough and the darkness so intense they had no exact location to target. At one stage the yacht came to within 200 metres of him, but while Quinn could see it, the crew had no hope of spotting him in the maelstrom. His panicked shouts also went unheard. He was then 50 nautical miles offshore.

The crew had already sent out a May Day and within minutes other race yachts that were in close proximity changed course and set about assisting the search. Back on shore the race organisers, who were also aware of the drama, had activated a greater search effort which would involve any commercial shipping in the area. Even so, everyone working towards finding Quinn knew that in such horrendous conditions he would have virtually no chance of surviving. An added concern was that those aboard the yachts making the search were themselves exposed to great danger. Every 15 minutes or so they would have to contend with a rogue wave more than 12 metres high that was near vertical on its face and capped by a powerful and churning crest of white water.

After four hours of fruitless searching it was becoming increasingly likely Quinn had perished: officials even discussed writing his obituary.

At that moment though, Quinn, aided by a light buoyancy vest he was wearing, and backed by an incredible will to survive, was still alive. Almost to his own amazement, he was able to devise a technique where as each monstrous and breaking wave threatened to claim him he would duck-dive under it, escape its full fury, and pop out the other side for a frantic gasp of air. 'The only time I really started to get a bit desperate was right at the end and that was for a very short period of time,' Quinn said. 'At that stage the buoyancy vest I was wearing was losing some of its buoyancy and I was starting to swallow water and get tired.'

Then it happened: 'A while later, as I rode to the top of one big wave, I saw it – the most beautiful Christmas tree you have ever seen. It was a bloody big ship with all lights blazing coming ever so slowly towards me.'

In a stroke of extreme good fortune it happened that the oil tanker *Ampol Sorrel* was about 30 miles away from *MEM*'s position when Quinn went overboard. The captain, on hearing the May Day call, changed course and headed for the search area. He very astutely assessed that the most effective contribution that could come from the ship would be if he steered it to the exact spot where Quinn was lost, then shut down the engines and allow it to drift downwind on the path he assumed Quinn would travel in those conditions. He also called all available crew to the ship's bridge, which was the highest point of the superstructure and near the stern. Once on site *Ampol Sorrel*'s powerful searchlights were turned on so the crew could scan the storm-driven seas. At the same time four of the race yachts which were part of the search were requested to fall in behind the ship and follow it on the drift.

For Quinn, the elation that came with sighting the ship was quickly disappearing: he realised that the huge waves were actually moving the ship away from him. He had by then survived more than five hours in the atrocious conditions, but now his one chance at being saved was about to disappear.

'I thought the ship was going to pass me without anyone spotting me because it was coming down the drift at an angle, and the stern – where all the lookouts were gathered on the bridge and using the searchlights – was the most distant point from me.

'My heart began to sink, but as it did a big wave picked up the stern and washed it sideways towards where I was. Suddenly the ship was right there, just metres away. I started to yell my lungs out. "Hey, hey, hey," I shouted.

'Brent Shaw, who was manning the searchlight, heard my yells then spotted me. He was fantastic. After hearing me shout he locked the beam of the searchlight on me and started to shout out, "I've got you. I can see you.'"

Shaw held Quinn in the full glare of the searchlight while the crew of the race yacht *Atara*, which was immediately astern of his position, was advised that the target – that is, Quinn – was in the water right where the beam of the light was hitting the surface.

Atara accelerated to that spot and sure enough, there was an exhausted Quinn struggling to believe his luck. Conditions were so rough, however, that the crew were unable to drag him aboard, so two of them donned harnesses, leapt into the sea and put a line around him. The others on deck then dragged him to the side of the boat and completed the recovery.

Quinn, who was suffering from hypothermia and had been stung badly by bluebottles, particularly on his face, was immediately taken below, stripped of his soggy clothing and put into a bunk. Crewmembers realised that the quickest way to get heat back into his body was to share their own body heat with him, so they took it in turns to crawl into the bunk and envelop him.

The effort by the *Atara* crew in the search and recovery received high commendation as it was only realised later that it too had been in survival mode; not long before Quinn went overboard, it had been heading for shore after being dismasted and suffering severe structural damage. The broken mast had punched a hole in the hull and caused the topsides to bulge inwards. To save the vessel the bunks in the area where the damage had occurred were ripped out then six of the 12 crew locked their backs against sail bags that were put over the damaged area, just to ensure that the hull did not cave in.

This led to one of the crew joking with Quinn that while he had been rescued there was still a chance *Atara* would not reach shore. 'Do you realise that you might have to be rescued for a second time?' the crewman asked.

'No,' Quinn replied. 'If I'd known the ambulance was sinking I wouldn't have got aboard.'

FOOTNOTE: There was an ironic link between this incident and the inaugural Hobart race in 1945. John Quinn's father, Harry, bought Rani from Captain John Illingworth soon after it won that first race. A little while later he took John and two family friends on the yacht for

a fishing trip to Port Stephens, 90 miles north of
Sydney.

A storm moved in while they were there, so they
anchored Rani off the deserted Broughton Island and went
ashore to spend the night in an old fisherman's hut.
Unfortunately, Rani dragged its anchor overnight and was
wrecked on a coastal beach a few miles away. There was
no sign of survivors when the wreck was found, and the
worst was feared. However, an aerial search for them
eventually spotted the four on Broughton Island, but the
conditions were so severe they had to wait there another
four days before they could be rescued by a boat.

CHAPTER 4

LEGENDARY AVIATOR, DEATH-DEFYING NAVIGATOR

*K*eith Thiele has defied death probably more times than anyone on earth. If he was a cat he'd be telling you he'd had at least 40 lives, but in reality there have been countless times for him in more than eight decades where there was the finest of lines between life and death, both in the air and on the open ocean.

Now 88 years old, his life story includes some incredibly heroic, almost unbelievable, deeds as a bomber and fighter pilot during World War II. Then, over the past 35 years what had already been an adventurous life, continued under sail, and on more than one occasion the odds were that he wouldn't make it back to shore.

Keith Thiele's colourful saga matches his robust character. It is also full of high drama.

It started in 1939 when as an 18-year-old he joined the Royal New Zealand Air Force to train as a World War II pilot. By war's end there was no other airman in the RNZAF who had received such high distinction as a pilot of both bombers and fighters: Keith Thiele held the Distinguished Service Order and the Distinguished Flying Cross with two bars. As well as recognising his amazing skills, these commendations could also be seen as a 'thank you' from the significant number of allied airmen who were still alive at the end of the war thanks to Keith Thiele, the extraordinary pilot who incredibly survived more than 50 bombing raids across Europe.

A career in commercial aviation followed the end of hostilities.

When his life turned to offshore sailing he crossed the notorious waters of the Tasman Sea between New Zealand and his adopted home, Australia, on 12 occasions, three of those times single-handed. When age finally caught up with him and he stepped ashore for the last time just a few years ago, he had cruised more than 200,000 nautical miles along Australia's east coast, around New Zealand and to the islands of the South Pacific.

Both in the air and on the sea it has been supreme skill laced with bravado, daring and heroics which have so often seen him live another day. But if you ask him what has been the key to his longevity, his modesty has him tell you that the only way to stay young in today's world is to laugh a lot, so that the endorphins keep flowing – and to 'scare yourself shitless as often as possible so that the adrenalin keeps pumping'.

This same man has a delightful element of rogue about him: he's a highly successful and entertaining practical joker, albeit in a non-malicious manner. It's all been built around getting a laugh.

Keith Thiele's story is one only he can tell. It starts with his time in the Royal New Zealand Air Force:

I was born in Christchurch in February 1921 and when I left school I became a cadet reporter on the local newspaper, *The Christchurch Star*. But once war broke out I could only think about becoming a RNZAF pilot even though I had never flown before. My interest in flying was ignited the day I jumped onto my bicycle and rode out to the local airport to see Charles Kingsford Smith land after crossing the Tasman.

I enlisted in 1939 but I had to go to night school for a year and study before they would accept me. Once I was in and suitably qualified I was sent straight to Europe as a brand–new pilot officer, then I became a flight lieutenant. I started flying Wellington bombers, then halfway through that first tour I went over to Halifax bombers. This second squadron had been going for only two years and at the end of the 30 bombing missions I did over Europe I was the only airman to have completed the lot: everyone else had been shot out of the sky at some stage.

Sadly, for all the wrong reasons, this was a time of rapid promotion, one where you were, as they said at the time, 'stepping into dead men's shoes'. It seemed in no time at all I had become a squadron leader, but then unfortunately for me, because I was apparently showing a high level of talent, it was decided that I should become an instructor. It took me no time to realise I hated it – I was missing the real purpose for me being there. So I went back to flying, but I had to drop back a rank to flight lieutenant because there were no operational postings available for a squadron leader. I finished up with the Australian 467 Squadron which was being formed at the time at Bottesford Air Base in Nottinghamshire, and became a squadron leader. We flew Lancaster bombers over Europe and that's when I received most of my gongs – gongs which came from getting shot up but still managing to keep the plane in the air.

One of the raids I did with the squadron was on a dry dock in Kiel where the target was a large ship in the dock. Not long after we took off it was decided by Bomber Command on the ground that the mission should be recalled because of bad weather over Kiel. But my radio operator didn't receive the message, so we pressed on unaware. We finished up being one of only two aircraft that continued and we got through. We bombed the place and blew the ship to bits!

On the last two sorties I did to Europe I got home on just two of the four engines. On the first of those trips I had to land on one wheel and with no hydraulics operating, and on the second I just crash-landed because I had been wounded in the head and the plane had been shot to bits – it was more like scrap metal than an aircraft, thanks to ground fire and enemy planes. Those were my 19th and 20th trips. On another occasion I had no option but to land a Lancaster at night the wrong way onto the runway when I got back to England, because we had been so badly damaged that I wouldn't have been able to circle and land the right way. I called up and told the base what I was going to do but unfortunately as I touched down there was a surprise waiting for me – another Lancaster on the runway. I crashed head-on into it but incredibly there was no fire and both crews walked away uninjured.

We had a tradition before every bombing mission over Europe where each crew would go up to the mess and be offered an egg before we took off. You could either have it then or when you came back. I was always the optimist – I chose to have it when I came back because I knew I would enjoy it more.

I had always wanted to fly fighters but the first time I actually tried to get into a fighter squadron I was stopped by Sir Arthur Harris, otherwise known as Bomber Harris, or in flying circles Butcher Harris: I was told I was to be taking over Guy Gibson's Dambusters' Squadron. This was just after Gibson had received his VC, and when I went over to see him I was fully expecting to be told what my role would be. However, when I walked in the three WACs (Women's Army Corps) in the office let it slip that there had been a change of plan: I was in fact not going to be joining that squadron but going to fighters instead. I couldn't have been happier.

I started flying Spitfires in 1943, doing sweeps over France and shipping patrols along the coast. I also operated over the beachhead on D-Day. It was wonderful flying.

New challenges came for us as Spitfire pilots when the Germans introduced the V-1 'Doodlebug' jet-propelled rockets. We patrolled for them but they were so fast we couldn't catch them. The only way we had any chance to hit them was to fly at 8000 feet and then dive on them. I think I nailed two of them, but in that situation you just never knew.

After the Spitfires I flew Mosquitos then went into a Tempest Squadron based in Holland. These too were one-man aircraft and our prime target there was trains: we got a hell of a lot of them. It was nothing to go out and blow six of them off the tracks in a day. It was easy hunting, but on one particular day in

February 1945 one of our targets brought my undoing. Four of us had already taken out six trains when we spotted another one trickling along the tracks. I was almost out of ammunition, but I had a new boy with me and he hadn't fired his guns much, so I thought I'd take him down so he could have a shot at the train and get some more experience.

I told the two other blokes to stay high and cover us while we went down and had a crack at the train. On the way down I sensed the place was pretty well defended because there was a built-up area around the railway siding and station – and I was right. What I didn't see was a well-camouflaged flack train which was parked in the siding to protect the area from Allied aircraft.

We attacked the train as it approached the station and hit it, but as we pulled away all I heard was 'bang!' – a big bang – then there was complete silence. Suddenly there was soot floating around in the cockpit and I looked down and saw yellow flames all around my boots. I thought, 'Hell, I'd better get out of here,' but I had no engine, so I pulled up as high as I could – to about 800 feet – and that's where I made a boo-boo:

that's why I got a bit burnt. I pulled my hatch lever so the hatch would fall off and the door at the side of the cockpit would open, then I rolled her on her side so I could literally fall out the door. But I forgot to undo my safety harness, so the instant the cockpit hatch blew off the cockpit turned into a blast furnace and I was burnt all over my face. I then managed to unclip my safety harness and bail out, knowing that I would have to pull the rip cord on my parachute as I went because I was so close to the ground. The 'chute went bang as it popped open, I did one big swing underneath it, and next thing I hit the ground.

I landed right next to the railway station where there were 200 people waiting for the train I had just shot up. There it was belching smoke and steam and blocking the track just down from the station, and it was going to be a week before another train could get through. The 'ack ack' guys who'd shot me down ran over and grabbed me. They were taking me back to their unit, but to do that we had to cross the railway line and then the platform where there was a very angry mob of would-be passengers waiting to get at me because I'd wrecked their train. As we stepped onto the platform the station master rushed out and wanted to kick me in the bollocks, but the Luftwaffe blokes tightened the circle around me and somehow got me through.

By the time we reached their unit I was in agony: my face was all swollen from the burns and I thought I was going blind. Before long I found myself in a prison camp in Frankfurt where I was thrown into solitary confinement and interrogated solidly for a week. Not long after I went into this POW camp it was obvious that the allies were approaching and the Germans were on the run, and when they left they decided to leave 16 of us behind under the control of two old German guards because we were too unfit to travel: I was still badly burned and had a bad bout of tonsillitis. Terry Spencer, one of my cohorts in the camp (and who later in life became the official photographer for the Beatles), was as concerned as I was that the SS might be retreating ahead of the British Army, and that if they came our way we might be in a bit of strife, so we set about planning an escape. We succeeded and immediately headed for town where our plan was to pinch a car so we could drive to the British frontline, but we couldn't find one so we went to a farmhouse and pinched a motorbike instead.

I had a shirt collar stud which had a compass concealed inside, so we used it to make sure we were heading east. Fortunately, I had managed to hide this stud between my toes every time we were searched while in the POW camp, and it was to be our saviour. Our intention was to get ourselves to Cologne, which was a bit more than 100 miles away and by then in British hands. The roads were packed with refugees and there was great confusion as many of the bridges along the way had been blown up. Before long we found ourselves in Cologne, but when we got there it was apparent that only half the town had been taken by the British and that was the half we were looking at across the river. Unbeknown to us until then, we had crossed the German frontline on three occasions while we were making good our escape. We rode into an intersection and spotted an American army guy standing there directing traffic, so we asked him where we were. He simply said, 'I don't know but there's a convoy coming through here very shortly.'

Sure enough, the Yanks arrived but initially didn't want to know about us because they thought we might be spies, until they realised I was a squadron leader; then we were okay. They lent us a jeep and we drove ourselves back to our headquarters. We arrived about 6 pm and found everyone standing around inside the mess 'chewing the fat', so we walked in and went up to the squadron leader, who I tapped on the shoulder then said, 'Buy me a drink!' It was a great reunion.

In 1946, when the war was over, I got a job in England as a pilot with a charter company, London Aero & Motor Services, initially flying food as cargo between India and Mecca. One Sunday when I was back in London we were all having a drink in the pub when my boss came along and told me he wanted to take three aircraft to Australia and set up a base down under. We already had a base in South Africa and for this new business in Australia the plan was to operate an air freight business transporting beef carcasses from the outback to Adelaide from where they would be exported. He told me that he wanted to take one of the planes in England to Australia, so I put my hand up for the job, and sure enough he made me chief pilot for the new business.

We decided it was best for us to fly against the prevailing winds from east to west, but not surprisingly it turned out to be a quite horrific trip: we should have researched it better. We flew up to Scotland then across to Iceland where we had engine problems and got stuck for a few weeks. From there it was about 1700 miles over the ocean to Gander, in Newfoundland. Everything was going smoothly until almost the moment we reached the point of no return for us to get back to Iceland. We were confronted by this incredible wall of bad weather – a savage storm – the likes of which I never saw again in all of my years of flying. It went straight up from the ocean to as far as you could see. My only option was to try to climb over it but we didn't carry any oxygen, so at about 30,000 feet, when we still hadn't reached the top of the weather, I had no choice but to dive into it. Straight away the plane started to load up with ice, so down we went, diving in a bid to get to a level where we would get rid of the ice. By then we had all put on our life jackets because we had no idea what the outcome was going to be. Incredibly, at just 600 feet above the Atlantic we broke out of the storm and flew into light rain which was enough to wash the ice off the wings. We stayed at 600 feet because we didn't want to risk the ice again, but that meant it took us even longer to get to Gander. It turned out that my radio on the plane wasn't the right one for communicating with Gander, so I was unable to contact the tower there to tell them we were coming in to land. I was able to see the windsock at the field during our first pass so I decided to just go round and land. But it wasn't that easy: on the first three approaches I wasn't making the strip, so the only thing I could do was to then make a very high approach and see how I went from there. This time it worked, but when we hit the ground I realised why we'd had so much trouble getting in. It was blowing at about 80 knots, so hard that the guy in the control tower was unable to get out because of the pressure of the wind on the door. It was a horrific scene all round and we were bloody lucky to be there.

We had another shemozzle when we came in to our next stop. We were originally planning it to be

New York but we were diverted to Boston. When we arrived there the weather was again atrocious and the tower told us to hold at 9000 feet because of the number of aircraft stacked below us still trying to land. I told the Yanks in the tower that I was operating with only one radio and that I would be unable to monitor other channels, but they refused to believe me. After an hour of circling I'd had enough. It was as though they were just ignoring me, so I got on the radio and declared an emergency. I told them that I was simply descending over the sea so that I could get a visual on the airport under the clouds and would be coming in. They didn't know quite what to do about that so down we went. It turned out when we landed that we were the first international aircraft to land at their airport. By that time our survey of a possible east to west route to Australia and on around the world was not looking good.

As it turned out the planned business venture in Australia failed. It just wasn't viable, so the boss, who was with us, decided the same crew would fly the aircraft back to England. To help defray costs, the boss had six tons of lard put aboard the plane, the plan being to sell it when we reached England. I told him six tons was too much for the plane: we wouldn't be able to get the range we needed, especially for the leg from Darwin to Surabaya, in Indonesia, but he insisted we try. Well, the fact that we were overweight was obvious even when we went to take off from Sydney's Mascot Airport. I was lucky they still had the old railway line across the strip there because the bounce we got from it as we went down the runway was enough to just get us into the air. We even had trouble getting over the Blue Mountains and twice before we reached Darwin we had to land prematurely to refuel before we could continue. By Darwin I'd had enough of being overloaded and I insisted that we leave two tons of the lard there. We took it off the plane and dumped it in the bush off the edge of the runway. It's probably still there today, confusing people as to what it is and where it came from!

It was an eventful trip all the way but never more so than when, on the leg to Karachi, we were informed that the airport was closed due to torrential rain. That meant we had to divert to Bahrain, but when we landed there the only welcome we received involved officials impounding the plane and taking our passports. Eventually with four tons of lard still on board we made it to London and became the first unchanged crew to ever circle the world from east to west.

With this experience behind me I got a job as a pilot of a converted Halifax bomber flying migrants from Europe to Australia. Then I was one of the pioneers for air freighting fresh produce between Australia and New Zealand.

I joined Qantas in the late 1940s, became an Australian and got married in Sydney. I went straight into being a captain of Lancasters flying across the Tasman to New Zealand and to Japan. Then, during the Korean War, I flew troops and supplies there.

It was a fabulous lifestyle. We had great times flying the old Super Constellations and DC4s. It was a case of us flying from party to party while Qantas supplied the planes and some of the girls, who enjoyed it as much as we did. All that changed when they brought jets into the fleet in 1962. Three years later, with 18,000 hours of flying behind me, 1600 of which were during the war, I quit flying because I found jets were a boring aeroplane to fly. With jets you experienced a few seconds of terror on take-off and a few seconds of terror on landing, and that was it. The hardest job in between take-off and landing was staying awake. On a few occasions when I was flying them I would return to the cockpit after a break and find the entire crew asleep. I would just lean across and press the fire warning test alarm and suddenly they were all awake!

Once out of the airline I decided to set up a waterfront business with another Qantas pilot who had also retired. We bought a very dilapidated old wooden boatshed at the Spit, on Sydney's Middle Harbour, right beside the Spit Bridge. It cost us $22,500 and there we built Australia's first floating marina.

That experience lasted until 1974 when we bailed out of the marina. A short time before that I bought a famous little 31 foot yacht, *Cadence*, which won the Sydney to Hobart race in 1966. She was a tough little timber double-ended sloop which had a fibreglass cabin on top that resembled a blister. I had already decided that the cruising life was going to be for me; I think this was because since I was 19 years old I had led a life that had seen me roaming the world almost incessantly.

In 1975 *Cadence* was ready for her first cruise so I grabbed a mate and we headed for Lord Howe Island, 400 nautical miles east-northeast of Sydney. It was an uneventful trip on the way over and we had a great time on the island, but on the passage home the conditions were at the opposite end of the spectrum.

It might have been because I hadn't really sailed *Cadence* in rough weather, but the fact was I was driving her too hard in the conditions. We were about 80 miles off the coast. The seas were building and the weather was turning sour so we decided that we should reduce sail. We were both down below putting on our wet weather gear when we simultaneously yelled, 'HANG ON.' You just sensed the yacht was being launched into outer space – she was flying off the top of a huge wave and into thin air. She crashed down onto her side with a sickening smack. I went hurtling through the air and finished up head first into the galley. The toilet was ripped off its mounting and there was gear hurled everywhere.

The noise of the landing suggested serious damage.

There was a definite sound of splintering timber. We ripped up the floorboards to check the bilges. It wasn't what we wanted to see: water was pouring in. She was leaking like a busted drain.

We manned the pumps day and night in a desperate effort to keep her afloat while at the same time sailing her ever so carefully towards Sydney. We managed to make it and when I hauled her out of the water I realised just how lucky we had been: five of the hull planks had been really badly fractured.

I put it down to a lesson learned and set about preparing for the next cruise: to Norfolk Island via Lord Howe Island then into the South Pacific. I had the boat ready just before Easter so, with my mate Bruce Chapman, we made plans to set sail on Good Friday. Now, as any superstitious sailor will tell you, you *never* set sail on an offshore voyage on a Friday. It just brings plain bad luck. But that didn't faze me. I wasn't superstitious, but I have to tell you that after what we experienced I am now when it comes to setting sail on a Friday.

There had been some bad weather brewing the day before but I wasn't overly concerned because it was coming from the south and the forecast wasn't for extreme weather. I was confident *Cadence* could handle it, but on the Saturday morning, when we were about halfway to the island, it quickly became apparent that we were in for a tough time: the weather was going to be a lot worse than originally forecast. A message crackled out over the two-way radio that a storm was developing 300 miles east of Port Kembla, at a point about 200 miles south of us, and it was heading in our direction. We were making good speed and on course, so I thought the best thing I could do was keep pushing on. But a few hours later, by mid-afternoon, the wind was already screeching through the rigging at up to 70 knots and the motion on deck was so violent that we struggled to move around.

By then common sense had prevailed: I had decided the safest thing to do was to take down all the sail and lie-a-hull, essentially setting the boat up in a survival mode so that it maintained the safest possible angle to the seas. I realise now that this was probably a mistake. If I'd set the storm trysail I would have been able to control the yacht and cope better with the seas: we would have been able to steer over the waves. Our problem was compounded by the fact that we were right over the top of the massive sea mounts that lie on the direct line between Sydney and Lord Howe Island. These underwater mountains come from the ocean floor 1500 metres down to just 110 metres below the surface at their peaks. In a storm the combination of the wind strength with the current that flows rapidly around these undersea mountains often causes horrendous seas, as we were to find out. Before long the seas were taking on alarming proportions – the height of five-storey buildings, and breaking at the top.

We were starting to feel some trepidation, which we soon realised was quite justified. Inevitably, the first of the real monsters arrived on the scene and got us. There was nothing we could do about it. It just broke over us; it dumped on the boat and smashed the self-steering gear. Then came the one I didn't want to see. It must have been 80 feet high. Mountainous! It was ugly and carrying a massive crest of broken white water. I knew we were in for it. There was little I could do but try to stick the stern towards it, but that was a waste of effort. I just looked up at this wall of breaking water that was crashing down on us, hung on and hoped.

It was as if we were about to be demolished. The yacht was literally buried under tons of white water. Bruce, who was below deck, was being hurled in every direction while I was being thrown around on deck at the end of my safety harness like a puppet on a string. I had no idea if we were right way up, upside down, or going sideways but it would become apparent later that the yacht was at least inverted and possibly rolled through 360 degrees. I can only guess that the mayhem lasted for about 30 seconds then the wave let us go and rolled on. I think it is quite possible that I was knocked out briefly because I was being smashed around so violently. I do remember her surfacing above the white water – she was coming up out of the water like a submarine – then I looked forward and realised what had happened: there was little more than the mast left. The cabin had been absolutely smashed off the deck; *Cadence* looked like a flush-deck sports convertible. There was a gaping hole into the hull. Worse still, the dinghy and liferaft were gone. We were on our own and if one more wave like that came along, we were dead.

I knew the only thing we could do to try to save the boat before that wave arrived was to cover the hole where the cabin had been. Bruce came up on deck while I dived below to find what I could to do the job. I grabbed the storm trysail, which was still in its bag on the cabin floor, and also the sun awning I'd had made to go over the boom. Fortunately it had solid timber battens in it so Bruce and I were able to roll it out along the deck and cover the hole, then spread out and tie down the trysail over the top of it. The yacht was then as waterproof as we could possibly make it. The good news was that the mast was still in place, but the boom had broken in half and was wrapped around the rigging.

Bruce then went below and when I followed him a few minutes later I found him sitting on the engine box in an absolute state of shock. He was shivering and shaking and just saying over and over again, 'We're not going to make it. We're not going to make it.'

I rummaged around under a bunk where I found a plastic bag full of old woollen jumpers which I had stowed for when I was sailing in cold weather. I got

Bruce out of his wet gear and put some dry clothing on him in a bid to get him warm.

Much to my delight the only bit of glass in the boat that wasn't broken was a bottle of scotch, so I tipped a couple of scotches into him, and before long he was coming good. But wouldn't you know it: just at that time another bloody great wave suddenly came out of nowhere, broke all over us and absolutely soaked him. Bruce threw his hands into the air, looked towards the heavens and shouted, 'Jesus Christ, can't you leave us alone!'

Fortunately our efforts to cover the hole in the deck had been pretty successful because only a small amount of water found its way below deck with that second wave.

What amazed me was how little water there was inside the yacht after it was hit by the first wave, even though the cabin was ripped off. I can only think that this happened as a result of the incredible pressure that came inside the hull when the yacht was buried by the wave; the pressure was so powerful that it was like an explosion that kept the water out. What made me more certain of this was that the companionway slides, or storm boards, that I had in place at the entrance to the cabin were bowed outwards and jammed into their tracks: fair evidence of the massive pressure of air that was experienced inside the hull.

Bruce had been really lucky to survive down below because bottles, tins and anything else that wasn't secured went hurtling through the cabin as if they were particles of a bomb. The force of this rollover was then made more apparent when I went to check the engine: it had been ripped off all of its mountings. But the most amazing thing of all for me involved the new tub of margarine that had been unopened and stowed in the small icebox I had in the cabin. I never did get to find the container that the margarine came in, the lid of that container or the paper seal on top of it, but every bit of that lump of margarine was jammed through the two-way radio that was on the opposite side of the cabin. There was just this yellow gooey mess through every part of the radio and around all the valves. Not surprisingly, as incredible as this appeared, the margarine rendered the two-way radio useless, so there was then no way for us to send out a May Day call.

The conditions remained extreme as night fell and it was not going to be possible for us to set any sail until things improved. The only thing the two of us could do was sit in the cabin looking at each other while praying under our breaths that another horror wave would not come along and claim us.

By 4.30 am we sensed that the wind was starting to ease and the seas were beginning to abate. By 7 am things had improved to the degree where we could set some sail and turn back towards Sydney. You would have thought that our problems were over by then, but no: during the morning one amazingly steep wave came out of nowhere and we took it bow-on. *Cadence* went up and up, over it then speared off into mid-air before crashing into the trough behind it. As she landed there was an all too familiar sound of cracking: she had split another plank and was leaking. We were still 12 hours out of Sydney so all we could do was take it in turns to steer and man the pumps.

It was late at night when we finally found our way into our berth at the marina in Mosman Bay. We collapsed into our bunks then woke up the next morning to hear the marina manager shouting down at us, asking what we were doing in that berth. I went up into the cockpit and he suddenly realised that he was looking at the 'much modified', flush-deck *Cadence* sitting in her proper berth.

Today, Keith Thiele still lives life to the fullest. Even though he is in a nursing home in North Queensland his wicked sense of humour remains as strong as ever, much to the delight of all those around him.

The second round of dramas with his yacht Cadence *in the mid-Tasman finally convinced him it wasn't the ideal yacht for cruising, so he sold it and decided to try farming, buying a property in Queensland. But his enthusiasm for that quickly waned and in 1983 he bought a more suitable fibreglass 33 foot yacht, which he appropriately named* Spitfire. *After that there was no stopping him.*

'I couldn't stop because I dreaded the thought of living in a house,' he explained.

CHAPTER 5

THE MISSING MEXICANS

Historic San Blas is an unkempt and sleepy village on Mexico's west coast where time has all but stopped for its 9000 inhabitants. It is said that this isolated town is still the way Mexico was before the tourist invasion came from north of the border; it has been missed by the modern world. There are no condominiums, major resort hotels, fast food outlets, shopping malls, freeways, golf courses or stoplights. And, apart from some historic buildings and ruins, its principal claim to fame is that it's a haven for bird-watching in nearby jungles and wetlands. Even more memorable though are the *jejenes*: notoriously brutal, blood-sucking sand fleas which are so small they could best be described as 'no-see-ems'.

The financial spine of San Blas comes from its fishing industry. The waterfront is crammed with large, professional looking ocean-going shrimp boats, and also littered with rusty, dilapidated and derelict hulks, all of which confirm business hasn't always been good. More numerous are the pangas, a much smaller open dory with bench seats that the locals use for three- or four-day shark fishing expeditions to nearby islands. This industry, which thrives on the demand in China for expensive shark fin soup, can be a lucrative occupation for the boat owners and crews based in San Blas, but like almost every venture involving the sea, there can also be a significant element of danger attached to it.

The career path for most young men in San Blas leads them to the sea and some form of fishing. And with household incomes being so meagre, families often place pesos ahead of education for their children: many are working on the boats before their years have reached double digits.

Such was the case for Salvador 'Chavita' Ordonez, who for 27 of his 36 years had worked as a fisherman, or *pescadore*, along this coast. Small in stature and stocky in build, he had a big reputation in San Blas as a shark fisherman, so there was no surprise when a relative newcomer to the business, Juan David Lorenzo – who was in town looking for three crew for his 8.2 metre long fibreglass panga – was directed to Salvador.

The pair negotiated a deal and Salvador signed on. This led to his fishing and drinking buddy, 27-year-old Lucio Rendon, also agreeing to join the crew, along with Jesus Vidana, also 27, who had left his pregnant wife and young son in the northern coastal town of Las Arenitas while he went to San Blas looking for a job that would earn him around 200 pesos, or $20, a day.

Their role on this shark fishing expedition involved them preparing, casting and retrieving the longline that is used to catch the sharks. It is a laborious and very demanding task where skill so often makes the difference between success and failure. And the rotund Señor Juan, who made his money operating an internet café in nearby Mazatlan, certainly didn't have that skill, even though he was a keen angler.

Regardless, his boat certainly looked professional: the grey hull, which like so many pangas had no shelter from the elements in the form of a canopy or cabin, was obviously in good condition, and it was propelled by twin 200-horsepower outboard motors, which was the maximum for this style of boat. Such powerful motors carried a promise of high speed – up to 35 knots – for the 60 nautical mile passage offshore to the Islas Marias archipelago, a place where the sharks were found in the sea and Mexico's worst criminals were jailed on the island.

When Salvador, Lucio and Jesus arrived at the dock at first light on the day of departure they were surprised to discover they were to be joined by a fifth man, a friend of the owner who they came to know only as El Farsero – which, roughly translated into English, meant that he was considered to be a bit of a farce or a trickster. From the moment they were introduced the trio realised El Farsero knew nothing about fishing, and that he had experienced what could be best described as a charisma bypass when it came to personality: he ignored the crew and would only communicate with Señor Juan. It wasn't a problem because for them the captain was king. El Farsero was obviously there for the ride, and Salvador, Lucio and Jesus were there to work.

Señor Juan had provisioned the boat well by Mexican standards with ample food, fuel, water and equipment, but while there was a compass there was no actual safety gear, like a VHF radio or mobile phone for communication, navigation charts, GPS plotter, life jackets or oars. That would have caused concern in most other corners of the world, but in Mexico it was considered the norm. Also, if those on this voyage had been superstitious seafarers there would have been cause for additional concern: there were bananas on board – an omen of misfortune in the eyes of many mariners.

Most prominent on the boat was the cimbra containing the longline that was hundreds of metres long. When set it became a floating banquet for the unsuspecting sharks – 80 to 100 hooks, each one baited with a lump of fish and suspended on a light line about a metre below the surface. Each line and bait was attached metres apart along the heavy nylon longline over its entire length, and each end of the longline was marked by a large float. Normal procedure in shark fishing was for it to be set at around nightfall and retrieved between 12 and 24 hours later.

It was 28 October 2005 and the early morning sun was warming the men's backs as Señor Juan guided the panga slowly away from the dock, before accelerating to more than 20 knots for the two kilometres they would cover down the bay to the open sea. Once outside, the course was changed to the west and the panga came to life; it was showing why, over lifetimes of evolution, this style of boat had become a highly refined and seaworthy workhorse for Mexican fishermen. Its fine bow carved effortlessly through the choppy seas, and the ride remained relatively smooth. When fully laden a large panga can carry up to five tonnes of fish and still maintain good speed.

San Blas was quickly disappearing below the eastern horizon as they headed off on what was scheduled to be a three-day trip. But fate had other intentions: *los pescadores* were destined to become *los perdidos* – the lost.

Some four hours after leaving San Blas the panga arrived at the island where Salvador, Lucio and Jesus knew they could use handlines to catch the tuna needed as fresh bait for the shark fishing that evening. It was a successful mission and once there were enough tuna in the hold of the panga Señor Juan started the engine and headed the boat for their preferred shark fishing spot. The others, excluding El Farsero, baited the hooks and prepared the longline.

Darkness was descending when the trio began setting the line. Salvador, Lucio and Jesus were determined to ensure that every hook was baited properly and that each down-line was not tangled as the longline entered the water over the stern. The relatively calm weather made the procedure easier, even for Señor Juan, as he moved the boat forward at a low rate of knots. Once the entire line was set it was secured at the back of the boat and the motors stopped. The boat would then drift with the wind and current.

Then it was a waiting game, so for the rest of the night the five men would lie on the floor of the boat and try to get some sleep; they were hunters resting before they got to check their traps.

All was peaceful until around midnight when the five were roused from their sleep by a sudden blast of wind and a rapid change in the motion of the boat. A storm had charged in like a drill sergeant marching into a dormitory unannounced and calling everyone to a pre-dawn reveille. The three *pescadores* knew that the rising seas would make the retrieval of the longline extremely difficult; however, instinct was already telling them something wasn't quite right – the motion of the boat was different to how it should be with hundreds of metres of heavy longline trailing astern. They realised it was more lively; it wasn't riding over the waves as you would expect. They went to the stern and saw a sickening sight – a very short piece of nylon line that had been chafed through by the motion of the boat. The longline was gone. And, as if that wasn't bad enough, the trio knew that the standing rule in fishing was that they would have to share in the cost of the lost equipment. It was worth more than $1000, and that represented a fortune to these men.

The captain immediately became as anxious as the others to find it, but it was virtually a waste of time trying before first light. They didn't know how long the line had been gone or in what direction, so they didn't know where to start looking. Señor Juan fired up the engines and a low-speed search was initiated in the form of an ever expanding circle from where they were located, but without a chart or Global Positioning Unit, or having any visible reference of the islands, it was near impossible to plot an accurate course. Later, as first light began to emerge in the eastern sky, it became apparent that even if they were in close proximity to their quarry, it would still be extremely difficult to spot the buoys on the longline bobbing along on the windswept and rough seas that were reflecting the hues of the leaden sky. Worse still, if there were any sharks attached to the longline they could be dragging it whichever way their inclination took them. It was like trying to find a tadpole in a torrent.

Throughout the day the search continued relentlessly – five sets of eyes scouring an ocean laced with steep and nasty seas while the thirsty engines droned on, all the time consuming valuable fuel. At that stage Islas Marias looked like a grey smudge low on the horizon, but Señor Juan gave no thought to heading there to top up the fuel tank. His fixation was on finding the longline and avoiding the humiliation associated with returning home without it. The search continued into the night, and by next morning, with the fuel getting low and there still being no sign of the longline, Salvador respectfully tried to reason with Señor Juan about the predicament they faced. They no longer had enough fuel to return to San Blas, and they would be lucky to even make it to Islas Marias.

The captain would not accommodate such a suggestion; the search would continue. It was a decision that held fatal consequences.

When Señor Juan finally accepted that their fuel – or lack of it – held priority over finding the longline, it was too late: a short time later both engines made their last gasps for fuel then died. Even so, all five on board were relatively unperturbed by their situation. They could see another panga in the distance and they expected that it, or another boat working in the area, would eventually come by and tow them to safety. But that balloon of hope soon became laden with lead. Twenty-four hours later their anticipation of pending salvation was on the wane. There were no boats to be seen and they were drifting away from the islands – away from the region where the pangas worked. The one consolation was that the weather was improving and the sky had cleared, but that wasn't going to help them, save for the fact that they would be more easily spotted from a passing boat.

They also knew that it was improbable that a search for them would be mounted from San Blas as it would be days before anyone became concerned about their whereabouts. Everyone tended to mind their own business around the waterfront; no one kept note of when fishing boats departed or returned, and families were never sure when the fishermen would actually be home.

The five continued to live on fading hope until the fourth day of their drift. That's when a serious realisation came home to roost – they were now at the mercy of the elements and in the hands of God. The lack of food was already a problem. Their previously held belief that they would be rescued had led to them consuming most of their food and water. They remained confident that they could cope without food for some days, but as there was no shelter on the boat, and with the sun beating down relentlessly on them each day, dehydration was going to be the major issue.

Within 24 hours their supply of fresh water was completely exhausted, and from that moment their rapidly accelerating bid to survive led to them consuming small amounts of seawater. However, the cramps and headaches that came as a result of this left no doubt that drinking from the ocean could only be a last resort over a very short period. (The consumption of seawater by humans to maintain hydration over a period of time impacts the function of the kidneys. Because of the levels of sodium chloride, or salt, in seawater the concentration of sodium in the blood rises to toxic levels, and this can lead to an irregular heartbeat and fatal seizures.) Salvador took another option – drinking his own urine. Initially the others refused to follow his lead, but before long they realised they had no alternative.

The deeply religious *pescadores* soon turned their attention to the heavens. They had been drifting aimlessly away from the coast of Mexico for almost a week and were in dire need of rain for drinking water. For them, prayer and a battered old Bible that Salvador had brought with him represented their only hope for communication with the outside world. Incredibly, be it through divine intervention or simple good fortune, the much-needed rain came within 48 hours, and everyone worked desperately to catch every drop. With no canopy on the boat to act as a catchment for the rain they looked to the small foredeck at the bow of the panga. By hacking into their plastic fuel containers they were able to create a makeshift dam on the fibreglass deck and channel every possible drop of the precious fluid into the containers they had on board.

Back in San Blas there was growing concern, particularly from Lucio's family, for the safety of the five fishermen, yet the Port Authority showed no desire whatsoever to initiate a search. It was left to the local fishermen to try to find their friends, and that's what they did. The extensive search proved fruitless, and somewhere around a week later the effort was abandoned. While family members continued to live with the hope that their brethren would be found alive, the majority of fishermen in San Blas were convinced after a week of searching that five more of their community had joined *los perdidos*.

Back aboard the boat the pangs of hunger were ripping through each man's body with unabated vigour; the water they continued to catch from the now regular rainfall was their lifeblood for the two weeks that passed without food. The sea was obviously their only hope for a harvest, but there was nothing to be had; it was devoid of any activity – fish or bird life. The only occasional sign of there being another world outside their own was the sighting of an aircraft at high altitude heading for an unknown destination – as were they. That's when their minds turned to their homes and what might be happening there.

Each day, when the burning sun was arcing through its zenith, they took it in turns to achieve some respite from its punishing heat by squeezing into the little shade that was available under the small foredeck. When they were up and about each man kept a casual eye on the horizon, always looking for any sign of a ship. They had seen two pass by within 48 hours of their odyssey beginning, but they were unable to attract the attention of those on board. They were also hoping that they might at some stage see a sign of sea life – a possible meal!

They were able to keep track of time because Lucio had a watch that featured a calendar, so they knew that it was two weeks after they had tasted their last skerrick of food that an inquisitive turtle surfaced just off the bow of the panga. The quick and agile Salvador knew he had just one chance to put turtle on their menu that day, and in a flash he had sprung onto the side of the boat and dived onto the back of the turtle like a cheetah leaping onto its prey. He grabbed it, resisted its desperate efforts to escape, and dragged it back to the boat. They had food, glorious food, even though it had to be eaten raw.

Salvador, Lucio and Jesus filleted the flesh and rinsed it in seawater, and during the process they drained the blood into a bucket so they could drink it. (Salvador had learned at a survival course he attended only months earlier that in dire circumstances you could drink blood and gain energy.) But while they ate the meat as well as the turtle's intestines, neither Señor Juan nor El Farsero could. For physical or mental reasons their bodies rejected the repast – they gagged each time they tried to eat and couldn't keep the food down. It was a sign that didn't bode well for their survival.

The turtle provided the only two meals they would savour during the entire month of November, the second one being a small seabird that landed on the side of the panga. Again Salvador would prove to be a successful hunter, and again the captain and his mate couldn't eat the raw flesh.

Salvador's unfaltering faith had him convinced that they weren't going to die, even though he had no idea where they were headed or how long they would be drifting on their tiny island. However, in late December – two months after their plight began – both Señor Juan and El Farsero were showing alarming signs of decline. The captain was vomiting blood and bile, probably because of malnutrition, and the emotion of the situation continued to tear at El Farsero's mind: he still refused to communicate with the crew and spent most of his days huddled in a corner of the boat crying. It was the start of a mental breakdown. Lucio was also suffering with a painful inner ear infection. He joined Señor Juan in what had become the sick bay – the small area under the foredeck.

Despite his best efforts to prove he was fit and healthy, Señor Juan continued to slide. He had gone for more than a month without food and at times was becoming quite irrational in his behaviour. He was then far from capable of being responsible for the boat and those aboard, so it was not surprising that the still energetic Salvador assumed greater responsibility. He was the most emotionally stable and fittest of the five; even Jesus was at times bedevilled by emotion and broke down and cried.

As the panga continued on its meandering course to nowhere, its hull below the waterline became a haven for crustaceans, particularly barnacles. This would prove to be of major benefit to the crew as they struggled to secure what food they could from their only source – the ocean.

The barnacles provided ideal bait for fishing. However, the fishing lines they had onboard had been damaged and were next to useless, and the hooks used to catch the tuna after they left San Blas were way too big for the fish that were beginning to congregate beneath the hull. It was time for improvisation, so Salvador, Lucio and Jesus took to raiding the defunct motors. With the few tools they had they were able to remove small clips, metal plates, rods and wires from the motors and fashion them into a basic form of fishing equipment. Their efforts were well-rewarded as on one single day in January they landed more than 60 fish, which supplemented their regular catch of sea turtle.

Obviously this represented an excess of food so they prepared what they didn't eat and dried it in the sun so they had food for many more days. Incredibly, they even managed on the odd occasion to strip slivers of timber from the boat and start a small fire using Lucio's cigarette lighter, then actually cook small pieces of fish. Their ingenuity and improvisation meant that while they had no idea where fate would take them, they had a surprisingly good chance of not starving to death or dying of thirst.

Sadly though, this was of no benefit to either Señor Juan or El Farsero. While Lucio regained his health, the other two continued to weaken. Neither could eat and this was taking a massive toll on their bodies. By mid-January Señor Juan was in a terrible condition. He was weak, bleeding internally and incontinent. His mind was wandering and it was obvious to the three *pescadores* that he was close to death. They did everything possible to ease his pain.

Death came on 20 January. Salvador, who was fishing at the time while the others slept, heard a muffled groan come from Señor Juan who was curled in a ball under the foredeck. By the time Salvador had got to him, he had died.

They kept his body aboard the boat for the next three days apparently in the hope that they would be rescued and the corpse could then be transported back to his family for burial. But when they realised there was no option but to consign him to the deep, Salvador, Lucio and Jesus blessed his body before slipping it over the side of the panga.

With Señor Juan gone, a dramatic change came over El Farsero. It was as if he realised he had to surrender his arrogance and become a part of the team. He began conversing with *los pescadores* and even took to helping them catch fish.

All the time though, his health continued to deteriorate. He had not eaten for many, many weeks, even though he had tried, and just two weeks after Señor Juan passed away, El Farsero's body went into a rapid shutdown and he died.

His passing went unnoticed. His death was only confirmed when one of the trio went to check on him: he was huddled in the corner of the boat. Being unsure as to when he had died, they opted to keep the body aboard the panga for three days; then they decided it was time to pray for him and place his body into the ocean.

Incredibly, the more-than-modest lifestyle that came as a consequence of them being lowly paid fishermen meant that none of the *pescadores* had ever been on an aircraft, and Salvador was the only one to have ever crossed a border. So it was safe to say, at that stage of this experience, they had travelled further in the previous months than at any other time in their lives. They had also endured a daunting level of emotion by accepting that they were the only people on the planet who knew they were alive, and that back in San Blas the rest of their world had moved on.

Beyond this the only certainty they held was that the aimless drift was taking them in a westerly direction.

Their desperate bid for survival became a near monotonous but vital procedure. Fortunately the rains came regularly and they were able to catch fish and turtles, which were plentiful in the warm waters: by their calculations they would catch more than 100 turtles during the ensuing months. The hour of the day became meaningless: they slept when tired, and when it was cold the trio curled up together in the claustrophobic area under the foredeck so they could benefit from body warmth. During their waking hours, when they weren't fishing, they tried to remain sane by reading the Bible, praying and enjoying basic forms of entertainment, like playing the air guitar and singing hymns. There was nothing else to do.

They were also on a weather alert as this would prove to be no fair weather passage. On many occasions during their unwanted wanderings towards God knows where, they had to battle the elements as much as hunger and thirst. Storms and rough seas were not a rarity and in such a small open boat the possibility of capsize by a large breaking wave was very real. This was where the seafaring skills that had been ingrained in *los pescadores*' lives came to the fore. In the roughest weather they set a sea anchor on a rope which they trailed from the bow of the boat. It comprised whatever bulky material they could find aboard – including the cowlings off the engines – all tied to one end of the rope then put over the side. The drag this created was sufficient to hold the bow of the panga into the wind and waves so that the chance of a roll-over was minimised. Still, there were some hairy moments, particularly when, during one savage storm – which probably occurred when they were near Hawaii – the rope holding the sea anchor broke and the panga turned side-on to the eight-metre breaking waves. Prayer and panic went hand in hand and they somehow weathered the storm.

At other times, in good weather, they would set a crude sail as a jury rig. It was made up using the seats from the boat (the mast) and tatty blankets (the sail). This enabled them to harness the prevailing tradewind and propel the panga at a higher rate of knots. The fact that they were making progress was mentally stimulating, it broke the monotony of a 'regular' day, but they still had no idea where their course would take them. Jesus even dared suggest that their destination might be China, which he always knew was somewhere over the horizon to the west, where the sun set. Rough calculations had them moving through the water at anywhere between 12 and 28 miles a day; however, due to variable currents and changes in wind direction, this would not have been a straight course. The prevailing conditions could well have taken this boat in large and irregular-shaped loops across the ocean.

Inevitably the stress associated with their seemingly endless odyssey took its toll to the degree where heated exchanges were easily triggered. However, all knew that if they were to see San Blas ever again there was no room for such dissension. They had to pull together as a team. They needed to continue catching fish and rainwater if they were to survive. They were forever struggling to cope with the unavoidable sunburn and dehydration that came in the sauna-like heat of the tropics. At the same time their search of the horizon during daylight hours for any sign of civilisation in the form of land or a vessel continued unabated. They were tormented on countless occasions at sunrise and sunset when the low angle of the sun highlighted the clouds on the horizon and made them appear to be land. On every occasion there was hope, but within minutes it was gone.

For month after month one day blended into the next while their proven procedures for survival continued. They realised at one stage that, according to the calendar on Lucio's watch, they had been at sea for longer than the entire time it took Christopher Columbus to sail to the New World and back to Spain. That brought great mirth. What they didn't know at the time was that they had actually survived at sea longer than any other human being – by a long shot.

On the morning of 9 August 2006, more than nine months after they had stepped aboard the panga in San Blas, *los pescadores* were roused from their sleep by what they thought was the sound of a motor – but was this real, or was it a hoax like those they had experienced on so many previous occasions? Salvador had to know immediately. He leapt to his feet and strained his still bleary eyes in the direction of the sound, and sure enough there was a large ship a few hundred metres away ... and a launch with two men on board approaching the panga! This was not a mirage. After 289 life-sapping days their incredible ordeal was about to end!

The launch had come from the Taiwanese trawler *Koo's 102*, which was standing by in the background, and despite there being no common linguistic ground between the Mexicans and the Taiwanese, it was very obvious to the launch crew that Salvador, Lucio and Jesus were overjoyed to see them. Sign language mixed with overwhelming emotion was enough to have the boys from San Blas soon clambering aboard the launch and the panga being towed back to the mother ship where, from the moment they stepped aboard, one of the all-time great stories of survival at sea began to unfold. However, fractured communications between Salvador, Lucio, Jesus and the captain of the trawler contradicted a logical belief the trawler crew held — that the men they had found were extremely fortunate Pacific islanders who weren't far from home. The Mexicans persisted with scrawled sketches indicating where they had actually come from, but these and their animated gestures regarding their amazing voyage did nothing to convince the captain otherwise. It was not humanly possible for the men to have drifted an amazing 5000 nautical miles to the west of San Blas over a period of nine months, to a point where they were 2700 miles northeast of Australia and 600 miles from the Marshall Islands, where the *Koo's 102* was based.

In a bid to make sense of their story, the captain contacted the Ministry of Foreign Affairs in the Marshall Islands, which in turn contacted Mexican Government officials in New Zealand. Within 48 hours the information, including photographs of *los pescadores* aboard *Koo's 102*, had filtered through official channels to San Blas, where all was confirmed ... and from that moment the world had a story that was nothing short of a miracle.

CHAPTER 6

TO THE EDGE OF HELL AT HIGH SPEED

It was a superbly sunny Sunday sometime in late 1973 when there was an unexpected knock on the door at my home in Mosman, on the north side of Sydney Harbour.

When I opened the door I welcomed a friend: a 34-year-old guy with a dark and scrawny beard who was wearing his signature wide-brimmed, weather-beaten felt hat – the style you'd expect to see perched on the head of an old drover in the dusty Australian outback.

'Warby,' I said with an element of surprise. 'What brings you here?'

The massive smile that flashed across his face should have been a clue, but it didn't register.

'Follow me,' he said as he walked in and headed for the living room at the front of the house where large bay windows provided an unfettered view down to the street below, and out to picturesque Mosman Bay.

He said no more; he just kept smiling, then pointed to the street.

I followed his aim ... and there was his well-used, seven-year-old Ford Falcon sedan; but it was what was on the flat-bed trailer behind it that was cause for his excitement.

'Holy hellfire,' I said.

Then, before I could utter another word, Warby made a statement that has remained with me for more than four decades: 'Mundle,' he said, 'I am going to break the world water speed record with that!'

What I was looking at was a 30 foot (8.22 metre) arrowhead-shaped sled which had a monstrous jet engine strapped to it.

I couldn't get out the door and down to the street quickly enough, just to get a close-up look at this 'thing'. It was a classic case of 'I see it, but I'm struggling to believe it'.

I had been aware for a long time that Ken Warby had a burning desire to be the world's fastest man on water, and that he was building a boat to his own design to pursue that goal. But until that moment I could have been forgiven for believing that it was little more than a fantasy. Yes, Ken Warby was a champion speedboat racer, and an intelligent and creative character. But would he be the fastest man on water? No way!

My theory on the man was shared by many others. It was based on existing evidence regarding the magnitude of the challenge: England's Donald Campbell had died almost a decade earlier when trying to best his own world water speed record of 276.33 mph (444.71 kph); and American Lee Taylor's similarly mega-expensive effort had raised the bar by just 8.88 mph (14.29 kph) less than three years later.

Besides, this was among the most dangerous sporting endeavours the world had known: since 1940 the fatality rate among those who had tried to go beyond the record was a staggering 85 per cent.

But Warby soon had me convinced he was as undeterred about that figure as he was determined to better the existing mark. As he took me through the features of his design it became increasingly apparent that he wasn't being an effusive egotist who was clinging to the long coat-tails of an impossible dream. Instead, there was a pragmatic and mature individual who, through the application of common sense and creativity, was at the helm of a project that just might outclass big bucks and bravado, even though this somewhat crude-looking boat gave the impression that it had as much chance of being a skyrocket as it did a sleek, on-water missile.

The basis for what would become known as *Spirit of Australia* was as bold as it was simple when compared with what we knew of Campbell's and Taylor's designs. But the more Warby told me of the boat's features and his plans, the more I became convinced that what he lacked in dollars would be outweighed by the mind of a determined and creative genius. Beyond that, he had one overwhelming advantage over his predecessors in this world of jet-propelled speed across the water: testicles the size of church bells!

Ken Warby was born on 9 May 1939, the middle child of five born to Neville and Evelyn Warby. They lived in an old, Edwardian-style timber residence in New Lambton, an old coal mining village which is now part of the City of Newcastle, 100 kilometres north of Sydney. His upbringing was nothing out of the ordinary for those living in middle-class New Lambton, and his achievements at school certainly didn't qualify him for being dux of the class. As a 12-year-old he was forced to repeat 5th grade simply because of the high number of days he'd been absent that year caring for his ailing mother.

He wasn't the healthiest young lad either; he had what was referred to at the time as a 'tired heart', a condition that caused fatigue. Not surprisingly then, he wasn't the most successful participant in sporting activities, but he did have one very valuable natural asset: a photographic memory. He was also very skilled when it came to manual activities like woodwork, metalwork and technical drawing, so much so that, in his final year of schooling, he was awarded the highest marks in the woodworking exam in his home state of New South Wales.

Warby's life-changing experience came when he was aged just 16 — about the same time he left school.

He was wandering along a beach at a Boy Scouts' camp on the shores of Lake Macquarie, just to the south of Newcastle, when he spotted a 13 foot long racing speedboat pulled up on a beach. It was as if a bolt of lightning had struck him, or more appropriately a genie had wafted her way out of a bottle and beckoned him towards his future. The teenager was seemingly spellbound by the boat and the excitement it might offer: he had to have a boat just like that, and have it go as fast as possible. From that moment, his head was filled with dreams and he was determined to pursue them.

In no time, he was applying all three manual arts skills he had learned at school to his project – the end result being his very own 10 foot long plywood speedboat powered by a 21-year-old, four-cylinder petrol engine that had come out of a Ford Prefect motor car.

Unfortunately for the enthusiastic Warby, the project brought with it an abrupt reality check: there was nothing perfect about his design for the boat, or the choice of motor, but in the true spirit of a pioneer he persisted until he realised his efforts were futile. He had to accept there was no way of correcting the design flaws built into the boat he named *Hellcat*. He had made the mistake of designing hollow sections into the bottom of the hull, a feature that caused it to perform more like a bucking bull rather than a speedboat that would skim across the water at high speed. Each time he tried to accelerate, the bow flicked skyward and the entire unit threatened to do a bow-over-stern backflip. Interestingly though, his design did, in some ways, resemble the shape of a hydroplane, which *Spirit of Australia* would ultimately be.

There was only one solution – learn from the experience, sell the boat for whatever he could get for it and try again. He also had to accept there was no shortcut to success; youthful exuberance would not outsmart tried and proven formulas in the world of powerboat racing. It was then all about self-education, through reading boating publications and the American magazine *Popular Mechanics*, and becoming what the powerboat racing fraternity called a 'pit pest' – someone who is in the pits at race meetings, and who hounds all and sundry for information. He also researched everything he could relating to high

Calm before the storm: John Glennie's dreams of cruising around the South Pacific were built on images like this one of *Rose-Noëlle* resting serenely in a cove. However, those dreams were smashed by a savage storm off New Zealand's east coast. What followed was a 119-day fight by four men to survive in a world that was upside down.

Home, sweet home: Turn this main cabin upside-down and imagine walking on the ceiling in water waist deep: it gives you a small idea of what the sailors endured aboard the capsized *Rose-Noëlle*. The entrance to what became the 'cave' that they lived in during the ordeal is the small opening bottom left.

A death-defying midnight swim:
An enormous breaking wave
generated by a heinous storm caused
John Quinn to be lost overboard
from his 10.6-metre ocean racing
yacht, *MEM*, 50 miles offshore
during the 1993 Sydney–Hobart
race. Through a series of incredible
circumstances on a pitch black night,
he was rescued five hours later.

Quinn was steering *MEM*
during a storm-ravaged
night when a huge wave
loomed up like a cliff. It
broke into a fury of white
water and hammered
the yacht so ferociously
that it capsized. Quinn
was hurled overboard, his
safety harness snapped
and he disappeared into
the maelstrom.

Nine lives: Both as a legendary wartime pilot, and later in life on the sea, it was supreme skill laced with bravado, daring and heroics which so often saw Keith Thiele live another day.

Survivor of the heavens and high seas: Squadron Leader Keith Thiele (right), aged 22, became New Zealand's most highly decorated bomber and fighter pilot in World War II. He is seen here at RAF Station Bottesford, in England, in 1943 with RAAF Flight Lieutenant EK Sinclair, from Melbourne.

Dangerous liaison: In 1974, eight years after the tiny 9.1 metre long sloop, *Cadence*, became the smallest yacht ever to win the Sydney–Hobart race on corrected time, Thiele bought her so he could take up a life of cruising. It would be an adventure that almost killed him.

In his element: At just 12 years of age Damian Langley was working enthusiastically as a deckhand on trawlers operating out of Brisbane's Moreton Bay. From childhood, he was renowned for his skinny legs, as the quote on the photo suggests.

Still fishing: Langley, a real-life Crocodile Dundee on Australia's tropical east coast, shows off a big Maori wrasse that he caught. These fish – which today are a protected species in the Great Barrier Reef Marine Park – can grow to two metres in length and 190 kilograms.

Peter Meikle

Their time wasn't up: An incredibly lucky John Campbell with his three rescuers from Victoria Police Air Wing: David Key (left), Barry Barclay (centre) and pilot Darryl Jones (right). Their helicopter, with Campbell aboard, went within an ace of ditching in atrocious 25 metre seas during the massive 1998 Sydney–Hobart race search and rescue mission.

Steve Pyke

Missing Mexicans: After surviving nine months in an open boat near identical to the one behind them, the Mexican miracle men Lucio Rendon, Jesus Vidana and Salvador Ordonez pose for a photograph back home in San Blas. Vidana's T-shirt seems to say it all: Ask me if I care.

On a prayer and a cushion of air: Ken Warby, and his jet-powered boat, *Spirit of Australia*, blast across Blowering Dam and towards a remarkable world water speed record of 317 mph (511 kph).

The inspiring Kay Cottee went to the brink on the world's wildest oceans when she became the first woman to sail solo, non-stop and unassisted around the world.

Still a long way to go: Elinore and Ben Carlin pose with *Half-Safe* in Paris in June 1951 after taking 63 days to cross the Atlantic.

Circus parade: The rebuilt *Half-Safe* cruises through London's Piccadilly Circus in 1955. The huge waves the amphibious jeep somehow survived during the hurricane in the Atlantic were almost as high as the building behind it.

Winston Churchill was a classic timber yacht dating back to the first Sydney–Hobart race in 1945, but the tragic 1998 Hobart would be her last. Her aging bones could not cope with the magnitude of the storm that hit the fleet: *Winston Churchill* sank and three crew lost their lives.

Haunting image: Richard Winning walks away from a rescue helicopter after spending 24 hours in a liferaft, battling to survive the storm that ravaged the 1998 Sydney–Hobart race fleet. His yacht, *Winston Churchill*, was smashed and sunk by huge seas and only six of the nine crew survived.

performance speedboats, in particular Donald Campbell's world water speed record holder, *Bluebird K7* ... and it was this radical boat that fostered his thoughts about becoming the fastest man on water.

Almost every time there was a speedboat race meeting being staged out of the Royal Motor Yacht Club at Toronto, near Newcastle, Warby would be there to share in the excitement and feed his dream. By 1958, he had saved enough money to buy a speedboat, a clinker–hulled runabout which he named *Rebel*. It had a top speed of around 40 mph (64 kph), which wasn't enough for Warby, so he replaced the six-cylinder engine with a far more powerful V8. It was about this time, in 1959, that he also found employment: like so many other local lads he began work with one of Australia's largest companies, BHP, an industrial organisation that had a large facility in Newcastle. He took up a position as an apprentice mechanical engineer, a job that would set him on a career path which, as well as giving him an income, would provide expertise that would benefit his sporting pursuit. Four years after starting work with BHP, he married Jan, a shy and unassuming lass from

Sydney, who would years later struggle to cope with Warby's pursuit of his dream and the escalating profile that it brought.

Over the next decade, considerable success saw Warby's image in the sport of speedboat racing increase proportionately, his reputation being that of a perfectionist who was careful but seemingly fearless when it came to high speed on the water. By the mid-1960s he was experiencing the thrill that came with exceeding 100 mph (161 kph) in a hydroplane which he had rebuilt for its owner. This was a design concept that would also influence the shape of Warby's world record-breaking *Spirit of Australia*.

In 1967 he made the big time, winning the New South Wales Championship in a high-speed racing skiff which he had bought, tinkered with and re-named *Monte Cristo*. That was also the year in which he left BHP and established his own business, which sold a diverse range of commercial and industrial equipment.

In Bill Tuckey's biography of Warby, *World's Fastest Coffin on Water*, Warby's mate from this era Ross Morgan described him as being '... probably an extrovert – he gets an idea in his head and nothing stops him. He's a very self-reliant sort of person, prepared to give up jobs to stay involved in racing'.

Warby's ambition to become the fastest man on water was all-consuming for him by 1969, so much so that he had started to draft plans for the design of his boat on his kitchen table at home. It was a determination that had been fired by news which came on 30 June 1967: American Lee Taylor had driven his very expensive jet-powered hydroplane, *Hustler*, to a new world record speed of 285.21 mph (459 kph) – just a smidgen above Campbell's record.

However, you can't spend enthusiasm and desire. Warby was funnelling every possible cent into his project, but compared to his foreign counterparts, it represented a drop in a bucket. The fact that money wasn't readily available to finance the project no doubt influenced the design: it had to be inexpensive, simple, efficient and as easy as possible to build.

The next step towards achieving his goal came in November 1972 when he found a better paying job in Sydney. In no time, he had moved Jan and their three children to the North Shore suburb of Gordon, where he found a family home that met his one essential requirement: it had a backyard big enough for him to build *Spirit of Australia* – just.

Any doubt that Warby wasn't serious about this project was erased before the family relocated. He had already purchased two Westinghouse J34 jet engines from the Royal Australian Air Force for just $100 each, items which then had to be moved to Sydney along with the furniture and family. The J34 was seen to be the ideal form of propulsion for the boat, Warby's intention being to install one and use the other for spares. Soon after, though, the offer of a third J34 for just $65 proved irresistible, so it, too, became part of the campaign.

The move to Sydney also led to Warby gaining a higher media profile, especially in boating magazines; the November 1972 edition of the country's then premier marine publication, *Seacraft*, trumpeted the news of Warby's desire to become the fastest man on water in what was described as a '28-foot plywood jet-powered monster'.

Once again, the kitchen table became his drawing board for a design which he described as a drag hydroplane. A friend, John Biddlecombe, who was an amateur yacht designer, helped him with some of the finer calculations, but the concept was all Warby's. He was quoted in the Tuckey biography as saying: 'I'd got to the stage where I was tired of going around in circles [on a race course] and I'd seen photos of Taylor breaking world records and decided to build a drag hydroplane to do it. There was just one page of pencil detailed drawings ... I was sitting there fiddling with a pencil and I drew the boat. There were no secrets in it. People looked for things that weren't there. It was always going to be simple because I didn't want to go to aluminium, exotic carbon-fibre or fibreglass.'

As it would turn out, Warby's approach was as simple as the concept itself. The initial design came from gut instinct and experience. There was no wind tunnel testing, hydrodynamics or computer modelling applied to what would become *Spirit of Australia*. If there was any outside influence on the final shape, it came from Taylor's hydroplane concept, but Warby was convinced his boat would be better both aerodynamically and hydrodynamically. In particular, it would have the ability to remain safe on choppy water whereas both Taylor and Campbell required near glass-smooth conditions for their boats.

Before long, the campaign became an obsession for Warby. He quit work so he could concentrate on it 100 per cent, while Jan continued to work to support the family and provide what dollars she could for the boat.

As *Spirit of Australia* began to take shape, an increasing number of friends became enamoured by the project and offered what help they could. Warby spent every available moment at the coal face, with the sound of pieces of timber being hammered, sawn and drilled filling the air. His exceptional woodworking skills brought big dividends when it came to the strength and accuracy needed to build a boat strong enough for the high stress loads to which it would be subjected. His one big problem was that there was not enough room in the backyard for the boat to be turned right way up during the building process but he quickly devised a solution. He called on as many friends as possible to help carry the upside-down hull out of the yard to a nearby park where it was rolled over then carried back into the yard so the deck could be fitted.

A considerable benefit came when two jet engine specialists working at the Richmond RAAF base, on the outskirts of Sydney, provided their expertise free of charge so that the engine could be set up properly.

In mid-1974, Warby decided the boat was sufficiently advanced in design and construction – even though it didn't have a cowling over the engine or a protected cockpit – to have its first test run, so he towed it 500 kilometres west-southwest of Sydney to Griffith, where he knew there was a suitable well-protected lake. It was a successful launch, the boat reaching somewhere around 160 mph (257 kph), a speed that would have been good enough to see him break the Australian water speed record first up had he been trying for it officially. Warby would say after the run that he was more than happy with the way the boat performed during its acceleration period and that the only reason he came off the pace was that he was going to run out of water if he didn't stop – and as supporter Ken Evans recalls, that was the case on one occasion: 'Ken Warby turned up with the boat and launched it while we all watched from the shore. It took a lot of messing around to get the jet engine started, and when they finally got it going, Ken went to the end of the lake, lined the boat up and hit the throttle. It took off and after about 10 seconds he de-throttled to stop before the water reeds at the end of the lake. No such luck. He didn't realise that with nothing in the water to stop the boat it would just keep going. *Spirit* speared straight into the reeds and sent water birds flying everywhere. The boat finally stopped when it nudged the dirt bank. There was no damage only heaps of laughs from the crowd that was watching.'

For the purists this run was an impressive first effort, but for some so-called media experts, Warby provided good 'meat' for copy. They became sceptics and described *Spirit of Australia* as 'Warby's white elephant'. They were provided with more fodder when *Spirit*, travelling at more than 150 mph (241 kph) on Lake Munmorah, north of Sydney, hit a beer can that was floating in its path. As light and flimsy as the can was, the force of the impact was such that it split the timber hull and the boat began to sink. *Spirit of Australia* got to the shore and was beached, but not before water in the hull damaged the extremely hot turbine blades of the jet engine.

Negativity from some quarters continued until Warby claimed the national speed record on Lake Munmorah with an average of 167 mph (268.7 kph). In looking back on this period, Warby was quoted in Tuckey's book as saying: 'I was pretty much the joke of the town ... the boating media was having a field day. The boat wasn't finished, there was no engine cowling, and the Maritime Services Board [the waterways authority in NSW] refused to let me run until the registration numbers [on the hull] were made bigger and I had passed a noise meter test.' With the Australian record to his credit, the sniping diminished. There was then a growing belief that Warby might just have the projectile needed to achieve his dream.

While *Spirit of Australia* left little doubt she could be a contender for the world record, Warby had to curb his zeal and become a realist. There were two major problems: the boat still required considerable refinement, and there was no major sponsor on the horizon who would provide the funds needed to mount a full-blown assault on the record. By this time he was back at work, but he still did not have the income needed to fund everyday life and simultaneously pursue his goal.

Such was his determination that he abandoned his employment as a sales manager and went into a profession few, if any, would have expected. He discovered he had a talent for painting miniature artworks, and this led to him going into shopping centres far and wide and doing 'paintings while you wait'. They were primarily landscapes and were painted on small pieces of timber, including bark. (Like many, I wouldn't have believed this until I actually saw him painting.) It was work that proved profitable, so before long the *Spirit of Australia* project was back on track.

Making things considerably better for Warby was the fact that he had experienced even greater inspiration for the project through a meeting with Professor Tom Fink, an aerodynamic expert from the Imperial College in London, who had worked with Donald Campbell on *Bluebird K7*. Fink was the then dean of engineering at the University of New South Wales in Sydney.

Tuckey's biography of Warby records Fink's first impressions of him: 'I hadn't heard of Ken until he walked into my office at the University of NSW. He said he had read about me in Campbell's book. I think … he thought I might give him some advice on the next phase of development of his boat and I said something like, well, it's always interesting to meet somebody who intends to kill himself and he said something like, well, that's why I've come here – to avoid that.'

Warby's recollection of the meeting was that, on learning about the project and the design of *Spirit of Australia*, Fink had become quite excited and consequently asked to see the wind tunnel model data for the design. Warby explained he didn't have a model or data, it was simply a home-grown concept, but he would make a model so it could be tested. When Fink got to test that model in a wind tunnel, then analysed the numbers, he declared, much to Warby's delight, that *Spirit of Australia*'s test figures were better than *Bluebird K7*'s. However, while saying this, he stressed that the boat's engine needed to be moved forward one metre to provide better fore-and-aft stability at speed.

Further reinforcement for the potential of the project came with the declaration that *Spirit of Australia* would be safe in conditions that would have been deemed extremely rough and dangerous for Campbell's *Bluebird K7*. Interestingly, after *Bluebird K7* became airborne on Coniston Water, disintegrated and sank, taking Campbell with it, Fink, who was in Australia at the time, declared that Campbell had obviously ignored all the rules he had been given for his record attempt. Tuckey wrote in his book that Fink attributed the crash to Campbell's decision to make the return run immediately after the first run where he had clocked 328 mph (527.86 kph). The problem was that he made the second run before the wash from the first had dissipated. Fink believed that hitting the choppy water caused *Bluebird K7* to exceed her safe pitching angle of just 5.5 degrees, the point where the aerodynamics of the boat changed dramatically. In an instant the boat took off like a jet fighter then cartwheeled down the course. In addition to this theory, Fink also stated that while the *Bluebird K7* design could travel safely at around 280 mph (450.62 kph), he had expected Campbell would be killed should he ever reach between 315 and 325 mph (between 508 and 523 kph). He added, 'It all looked quite suicidal really.' Incredibly, the same man was described in Tuckey's book as saying the *Spirit of Australia's* design was 'very cunning'.

The most obvious change to *Spirit of Australia* that came from Fink's involvement was the addition of a tailplane – a vertical fin mounted at the back of the boat which carried short wings at the top. It was a feature that would better control the balance and direction of the boat when it was travelling at high speed. This tailplane was built by an aircraft component specialist using second-hand wing tips that came from a Cessna 182 aircraft.

While Warby and his associates continued to search for sponsorship, he also spent time looking for a suitable venue for his record attempt. Eventually, he chose Blowering Dam, near Tumut in southern New South Wales. The relatively straight and narrow waterway, more than 15 kilometres long, came into existence when the Tumut River was dammed as part of the Snowy Mountains hydroelectric scheme, a project which the Australian Government initiated soon after the conclusion of World War II.

He made his first trial run there in March 1976, when *Spirit of Australia* was still far from fully developed aerodynamically. For example, the streamlined engine cowling and tailplane were not fitted. Even so, Warby satisfied himself by creating a new Australian water speed record with an average speed of 177 mph (285 kph). This run also contributed to the learning curve confronting him and the development of the boat: he came away from it concerned that the boat showed signs of wanting to become airborne when travelling at near 200 mph (322 kph).

In September 1977, Warby decided everything was in readiness for a record attempt, but it would be a short-lived 'readiness'. A few weeks later, when he was at the Fairbairn RAAF base in Canberra to give the boat's jet engine a test run, a screwdriver which he had inadvertently left in the boat caused major problems. It was sucked into the engine and became shrapnel, destroying the turbine blades as it went.

The only solution was to retrieve the $65 jet engine that was lying in the open air in Warby's backyard in Sydney and install it in the boat. It was an overnight round trip which led to the replacement engine being fitted within 24 hours. But when it was installed and fired up, there was another setback: the afterburner, which had been added to provide additional thrust, exploded into a ball of flame and destroyed itself after a fuel line failed. Warby had no alterative then but to make the record attempt without the benefit of an afterburner.

On 30 October, after a damaged rudder mounting was repaired (the result of a high-speed impact with a duck during one trial run), Warby had *Spirit of Australia* skimming across Blowering Dam at an Australian record speed of 245.82 mph (395 kph) – only 40 mph (60 kph) shy of Taylor's world water speed record.

That ended the current endeavour, but less than three weeks later, *Spirit of Australia* and the entire support team, including Tom Fink, were back at the dam and ready to go once more.

Fink had obviously been doing some deep thinking and complex calculations to determine what level of thrust would be required from the jet engine if the boat was to challenge the world record without the benefit of an afterburner. One of his calculations revealed that the drag – i.e. water friction – that came from the rudder amounted to 2400 lbs (1087 kilos) when the boat was travelling at 300 mph (482.8 kph). At the same time, if just two inches (five cms) were cut from the bottom of the rudder, Warby would still be able to maintain directional stability, yet the drag would be reduced by 400 lbs (181 kilos). This, in turn, converted to the equivalent of 400 lbs of additional thrust. Warby's own 'fly by the seat of your pants' calculations were complete in no time: he agreed with Fink. Within minutes the boat was on the trailer and being towed to a service station in the nearby town of Tumut, where far from high-tech surgery would be carried out. The plan was to cut the two inches of metal from the bottom of the rudder blade using an oxy-acetylene torch, but, unbeknown to Fink, Warby took matters into his own hands and cut off an additional half-inch from the bottom of the rudder because he believed that the boat would benefit even more. This crude attack on the metal appendage was finished off with the use of a rotary grinder. There was no doubt in Warby's mind about placing his faith in that ultimate modification to the rudder, as he would soon after explain how vital it was to controlling the boat: 'I know that if the rudder turns more than one-quarter of a degree, the stern of *Spirit* will try to meet the bow and I'll meet my Maker,' he told a journalist.

The surgery to the rudder certainly delivered the desired results. On 20 November 1977, *Spirit of Australia* made two blistering runs across Blowering Dam, going through the timed one kilometre distance at more than 290 mph (466.71 kph) one way, and up to 300 mph (482.8 kph) the other. This was enough to convince Warby that the average speed for the two runs would make him the holder of the world water speed record, but within minutes his simmering elation had turned to deflation: his average was 10 mph (16 kph) under Taylor's world record. While certain the timers had got it wrong, Warby had no option but to accept the jury's decision. Consequently, there was only one thing to do: have another crack at it there and then.

With his adrenalin pumping and his determination at a level never before seen, Warby did an about-turn and headed back to the boat. As he went, he declared for the benefit of all around him, 'Well, we've got

Campbell, now let's go and get that other bastard!' He was referring to Taylor's record using a word which, in Australia, is more often than not seen as a term of endearment.

Adding to his frustration was that it had started to rain. He made one run, but it was a 'slow' 266 mph (428 kph), so he decided to have that erased by officials and wait for the weather to clear. An hour later, *Spirit of Australia* was lined up and ready to go once more – and the result was something special. Warby had clocked 302 mph (486.02 kph), making him the first man in the world to officially exceed 300 mph (482.8 kph) on water. Quick calculations by his team told him that that he only needed to do 287 mph (461.88 kph) on the second run to claim the world record. (To achieve the record, two runs – one each way across a one kilometre timed distance – must be completed within one hour.)

However, drama quickly followed. Some of the locals, who used the lake for water skiing, had had enough of the Warby 'circus' having exclusive access to the waterway, so in protest a speedboat ran across the course area and created a wake which was likely to make it too dangerous for *Spirit of Australia* to attempt the second run within the one hour time limit. A tirade of abuse filled the air between the two sides on shore — those supporting Warby and those supporting the water skiers — but Warby remained oblivious to it. His only concern was that if *Spirit of Australia* was at record-breaking speed when it hit the wash, which was still rolling across the water, his boat could well become airborne.

It was a distraction he didn't need: he had enough on his hands simply controlling the boat under the best of circumstances. He explained that at high speed *Spirit of Australia* 'walked a lot' (rocked from side to side), adding 'there's more to driving a boat than sitting in the cockpit like a bag of wet cement'. During each high speed run he didn't simply steer the boat and operate the accelerator: he was as much a jet fighter pilot as a boat driver. At the start of each run the engine would be fired up until a blast of flame darted from its back end, then, after running it at idle speed for a short time, Warby would gently increase the pressure on the foot throttle so that the boat had sufficient momentum for it to be steered and lined up for the run. Once ready, he had about six kilometres ahead of him before he entered the one kilometre long stretch where officials recorded his speed.

On the return run, *Spirit of Australia* increased speed at a gentle rate initially, but as she gained pace Warby planted his foot down harder and harder on the accelerator, and the speed increased proportionately. Once the boat got onto the surface of the water and began riding on a cushion of air, there was no holding her back — she was off like a startled gazelle. Quite often, she could be seen to rock gently from side to side as she began to go through 100 mph then head for 200 mph and beyond. All the time Warby's concentration was at 100 per cent. It was vital that he held the boat on course while he watched where the needles were pointing on three important gauges: the indicators for the exhaust temperature, the oil pressure and the revs, which could reach 12,500 rpm. He also was in radio contact with his shore team, calling his speed which was being recorded via an aircraft-style Pitot tube and displayed on another dial.

With the timed section behind him Warby could start to feel excited: he knew it had been an incredibly fast run, but only the official timers could confirm it. Regardless, instinct told him his childhood dream was about to be realised. For the moment though, he could only guide his boat back to the base camp on the bank of the dam and wait. He climbed out of the tiny and tight cockpit, went aft and clambered up onto the T-section of the tailplane from where he gave a 'V' salute with each hand, all the time soaking up the adulation coming from his supporters. Once at the shore he leapt onto the land and immediately went up to his still trembling mother, Sal, and hugged her while his proud father looked on. However, his wife, Jan, and their three sons – Peter, David and Michael – were not there, as Warby had decided from the outset it was best if they weren't exposed to his death-defying exploits.

Eventually the official timers emerged from their huddle and stood before an anxious crowd. The announcement that followed brought a tumultuous roar echoing through the hills around the dam: *Spirit of Australia* had set a new world water speed record of 288.6 mph (464.46 kph), just 2.962 mph (4.77 kph) better than Taylor's time with *Hustler*. It wasn't much, but a record is a record: Warby's backyard boat, fitted with a $65 jet engine, had done it.

When asked how it felt to be travelling at such an incredible speed across the water, he replied, 'Geeze, mate, the land looks like it's coming at you real quick.' Of the many memorable quotes that Warby delivered for the benefit of the media at the time, this was among the best.

Bringing additional kudos to his remarkable effort was that he had just become the first person to design, build and drive his own boat to a world water speed record – and at a fraction of the cost of the other campaigns. Incredibly, the national and international media virtually ignored this amazing achievement, one that had come from the most basic foundation. It was a disappointment that Warby had to accept; he also realised that the lack of media mileage at this time would probably devalue any future record attempt in the eyes of sponsors, should he decide to continue.

It also rated little mention in America, but the previous record holder, Lee Taylor, knew about it almost immediately. He expressed no desire to hand over the world water speed record trophy, a solid silver figurine of Boadicea mounted on a wooden base which had originally been created as a yachting trophy for King Edward VII in 1870. Instead, Taylor wrote to Warby and asked him to send copies of his time sheets for the record run, and a photograph of *Spirit of Australia*. It would be another 18 months before the American finally relented and sent the trophy to its rightful owner down under.

Despite being pushed to a media backwater there was a degree of solace for Warby some six months after breaking the world record, when he was declared a Member of the Most Excellent Order of the British Empire (MBE). The award, recognising his achievement, was announced in the Queen's Birthday Honours List that year.

Now, for the first time in years, he had time on his hands, time to ponder his future. His greatest realisation was that the *Spirit of Australia* project had consumed his life for almost four decades. The quest for the world water speed record was all he knew: there had been nothing else. It was a mind-numbing reality check and he decided there was only one answer ... go again!

Within weeks Warby was declaring to anyone interested that he would soon make an attempt on his own water speed record, his intention being to raise the average speed to more than 300 mph (482.8 kph), a near inconceivable goal.

Around this time he also took his first ever trip to America, primarily to seek sponsors, but also to meet the man whose record he had beaten — Lee Taylor. This was before Taylor had agreed to relinquish the trophy to his Australian rival. However, there was a bonus for Warby: he managed to learn a lot about the boat Taylor intended to use in a $2.5 million campaign (about 25 times more expensive than Warby's project) to regain the crown. It was a surprisingly large and unusually shaped 40 foot (12.2 metre) long, rocket-powered hydroplane built from aluminium, which was named *US Discovery II*. Warby soon told friends he didn't like the look of Taylor's boat, which resembled a long arrow with small floats on either side of the bow. His prediction was that it would flip over at high speed.

Back home, sponsors began to emerge for Warby's new campaign including swimwear company Speedo, Channel 10 TV and the regional department store group Fosseys. The RAAF had also agreed to allow its apprentices to work on Warby's jet engine as part of their training program, and with this there came a surprise. When the youngsters started work on the jet engine that set the record, it became evident that it had been running well below maximum thrust.

Once that was fixed and his boat was better prepared than ever, Warby returned to Blowering Dam in early October 1978 to do what no previous world water speed record holder had done: raise his own record. All the others had died in the attempt! Unfortunately though, while he knew he and the boat were ready, the course was not: it was littered with snags, tree limbs and bits of foliage, any piece of which could spell disaster for *Spirit of Australia* when travelling at record-breaking speed. The course was eventually cleared of the dangers by supporters who took to the water in small boats.

The first record attempt, which came on Saturday, 7 October 1978, was full of frustration, but even so Warby knew he was close to raising the bar, and he was right. The following day would prove to be *the* day.

Conditions were ideal for *Spirit of Australia*, with ripples between three and four inches (between seven and 10 cm) high spread right across the course: the ideal surface for minimising drag on the hull.

By this time, Warby had so much experience with the boat it seemed like just another day at the office for him. He said a high speed run seemed like little more than lining up the boat, putting his foot down on the accelerator, and 'letting her go' – and go she did! Perfectly trimmed and rocking ever so softly from side to side, *Spirit of Australia* flashed through the one kilometre timed distance at a stunning speed – more than 300 mph (482.8 kph), a time that meant it had taken little more than seven seconds to cover the measured kilometre. Another similar run on the return would mean that Warby's record-raising effort was complete ... but drama lurked. The jet engine would not re-start after the boat had been refuelled, and with the one hour time limit for the two runs to be completed approaching all too rapidly, the pressure was on Warby and his mechanics. One more try and suddenly a flash of flame darted from the back end of the jet engine: it burst into life. The boat was ready to go.

Warby aimed *Spirit* down the course, accelerated and in no time had once again turned his boat into a projectile. Everything was on song as man and boat rocketed towards the timed kilometre, and the speedo was confirming the speed at around 350 mph (563.27 kph).

In a flash, little more than six seconds, the timed section was behind him, so Warby eased his foot off the throttle, and as he did a feeling of relief and euphoria flowed through his veins: he was confident a new record was with him. The support crew manning small boats moved in to help guide *Spirit of Australia* back to the shore where Warby's ardent supporters were waiting, including his emotionally drained mother.

On approach Warby extricated himself from the tiny cockpit, went aft and leapt up onto the top of the

T-shape tailplane – then, just like last time, thrust his arms in the air, simultaneously delivering a 'V' for victory sign with his fingers.

Once back onshore, with the official timekeepers wanting to make sure they had checked and triple checked the numbers, it became an agonising wait for what everyone believed to be an inevitable result. When the moment arrived, the roar confirmed that Ken Warby had done on water what no other person had before him. The average speed was 317.59 mph (511.12 kph) – a staggering 29 mph (46.67 kph) better than his previous record. The man with the battered felt hat and the bushy beard had this time become the first to take a boat through both the 300 mph and 500 kph barriers. His name, and that of his boat, would now be etched forever on the world water speed record trophy for a second time.

Two years later Lee Taylor decided everything was ready for *US Discovery II* to return the world water speed trophy to him, but sadly Warby's prophecy that the boat was a potential killer proved true. On 13 November 1980, on Lake Tahoe in California, *US Discovery II* suddenly veered off course while travelling at around 250 mph (400 kph), rolled over and exploded like a bomb, killing Taylor as it went.

Soon after, Ken Warby, the man who lived out a boyhood dream and built a boat in his backyard that proved to be the fastest in the world, was heard to say rather ruefully, 'I don't have to book a big function centre for old drivers' reunions.'

CHAPTER 7

TWICE TO THE EDGE

In little more than one hour John Campbell cheated death twice.

First, he was knocked unconscious and lost overboard from a yacht during a wicked storm. Then, after being rescued by helicopter paramedics in miraculous circumstances, and seemingly on the way to safe sanctuary on land, he and his rescuers went within an ace of crashing into a nefarious patch of ocean that was already a maritime graveyard.

Campbell's story was one of the more amazing among countless that emerged from the disastrous 1998 Sydney to Hobart yacht race. It was where a storm of cyclonic proportions created unprecedented conditions across Bass Strait, a notorious section of the 627 nautical mile course. It was a concoction of 80 knot-plus winds and a fast-flowing adverse current which, at the extreme, created gargantuan seas – some near 30 metres high and bearing a 10 metre breaking crest of white water.

Just before Christmas that year Campbell flew out of his hometown, Seattle, Washington, bound for Australia and on a mission. His father, Wally, drove him to the airport and during the journey they talked about the fact that this would be third time lucky in his bid to complete the Sydney to Hobart race. He held little doubt of achieving his long-held dream, especially after his friend Peter Meikle, from Melbourne, assured him the yacht they would be sailing, the 13 metre long sloop *Kingurra*, was very robust and seaworthy. Also, *Kingurra*'s owner, Peter Joubert, was the designer, and the yacht's long ocean racing record included 14 Hobarts.

The fact he had raced twice towards Hobart and not made it was like getting only halfway to happiness for 32-year-old Campbell. To complete the course had become one of life's pinnacles and he was determined this time to know what it was like to look down from the top. Besides that challenge, the Sydney to Hobart was a very different and far more exciting sailing experience to racing around the buoys on the protected waters off Seattle. Racing to Hobart was something he just had to do.

It was Christmas Day, the eve of the big race, when he arrived in Sydney, and the docks at the Cruising Yacht Club of Australia were the busiest part of town. Crewmembers who were staying aboard race yachts which were docked at the club were shuttling to and from the showers in the two-level brick and near perfectly square clubhouse. Breakfast was also on the agenda on the wooden deck that extended out over the waters of Sydney's famous harbour. For most it was bacon and eggs, a meal which for some helped absorb the liquid excesses they had enjoyed as part of their Christmas Eve celebrations at the club.

As he stepped aboard *Kingurra*, Campbell quickly realised what Meikle meant when he said this yacht would get them to Hobart. Its powerful shape and obviously strong laminated timber construction left no doubt that the designer was a man of the sea. Back in

1993, in what was a horribly rough Hobart race, Joubert and his crew had excelled themselves over a 28-hour period by rescuing another crew from a sinking yacht.

In 1998 conditions would be considerably worse. Still, after an exceptionally fast run south from Sydney under spinnaker *Kingurra* was coping well with the powerful change in the weather which had swept in from the Southern Ocean. She was powering along under a spitfire jib that was set from the inner forestay. The mainsail had been lowered and the boom was lashed securely to the deck on the windward side.

It was late afternoon on 27 December, and like all other yachts in that locale – between 30 and 60 miles into Bass Strait – *Kingurra* was close to the centre of what would become a weather bomb. And the crew didn't know it.

Soon the 43-footer was copping a thorough hiding from winds of between 60 and 70 knots and breaking seas that often popped up like pyramids more than 18 metres high. In some cases, even with waves so large, it was only six or seven seconds before the yacht had travelled from one wave crest, down 60 feet into the trough, then up another 60 feet to the crest of the next. Before long conditions had worsened to the degree where Joubert, having been a sailor and yacht designer for the majority of his 74 years, knew that of all the storms he had experienced, few, if any, matched the fury of this one.

'The spray and the spume were blowing about 60 feet into the air, straight off the tops of the waves,' he said, describing his most indelible memories of the storm. 'The waves were enormous. Many of them were very steep-fronted. A lot of them had breaking tops for the last two or three metres.'

Around 4 pm Meikle came on deck for his watch and was amazed by how threatening the conditions had become in the four hours he was below.

'How long has it been like this?' he asked one of the crew.

'A couple of hours,' was the response.

'I looked around and thought, "This is already at the top end of what they had forecast," and the information from the guys was that it was still building. I recalled what I'd heard *Sword of Orion* come on the radio and say, with some degree of urgency in the radio operator's voice: they had 78 knots of wind. They wanted people to pay attention to what they were saying because they thought this was a serious issue.

'I then knew what they meant.'

Meikle took over the helm and was quite surprised by how well *Kingurra* was coping: 'It was quite pleasant sailing, with the exception of the rain and spray. We were starting to consistently see 60 knots of wind on the gauge and it felt like I was being stabbed in the face with a fork.

'When the wind did get to 60 knots the noise increased to such a level that we couldn't communicate. It was really a low-pitched roar. We started to get some significant spindrift at that point and it was widespread. It was like spume; big, heavy spray just loaded with water.

'There were large white bales of it and it would extend downwind from the waves a long, long way. That was a little disconcerting because it was when the wind instrument stayed pegged on the maximum reading of 68 knots.

'Those of us on deck began to realise we had to be fairly sharp. For the first time I knew we had to really pay attention because the conditions were becoming so serious.

'The waves at that point were starting to break all around us. To me it was beginning to sound like trouble. It started to cross our minds that we were no longer really racing; all we were doing was keeping the boat as comfortable as possible, trying not to break it.'

Having twice invited Campbell to join him as a crewmember for the Hobart race then failing to reach the finish, Meikle was feeling somewhat obliged to get him to the line, and a ride on *Kingurra* was probably the safest bet you could have. So much so that Meikle had promised Campbell that if he didn't get his mate to Hobart he would pay for his return airfare from Seattle.

Now, here was Campbell sitting in the cockpit with Meikle, being plastered by spray, wind, waves and rain. He was uncomfortable, chilled, soaked to the bone and tethered by his safety harness, wondering what the hell he was doing there.

'I never really sensed danger because all I'd ever known of this race was that it blows,' said the sailor from Seattle. 'Also, everyone held supreme confidence in the boat, that it would be able to handle anything, so I didn't think there was need for panic or real concern. The boat seemed to be handling it really well and everything was completely under control. But I know I said to myself that afternoon, "Gee, we're going to have one tough, uncomfortable, wet and brutal ride for maybe the next 24 to 36 hours." The rest of the crew were just kind of hunkering down because there wasn't all that much to do, so I did the same.'

Every 15 minutes or so a great wave would crash right over *Kingurra*, absolutely drenching the crew and turning the yacht into a semi-submerged object. It reminded Campbell of a pre-start reply that came to his question about how dry it was in the cockpit in rough upwind conditions: 'You almost never get water here. Just a little bit of spray.' He was then thinking, 'This is a little bit more than spray.'

The next recollection for Campbell and Meikle was a sudden increase in wind velocity: 'It was as though someone had flicked a switch,' said Campbell. 'It went from your typical howling wind to screeching. It was very high pitched — just like a police whistle. I sensed there and then that the conditions had just stepped up a notch. It was as though it wasn't the wind whistling; it was just that we had gone into an entirely new situation. It was the most bizarre thing I've ever experienced.

'The noise was so loud you could no longer communicate with the guy next to you. You just stayed hunkered down in the cockpit, unable to look anywhere but at the floor. We were all concerned about the occasional big wave, so I spent most of my time making sure the cockpit drains were clear so the water would drain out.

'The next thing I remember is being half a mile away from the boat and wondering how the hell I got there!'

Campbell had been sitting hunched in the cockpit, just forward of the wheel and compass binnacle. It was close to 7 pm, and as it was summer it was still quite light. Conditions were murky, however; visibility was down to little more than half a mile for most of the time.

'The scene had a foreboding sense to it,' said Meikle. 'The spray was incredible and every now and then we started to see some really big waves; I mean sort of 50 to 60 footers and cresting. You'd be in a patch where by luck you were okay, but there would be other huge breaking bits all around you. You just thought how lucky you were not to be where a wave was breaking.'

By this time the crew had accepted that there were two options open to them – the finish in Hobart, or Eden, back on the mainland. They could see no logic in running off with the seas: it was far too dangerous. For Meikle there was little difference between being on the other tack and heading for Eden, or staying on their current tack towards Hobart: there would be no significant change in the angle of the course they would sail towards the waves.

'We all seemed to be quite happy,' said Meikle. 'I remember looking at one of the crew wearing my ski goggles for eye protection. The next instant I heard him shout out, "Shit! Watch out!"

'We just ducked our heads in expectation of a whole lot of water coming over us and into the cockpit. I thought I'd just keep my head down so water could run down my neck. I was so wet anyway it didn't matter.

'The next few seconds are a bit vague, but I must have spun around and grabbed my safety harness strop as I slipped off the side of the cockpit. At that stage we must have been over at 90 degrees and still going. I remember being sort of pummelled from side to side like I was in a giant jacuzzi and thinking, "This is a bit weird." Water was creeping up my legs then suddenly I realised things had gone quiet; there was less water action and it was dark.

'I had my eyes open and I was able to breathe but I couldn't work out where I was. I realised then that the boat was basically inverted and that I was actually in an air pocket underneath the cockpit. Then, after about five seconds the boat righted itself in one incredible hurry. White water was everywhere and I found myself sitting in the bottom of the cockpit. I leapt up and then I thought to myself, "Where the hell is everyone?"

In an instant Meikle felt gutted, realising there was no one to be seen on the yacht. He struggled to comprehend that a few seconds earlier there were four crew in the cockpit, and now there were none.

He also noticed that the boom, which had been lashed down, had been subjected to so much force that the large mainsheet winch used to control it had been ripped out of its solid mounting on the deck. Then came the first sign of life: a crewman appeared from around the side of the cabin down near the leeward rail. He'd gone out through the lifelines before being washed back on board again. Meikle then saw that Antony Snyders and John Campbell were suspended on their safety harnesses over the stern of the yacht. Snyders appeared to be okay, despite having shattered his knee, but there was immediate concern for Campbell.

'He was hanging there with his head just above the water and his harness strop was tight around his neck,' Meikle recalled. 'It was a horrible sight. I yelled down the hatch, "We need everyone on deck now!"'

What those on deck didn't know then was that there were actually two emergencies – one on deck and the other below. An immense amount of water had flooded the cabin and Joubert had been injured; he had blood coming from a nasty gash to his head and was badly shocked. There were even suggestions that *Kingurra* might be sinking.

Meikle knew he had to get Campbell back aboard, but there was no one to help. He straddled the pushpit rail at the stern and used all his strength to lift Campbell and managed to get his shoulders to the top of the lifelines, but then couldn't muster the additional energy needed to drag him over the lifelines and onto the deck. Meikle then realised Campbell was unconscious, but it didn't occur to him that he might be dead.

'At that point Tony Vautin came on deck and started to help me lift John, and that's when we got into trouble. John was wearing a wet weather jacket which had a slippery lining, and to our horror – and I will never forget the feeling – the jacket started to turn inside out as we lifted him, and he just slipped out the bottom of it. His right arm came out first and I grabbed his hand and held on to him. He was totally unresponsive. Then his other arm slipped out of the jacket. I desperately tried to hang on to his right hand, but he was getting washed around. He was facing me with his eyes closed just making these gurgling sounds. It was as if he was aware that he was slipping out of his jacket. I won't forget the noises he made as he slipped out. Then another big wave came along and I could hold him no longer. He was torn away from my grasp.'

Meikle shouted 'Man overboard' and called for someone below to note the yacht's position for a search area. He also took a bearing on where Campbell was last seen. Much to the horror of those on deck, Campbell drifted away face down. Lifesaving equipment had already been thrown into the water in a desperate hope that he might regain consciousness and get to it.

The engine was their next hope: it could help them get back to him. But the moment they were about to put it into gear it took a big slurp of the water that was washing around inside the cabin and died, refusing to start again. The only option then was to head the yacht into the wind as much as possible to slow its progress while the remnants of the tattered jib were lowered to the deck.

The next scene for the crew was almost unbelievable. The man given the task of acting as the spotter on Campbell saw his seaboots float to the surface as he crested a wave; then shortly afterwards his wet weather pants were seen to float away. Next there was a feeble wave of the hand towards the yacht.

Despite being badly injured, Peter Joubert had managed to stagger to the navigation station and grab the HF radio microphone. He pressed the red button indicating the desired frequency and called Lew Carter who was aboard the radio relay vessel for the race, *Young Endeavour*. 'This is *Kingurra*. May Day, May Day, May Day. We have a man overboard and we'd like a helicopter.'

'Who's gone overboard?' asked Carter. 'What's his name?'

'John Campbell.'

'What's he wearing? Has he got a life jacket?'

'Negative.'

'Has he got coloured clothing?'

'Negative. He's in blue thermal underwear.'

'Have you activated your EPIRB?'

'Not yet.' Joubert then collapsed. He had a ruptured spleen and countless broken ribs.

The EPIRB – emergency beacon – was then activated while Campbell drifted further and further away. The decision was to keep the EPIRB on the yacht as it was still not known if *Kingurra* was sinking. The trysail was then thrown up on deck but not set. It was decided that they might lose sight of Campbell during that manoeuvre, and they could well be blown even further away from him. By then Campbell was 100 metres away, but they could only see him when both the yacht and he were simultaneously on the crest of the huge waves.

It was then decided to try angling *Kingurra* at about 80 degrees to the wind, an angle which actually gave it some forward motion despite having no sails set. After a set time it would be gybed around, then it headed back up towards the wind and held on that course for the same time. This was the only way they could remain in close proximity to Campbell, who they could still see on the odd occasion.

A short time later crewman Alistair Knox popped his head up through the cabin hatchway and announced there was a ship being redirected and a chopper was on its way. It was then a waiting game.

The Victorian police helicopter *Polair 1* had just arrived in Mallacoota to refuel and join the huge search and rescue operation when they were informed of the *Kingurra* May Day situation. *Polair 1*'s crew was scrambled and the chopper quickly lifted off, bound for *Kingurra*'s position. Once in the air it raced towards its target as though flung from a catapult. It was experiencing at least 70 knots of tailwind so was travelling over the water at around 200 knots, and was in the search area within 10 minutes.

Time was rapidly going against Campbell and his would-be rescuers: it was early evening and it would be dark within 90 minutes.

'My first memory is of coming out of an unconscious state and seeing the boat in the distance,' said Campbell. 'I was completely disoriented. It seemed like the yacht was about half a mile away. I had no idea where I was, how I got there or why I was in the water. My initial thoughts were, "This is a dream. This has got to be a dream." Then a realisation washed over me that it was not a dream: I was in real trouble.

'A couple of things were going on in my mind. I wasn't really sure of my level of consciousness. The guys said they saw me within about 10 seconds of being lost, face down and apparently unconscious, but then I acknowledged the boat and waved madly towards them. I have no memory of that, but obviously I was conscious sooner than I remembered.'

Campbell believed the yacht was close enough for the crew to spot him and that they would sail back to pick him up. He assumed they were searching for him as the yacht appeared to be circling back and forth in a search pattern.

Before long he decided it best to swim towards the yacht: 'On the top of every wave I'd stop swimming and frantically wave my arms in the hope someone would see me, then they'd come cruising back and pick me up. But every time I thought I was on some kind of course that might bring me closer they would turn and go in the other direction. This chasing game went on for a while then I became somewhat depressed.'

He had no memory of taking off any of his sailing gear, but he was grateful that he had decided to wear oversize seaboots for the very reason that they would be easy to remove if ever he fell overboard: 'It's a decision that saved my life.'

Campbell saw his situation becoming more desperate as the yacht drifted further away. He was convinced he had to somehow get to it: no other form of rescue had entered his mind. But his determination to survive was being tested to the maximum by the 20 metre seas that were continually bearing down on him. Being upwind of *Kingurra* meant he was facing away from the waves, so he couldn't see them coming. The biggest waves repeatedly picked him up, sent him tumbling down the face and submerged him: 'They were massive waves and they'd break on top of me. I'd take a big, deep breath and tumble through the whole thing, then I'd come up for air. Incredibly though, I don't really remember being scared by the waves. Everything else, apart from watching the yacht, was an unnecessary distraction. I had no sense of cold and I had no sense of injury. Any of those other sensory things just slipped my mind. I don't know if that was a function of having a very cloudy mind or because it was a survival mechanism.'

Campbell was beginning to see the yacht far less frequently. He'd been in the ocean for 30 minutes, but to him it seemed like 10. He was beginning to think there was no chance of rescue when he thought he heard the sound of a helicopter above the roar of the wild weather. At the same time he saw a flare being set off from the yacht, and moments later a helicopter appeared overhead: 'They were there then next thing they cruised away. My heart sank. For the first time I was starting to think I was nearing the end of my endurance; that I might have just another 10 minutes of energy left.'

When *Polair 1* departed Melbourne's Essendon airport soon after 4 pm on 27 December in response to an AusSAR request to join the Sydney to Hobart search and rescue operation the crew was literally flying into the unknown. Senior Constable Darryl Jones was the pilot, Senior Constable Barry Barclay the winch operator and Senior Constable David Key the rescue crewman.

'I became well aware that we were flying into conditions I had never imagined – conditions we had never trained in or been trained for,' said Jones.

The 160km/h tailwinds pressing the twin engine French-made Dauphin helicopter towards the coordinates given for *Kingurra*'s position were the strongest winds Jones had encountered in 12 years of flying with the Police Air Wing.

As they neared the search area they were experiencing rain showers and continuous sea spray and a cloud base that ranged from 600 feet to 2000 feet. Below the chopper the ocean was raging – waves and swell combining to a height of between 80 and 90 feet, and an occasional wave which appeared to be up to 120 feet high. The winds were averaging between 70 and 80 knots (135–155km/h).

'We were then 65 nautical miles (125km) to the southeast of Mallacoota,' said Jones. 'I knew if we had any problems out there we were alone. We would more than likely die before help arrived.'

Wave height, wind, rain, low cloud and the horribly confused seas were making it near impossible for the crew of *Polair 1* to locate *Kingurra* and positively establish a search area. Jones commenced an expanding circle search pattern, turning to the north first. Just as the turn began Barclay spotted a red flare slightly ahead and to the left and Jones accelerated towards it. Within seconds Barclay called out that they were about to overfly the yacht. The helicopter was slowed as much as possible, the desire being not to lose visual contact. Barclay then made radio contact with *Kingurra* and *Polair 1* was advised that Campbell was thought to be approximately 300 metres to the west of the yacht.

They tracked to that position and shortly after one of the crew spotted an orange life ring which he thought contained the crewman, but on closer inspection it was found to be empty. However, while looking at it as the chopper turned away, Key caught a glimpse of something in his peripheral vision. It was Campbell frantically waving his arms. He was about 400 metres east of the life ring and 600 metres upwind of the vessel. They immediately prepared for a winch operation and reconfirmed the plan of action they had discussed during a briefing en route to the search area. Jones took up a 100 foot hover above Campbell and Barclay commenced winching Key down to him.

Campbell's emotions went into orbit: 'I was trying to tread water using one arm while waving frantically with the other. I was screaming, "Hey, I'm over here!" Then I thought to myself, "That's a bit stupid. They can't hear you. Just keep waving."

'They hovered over me and then I saw the guy coming down the wire. I was trying to swim towards where he was headed. I remember the pilot did a phenomenal job by putting who I now know was David in the water very close to me. I swam hard for maybe 15 or 20 metres towards the harness he was holding out. It was a beautiful target.'

Within minutes Campbell was aboard *Polair 1*, but both he and the crew were still far from being safe. They would go perilously close to ditching into the wild seas while battling incredibly strong headwinds on the way back to shore.

Eventually, with bright red fuel alarm lights flashing a dire warning that the chopper was on its last gasp of fuel, pilot Darryl Jones made a desperate life-or-death lunge at the first available landing spot and made it – just!

The story brought graphic emphasis to the heroism shown by the helicopter rescue crews involved in this tragic race, a heroism that prevented a sporting event from becoming the world's worst sporting tragedy, one where the death toll could easily have been 50 or more.

Ten years after the rescue Darryl Jones, who was still with the Victorian Police Force, but piloting a highway patrol car and not a helicopter, could all too vividly recall that death-defying flight home.

'I flew with the Victorian Police Air Wing until February 2001, when I got diabetes,' said Jones. 'Unfortunately that meant I couldn't hold my position as a pilot any more. However, as it turned out I was lucky to be in the Police Force because it meant I was then able to secure a "special consideration" transfer to the highway patrol, otherwise I'd have been out of a job and on the streets looking for work.'

Jones' efforts in 1998 led to him becoming the only pilot in the 30-year history of the Victoria Police Air Wing to receive a Valour Award. To this day his memories of the rescues he executed at the controls of the chopper are indelible, but it's the dramas that came after John Campbell was plucked from the ocean that remain the most vivid.

Jones recounted: 'As soon as we knew we'd actually located him, I said to the blokes, "Look, we'd better do this as quick as we can. I need to make sure we have as much fuel as possible for the leg home."

'We put "Keysie" on the wire and lowered him to the water. That wasn't easy to start with because of the strength of the wind. Everybody thinks, "Oh yeah, no worries; we hang him out on a wire and he goes straight down, vertically." But in that sort of wind he's like a rag doll on the end of a string – he's blowing out behind the chopper. Barry Barclay said to me on the intercom that he couldn't get Dave close to Campbell so wanted me to move the aircraft forward and fly through to the target – and that's when the big wave that everyone still talks about arrived on the scene.

'We were holding a 100 foot hover at the time, and the RADALT – the radio altimeter – was telling me we had 90 foot waves going through below us. Each time one went under us it showed 10 foot on the RADALT. But this time, when I looked ahead as I began to fly forward, all I saw was a massive wall of water coming at us. There was a huge wave building in the windscreen. I said to Barry, "Play out some cable, I have to climb." He said, "Okay, no worries," so I climbed up to 150 feet on the RADALT, and when this "thing" went underneath us the needle was showing 10 feet. Now Keysie says it was a 90 feet wave, and I can only say from what I saw on the RADALT, it was a lot bigger than that.

'It was a mountain of water and we actually dragged Dave straight through it. It was so huge and came at us so suddenly there was no way we were going to get him up and over it. If there was a plus it was that we made the experience a little bit quicker for him because we pulled him through.'

Key gave his version of events: 'I was in a trough when I saw a solid, vertical wall of water in front of me. It was a 90 feet wave. I was sucked up the front of it then the buoyancy of my wetsuit took over and I was tumbled back down its face. I was driven under the water for 10 or 15 seconds before coming out at the back section of the wave. I was completely disoriented and had swallowed a large amount of seawater. I was becoming concerned because I could not hear or see the helicopter or the male I was there to rescue.

'I was hit by another wave and driven under the water once more. Then, as I came to the surface, I was looking straight at Campbell. He was just a few metres away. He had a blank look about him and was ashen-faced. We started to swim towards each other. I grabbed him as we were hit by another wall of water and I held on to him as hard as I could as we were both pushed under the water. He was a dead weight; he had no buoyancy vest on and no strength. When we resurfaced I placed the rescue harness over his head then put his arms through the strap as he was unable to assist me.'

Key wasn't the only one thinking the helicopter had been taken out by the wave and crashed. The crew of another race yacht which, unbeknown to the chopper crew, was nearby was also convinced *Polair 1* had gone in.

'Apparently there was another yacht almost below us at the time,' said Jones. 'We did not see it but we found out six months later that the crew saw us in the hover and going into the rescue. Then they saw this mountain of water build up and come at us, and all they could say to themselves was, "They're gone." They were absolutely convinced we had crashed, until they saw our little helicopter still flying in the air after the wave had gone past.'

With Campbell secured in the rescue harness and being winched with Key up to the helicopter it was safe to assume that the worst was over, but that wasn't the case: 'In 14 years working with the Police Air Wing I'd never had a winch freeze, but that's what happened during that recovery,' said Jones. 'We got them a few feet below the aircraft and the winch froze – just stopped working. We knew immediately that if we couldn't get them into the aircraft then we were in serious trouble. I kept flicking the mission switch on the unit that supplies power to the winch in the hope that it would spark up, and after five or six tries it kicked in, so Barry was able to grab them and drag them inside. We found out a couple of days later, when the engineers checked the winch, that there was nothing wrong with the unit – the problem was that with so much moisture in the air the power supply to the winch was shorting out.'

With Campbell aboard and the chopper door closed Jones set a course for the nearest airport, Mallacoota. His calculations revealed that in the prevailing conditions the chopper had 80 minutes of fuel remaining, and according to the GPS, the flight time back to Mallacoota was 40 minutes: 'That was fine, but of course the GPS didn't allow for the extremely strong headwinds we were experiencing. From the moment we headed for home I was doing what all pilots do – watching all my gauges – and after a while I noticed that I'd flown for about 40 minutes, and the GPS was still telling me that I had 40 minutes to get back to Mallacoota. Basically it meant that while our airspeed was 120 knots there were times when I had a ground speed of about five knots – we had a 115 knot headwind!

'At that stage we were still over a very rough ocean. I could see land about 25 kilometres ahead, but even so I was starting to sweat a bit about fuel. I knew it was getting low, and sure enough, a short while later the solid red "low-fuel" warning lights came on, and then not much longer after that the red alarm lights started flashing and the emergency horn came on. So, with these lights flashing in my face, and almost empty fuel tanks, I'm thinking, "Maybe we won't make it to land." I was doing my best to wean the chopper by pushing the collective down to reduce the power requirements until I started to lose a bit of airspeed, then I would just tweak it back up to get back to speed. I was lowering my power requirements but keeping my airspeed up, just to stretch out as far as possible what little fuel was left in the tank.'

By now Barclay and Key sensed that something was wrong, simply because Jones had gone quiet. That was confirmed when one of them looked over Jones' shoulder and saw that the 'low fuel' warning light was on, and the fuel alarm light was sending a message no pilot wants to see. From their professional experience, Key and Barclay knew that there was then no reason to say anything to Jones; they just communicated among themselves about the problem, knowing that there was every chance they would be ditching the chopper, and when that time came they would have to be ready to go. Their preparation involved putting Campbell back into a harness, then taking out three safety straps and hooking themselves and the liferaft together. After that there was nothing more they could do but wait for Jones' call to abandon the aircraft.

'I was trying to work out when would be the best time for me to put the aircraft into the water,' Jones said, 'and when would be the best time to say to the crew, "That's it, guys. Prepare to get out." My plan was to get down as low as I could so they could jump into the water. Getting them out before I ditched would be much safer for them because that way the three of them would at least be together and with the liferaft.

'Once they were out my plan was to fly away downwind from them and put the machine in the water, or do the best I could. It was important to be some distance from them because once the chopper hit the water there would be bits and pieces flying through the air all over the place. I had to get the spread of debris away from them.

'I was very confident I wouldn't survive the ditching – the odds were absolutely stacked against me. The one good thing was that I was so busy right then I didn't have a lot of time to think about my fate.'

Jones explained there was a very simple calculation in his mind that led to him believing he would almost certainly die. Helicopters are top heavy, so once they hit the water and slow down the first thing they do is roll over and go upside down, then they sink quite quickly. In this model of Dauphin helicopter he was flying there was no door beside either the pilot or co-pilot seats at the front, so the only way to escape after ditching was for him to unclip his harness, squeeze between his seat and the side wall of the cockpit then fight his way back to the doorway – all as the chopper was going through its death throes in the water: 'That's why I was sure the aircraft was going to take me with it. I would be struggling to get out before it sank.'

While contemplating this awful scenario Jones still had not given up hope that a miracle might occur, that everything might just go in their favour and they would make it to shore: 'I had every possible scenario going around in my head. The fact that we were in a very light mode – I had only three people in the back, and very little fuel in the tank – was at least something going in our favour. We pressed on, and after a while I realised we were making headway. I began thinking, "I doubt we can get to the airport at Mallacoota, but if I can get over land I'll be a lot more comfortable – I won't have to ditch the aircraft, and then, if we do run out of fuel, I can at least do an auto rotation to the ground."

'I started to fly towards the nearest point of land, which was just to the east of Mallacoota, and incredibly we got there. From that point I just kept stretching it and stretching it, all the time looking for a landing location if I needed one. I was also thinking, "It's still going so I'll keep going."'

Jones kept pressing the chopper forward because if he landed on the eastern side of the inlet at

Mallacoota, where there were no access roads, one of the helicopters involved in the race rescue would have to be taken out of that operation so it could get fuel to *Polair 1*. That couldn't be an option when lives were still at stake offshore.

'There was no way I was going to try to get to the airport, which was about three miles ahead of us, so the moment I got over the inlet at Mallacoota and saw the football oval I knew that was where I was headed. I nosed down a bit and made a very shallow approach towards the oval, and the moment I got there I put the thing on the ground as quickly as I could – nothing fancy and certainly not a full and proper procedure. It had taken one hour and 22 minutes to get back to shore!

'Once you have landed a helicopter the procedure is to pull the engine throttle levers back to ground idle position, and let them run for a minute so the temperature and pressures in the engine settle down. I pulled the first one back, hit the stopwatch and 40 seconds later it stopped on its own. It had run dry! Then I pulled the second lever back, hit the stopwatch again and that lasted 20 seconds before it ran dry!'

Without hesitation Jones, Barclay and Key stepped out of the helicopter, walked a few metres away and stood in a huddle, all with a slight tremor and looking at each other in total disbelief. Nothing was said. They were in shock. They knew how close they too had gone to being victims: 'We stood there for what seemed like a little while, but it was probably more like just 30 or 40 seconds,' Jones recalled, 'and then an ambulance drove into the car park of the football oval and we just went snap, back into work mode!'

Campbell, unaware of the fact that he had experienced two incredible escapes in one day, was still lying in the helicopter. As he was helped from the cabin the 1000 or so holiday-makers who had rushed to the field from the nearby caravan park to see what was happening, realised that he had been rescued from the race, and a spontaneous round of loud applause and cheering erupted among them.

With Campbell on his way to hospital Jones, Barclay and Key called it a day, but their involvement with the Sydney to Hobart race rescue did not end there. After a few hours' sleep they were up and ready to go at 5 am the following day.

CHAPTER 8

'DAMO' DUNDEE

The exploits of Damian 'Damo' Langley in the rugged bushland of Far North Queensland, and in the crocodile and shark-infested waters along the adjacent coast, make that internationally recognised and legendary Australian movie character Crocodile Dundee look like a pup.

His almost unbelievable life is a tapestry of swashbuckling experiences that would put the fear of God into just about any other human being. He has confronted crocodiles that held just one intention: to kill him. In one case it was only his knife that was the difference between life and death. He's also been sized up as a meal by countless man-eating sharks; survived seven cyclones on the open sea, some where the waves charged in at 30 metres in height; he's been sucked into the cavernous mouth of a giant groper then spat out; and he's lived to tell the tale after potentially fatal encounters with stonefish, Irukandji jellyfish, and the horrendously toxic barb from a cone shell. And, oh yes, he's also been known to jump out of a hovering helicopter and tackle a live feral pig, just to get fresh meat for a bush barbecue.

He's a plucky and extremely fit bloke, now aged 40 and living in crocodile country north of Cairns with his wife and three young daughters. The sea remains his passion and fishing is his professional world.

It was a tough upbringing during his formative years; one where the torment and bullying that came because he was dyslexic generated an inner strength and provided him with a destination in life. An abusive father also delivered him the perfect example of where he didn't want to go.

It's an incredible story from start to end:

My parents separated when I was seven. We were living on Sydney's northern beaches and Mum had no option but to run away from Dad with my brother, sister and me after he became extremely abusive towards us. Mum was a real champion, a cool chick who loved riding surfboards; a bikini girl on Manly Beach before small bikinis were socially acceptable.

She bought an old yellow VW Kombi, shoved us three kids into it and headed north for Queensland. Mum was determined from the outset to keep us together as a family, so whenever we weren't living in women's shelters – which happened on many occasions – the Kombi became home for us over the next two years.

We eventually finished up in Brisbane, at Scarborough to the north of the city and on the shores of Moreton Bay. That's where I found my future. I got into surfing and became pretty good at it, so good that Mum had a vision of me becoming a pro surfer. When I wasn't surfing I was fishing. I used to fish off the jetties at Scarborough all day and all night, wagging school to do it, and I loved it. I wasn't big on going to school – I'm dyslexic, so I'm not really fancy at reading and writing. That made school really hard for me; no one believed in dyslexia back then so I was always being called an idiot. The other kids didn't like me much – which was probably partly my fault because I was having a blue with just about every one of them, all because they thought I was a dummy. Fortunately I was in a Christian Brothers school where the teachers turned a blind eye to me wagging, mainly because I was a really good swimmer and did well in competitions for the school. It put points on their board, so they didn't care about my schooling. I couldn't learn anyway.

Mum knew what I was doing and supported me. She said, 'I don't care what you do as long as the coppers don't bring you home. Don't break the law. Don't be a ratbag, and behave yourself.' I've always stuck by her rules.

When I wasn't fishing I still used to wag school, just so I could hang around on the local jetty and watch the guys unload their trawlers. Sometimes I'd give them a hand. Then one day this really nice bloke named Trevor, who had a crab boat, came along and said 'Do you want to come crabbing with me?' and I said 'I'd love to.' I was 10 at the time and worked with him on the bay for a couple of seasons, wagging school all the time until I got a pardon from the government to leave when I was 11 on the proviso that I had a full-time job. After two seasons this guy sold his boat, but before he left town he introduced me to a bloke named Mick Wicks who owned the 57 foot trawler *Silver Dollar*, the biggest trawler on Moreton Bay. Next thing I had a job as a deckhand on that boat, and I couldn't believe my luck because up until then I used to watch *Silver Dollar* go in and out of the river all the time, saying to myself, 'Look at that. That's a beautiful big boat.'

Mick had two older guys working for him, and when I jumped on he gave me the job of sorting one side of the catch tray after the haul was brought aboard while the other two guys worked on the opposite side. I touched them right up on the first night, finishing my sorting and cooking the prawns before they had even finished sorting, so I went over and gave them a hand. When the same thing happened on the second night he sacked the other blokes as soon as we got back to the jetty, saying to me, 'Why am I paying two other guys when I can have one good one do the lot?' So I became Mick's sole deckie.

I did that until I was 13; then one day Mick came along and asked me if I wanted to go north and work with him on the trawler. I was right into surfing at that time and looking for sponsorship so I could compete on the circuit, but I couldn't find any. Mick said, 'Come north, Damo, for a couple of seasons and you'll get enough money to go surfing. You'll kick arse.'

When I told Mum what I was doing – going north on the trawler – she was over the moon. She thought I'd be coming home with a heap of money to go surfing. What she didn't know was that I was never coming back, and neither did I.

When you go to places like Cape York as a 13-year-old it's all a new frontier. The fishing was incredible, and there were crocodiles and sharks everywhere. There was also great diving and surfing on the outer Great Barrier Reef – I took a lot of my boards with me; it was amazing. You'd be on the outer reef and paddle to catch this big wave and you had it all to yourself. There was no one to be seen and no one for hundreds of kilometres. Your only company would be more than a dozen big bronze whaler sharks riding that crystal-clear wave with you. You'd look down and there they were. But they didn't scare me. Sharks don't touch you if you've got no fear. It's only when you show fear that they will come after you. It was my world and theirs.

I lived that life until I was 16, the age when you could get your Master Fisherman's ticket so you can skipper a fishing boat. It was easy back then; I just put $50 in the mail and back came my ticket. A few years later a new law came in and I had to get my Skipper's ticket. I was lucky because I was granted an amnesty and didn't have to study for it as I had already been skippering for many years.

It was a fabulous life for me over the next eight years. Mick Wicks came along with a 45 foot trawler named *Brave Laurie* and said: 'Here you go, Damo. Get yourself eight crew, and as long as you fill that boat full of fish every now and then and send them home to us on our mother ship, you can do what you want with it. I'll cover all your expenses, you'll make some money and you'll have a good time.'

So that was me. We'd spend half of the year trawling and then the rest of the year we'd go fishing for coral trout. We started out of Cairns and the further north we went, the more exciting it got; more fish, more islands to see and more things to do, all the way through to New Guinea and Torres Strait. I fell in love with Torres Strait, and hung around the islands up there for a long time. We were the only white people to fish around the Murray Islands for many years; no one else was allowed there.

As I got older I decided I should get into diving for crayfish, but to do that I had to get the necessary qualifications by sitting for my tickets. Study is near impossible for someone who is dyslexic, but fortunately for me I have a photographic memory, and that meant I could answer what was required. I'm very lucky because it is said that every dyslexic is a genius at something, and while not wanting to blow it out of my own arse, I have to say that for me that something is fishing. That's what I understand better than anything. I breathe it. I eat it. I study it. But being dyslexic and not having a proper education became increasingly frustrating for me as the years went by, so when I got to around 30 I decided to do something about it and I started teaching myself whenever I had any spare time while we were at sea. It was an enormous challenge but worth every minute of effort.

The sea has really been my university, a place where I have had some incredible adventures and learned from remarkable experiences. It's all led to me being where I am today – fishing, mucking around on magnificent superyachts, working as a guide and sharing my stories.

You can imagine what it was like being up there in North Queensland when it all really started for me as a skipper: eight boys on a boat having a free rein on where we wanted to go and what we wanted to do. It was a great life, even though we never had a lot of food – except fish. Quite often we'd head into one of the rivers just to see what we could find for tucker. Crocodiles and turtles became part of our diet because they weren't protected all those years ago.

We had this young guy with us, Shorty, who was about 15, and one night we decided we needed crocodile for dinner. So I said to him, 'Go get us a lizard for dinner, Shorty.' He had an SKS rifle and he was a crack shot even at that age; he could shoot the top off a match at an incredible distance. So he jumped into the dinghy and had only gone about 100 metres into the darkness when his spotlight illuminated the eyes of a croc and he let loose. Next thing he's back at the boat saying, 'I've shot it but I can't find it,' so I said, 'Righto, we'll come and help you,' partly because I don't like seeing anything going to waste and dying unnecessarily.

We headed off in a dinghy and I asked him, 'Where did you shoot it from?'

'About here,' he said. 'It was about 150 yards away.'

'That's a fucking long way, Shorty. Are you sure you got him?'

'Yep.'

So we turned the dinghy towards where we thought we might find the croc and sure enough we spotted him, and he was still alive. Suddenly *booooom*, and Shorty's let loose with another shot at the croc. It was about five metres off the mangroves, so we raced in and just about got on top of it with the dinghy. Well, this thing's about five metres long, still alive and bloody angry. It leapt into the air, rolled over and disappeared: it'd gone mental and was heading for the mangroves. Shorty's got it in the spotlight again and gone *bang, bang, bang, bang* with the rifle. He dropped it cold, but as he did it disappeared under a mangrove head first. He wanted to make sure he'd finished it off, but couldn't get another shot at it, so there was only one thing to do: I'm first over the side with a knife, straight in there, to tackle it. I had another couple of guys behind me so we dragged this big lizard out while it was still thrashing around, just so Shorty could get another shot at it and finish the job. He did just that, and a while later there we were back on the trawler with this mother of all crocodiles for dinner. We carved it up, boned it and ate like there was no tomorrow or day after.

For some unknown reason that became a special moment in my life: I don't know why I did it, but I took one of the croc's teeth as a good–luck charm and I've worn it ever since. I have to say that every time I've taken it off something bad has happened, so now it stays exactly where it is around my neck. Many friends say it's my deal with the devil: it's why I'm still alive today.

I've had quite a few very close encounters with crocs, all of which could have gone either way.

One time I was pig hunting at night with a bunch of mates on a cane farm well away from a river. We took a lot of dogs with us and made them easy to see in the dark by putting glow sticks on them. The shooters were positioned so they shot away from each other and everyone carried a torch and a knife in a pouch. Normally you wouldn't take the knife out of the pouch until you were about to stab the pig, but my pouch had rotted so I carried my knife in my hand or in my back pocket, blade up, and the dolphin torch in my other hand. This time the dogs found a pig and went after it; *bark, bark, bark*. The pig made a run for it and jumped into a drain the farm owner had dug that led all the way down to the river. It was about three metres wide and four metres deep, and all the dogs went in there after the pig.

My mate's dog, Cinder, was a beautiful 60kg Great Dane-bull mastiff cross; it wasn't as quick getting to the pig as the other dogs, which were hanging off the pig barking at it and carrying on. Cinder went into the drain and I was about to follow so I could stab the pig when suddenly this croc, which had been hiding in the shallow water, came out of nowhere and grabbed Cinder in its mouth like a hamburger. Fortunately, Cinder was wearing a Kevlar chest-plate for protection, but even so, she was making a noise like you've never heard made by a dog that size before. It was horrible.

I had my knife and torch in my hands and I couldn't stop myself from going into the drain. I was on my way and had nowhere to go but feet first over the top of the croc, across its shoulders behind its front legs. So, there I am, embedded in the mud to my knees, and I've landed on the croc's back, which meant I've gone in nuts first, and I'm hurting, really hurting. I've shit myself. The only thing I could do to save myself was grab my knife and drive it in behind the croc's front legs. I nailed it and as I did the croc turned its head back at me and spat the 60kg dog out over my shoulder. The dog landed in the water and was starting to drown and I'm on the back of a giant and very upset lizard thinking, 'Oh shit! I'm in trouble here.' I can't help the dog because I can't get off the croc, and if I do get off it will get me.

My mates appeared on top of the bank, saw what was happening and began back-pedalling as quickly as they'd arrived. My torch was covered in mud so I couldn't see Jack Shit – absolutely nothing – so I screamed out to them, 'Get the fuck back here.' They came back, looked down at me and all they could see were two beady white eyes and thick black mud everywhere. I still had the croc wedged between my legs and I had both hands firmly on the knife, which remained embedded in its shoulder. The croc was thrashing around until it decided it had nowhere to go but forward with me on its back and my knife in its shoulder. The knife wasn't going to kill him because it only had a short blade, but I knew I'd hurt him. He continued to claw his way towards the river and was getting out between my legs with his tail thrashing around wildly. Next thing he'd gone, and fortunately for me he kept going. The guys got me back to the top of the bank and I was absolutely buggered, but worse still my balls were black and blue. They swelled up to the size of tennis balls and were so painful that I couldn't sit up, sit down or do anything. I had to hold packs of frozen peas on them for almost a week to ease the pain.

There were two other incidents with crocs that were worse than that one, both where I thought I could easily become crocodile shit.

The first one happened after we'd salvaged a yacht near Cape York, the northern-most tip of Queensland. It was 1997 and I was the skipper of a twin-hulled trawler, *The Wicked*. We were at Gallen Reef, around 70 miles south of the Cape, and about to go to sleep when we heard a May Day call which I answered immediately. This guy came onto the radio and said he'd sailed his yacht hard up onto the front of a reef that was only about 10 miles away from us. It was blowing about 25 or 30 knots from the southeast and I knew that if we didn't get there quickly they could be in all sorts of strife, so we upped anchor and steamed there pretty hastily. When we got there we found a beautiful 45 foot fibreglass yacht being pounded on the reef. The guy on board was an older and pretty cool Canadian gynaecologist who had two glamour 20-year-old French girls with him: they were prime! The boys jumped into one of our dories and motored to the yacht, got the three of them off and brought them back to the trawler. Then we immediately set about dragging the yacht off the reef because, with it being pounded so hard, it would be smashed to pieces by daylight.

We told the owner that it was our only option and he agreed to let us give it a shot. We anchored *The Wicked*, hooked one of our heavy cables onto the yacht, fired up our 1400hp engine that drives the biggest winch, then dragged the yacht across the reef and back into deep water. Incredibly, she hadn't been holed, so we towed her into nearby Margaret Bay where we could assess the damage the next morning.

The old Canadian guy wanted to know if he could continue his voyage back home, so the only option was for someone to get into the water, which was about four metres deep, and check out the damage. None of the crew wanted to get into the water that morning – they were chicken-shit scared, and I thought I knew why. We'd been diving for crayfish in that region for some time and had seen plenty of crocs around. We'd had a few run-ins with them but nothing really dangerous. Then I realised the real reason the guys didn't want to get into the water had nothing to do with the crocs; they didn't want to interrupt their chat with the saucy French girls!

So it was up to me. I set up the hooker (underwater breathing device) and jumped over the side into what was reasonably clear water – about four metres visibility, which was okay. The yacht was rafted up alongside our boat and the owner was sitting on the side of his boat looking down while I swam up and down the length of the yacht checking the damage. The keel and rudder were trashed and the propeller shaft was bent out at right angles to the hull: the yacht wasn't going anywhere soon. While I was in the water I noticed a lot of big shovel-nosed sharks swimming around on the bottom but that didn't worry me. They are easy to pick because they've always got golden trevally swimming around in front of them. I continued to check the yacht, looking at the damage to the fibreglass, and at one stage looked down to the bottom and saw what I thought was a big shark coming towards me. I took little notice of it because it had all these golden trevally swimming around it. I didn't even consider it might be a big lizard because I'd rarely seen any swimming around with golden trevally escorting them in front of their nose.

The next minute I glanced to one side and there it was in front of me, just glaring at me; a bloody big croc almost five metres long! I've immediately shit myself. I've spent a lot of time in the water with crocs so I knew there were things I had to do if I was to give myself any chance of getting away. You never arch your back when you're near a croc; that's strike mode and as soon as you do, they'll strike you. You always go level and calmly submit. They're different from sharks. You don't look them in the eye, and you never swim ahead of them. The first thing they'll do is head-butt you. It's a competition, not a fight or anything: it's just a show of aggression. So, if you go level in the water they'll do the same thing; you submit to them and keep submitting to them. That's all I could do. So there I was with this croc just a few metres away from me and I'm still shitting myself. I'm breathing through the hooker and slowly floating up towards the surface, submitting to the croc all the time, and it's coming up to the surface with me. My thought was that if I could hug the side of the yacht and slowly work my way round to the stern then get across the stern of my boat I might be able to get out of the water and onto the aft platform before the croc got me.

While I'm making this slow ascent to the surface
the old Canadian dude has looked over the side of his
yacht and seen what's going on – me with a big croc
right alongside, just below the surface.

He was by himself so he panicked. My crew and
the French girls were onboard The Wicked, so he
decided he had to save me. He's grabbed his fish gaff,
which has a bloody big sharp hook on the end: he
wanted to save me from the croc by gaffing me out of
the water! So next thing I've got a croc with me in
the water that's half-keen about eating me and I've
got this old dude up above trying to get this hook into
me. He was swiping the surface of the water even
though I wasn't anywhere near it. If ever I was
between a rock and a hard place that was it: I couldn't
go any closer to the surface in case he gaffed me, so it
was just me and the croc. It was bloody hairy.

I glanced over my shoulder and thought, 'Here we
go. I'm in serious strife now!' I'm still submitting to
the croc and hugging the bottom of the boat while
trying desperately to stay out of the reach of the old
dude who is running around the deck screaming,
'Crocodile.' Suddenly the boys started panicking,

thinking that the lizard had already got me, but when they realised it hadn't they were screaming at him to stop trying to gaff me. They rushed across and onto the bow of the yacht, but by this time I had managed to ease my way to the stern of *The Wicked* where the aluminium platform sat at water level. I couldn't shout out to them; I could only get myself up to the surface so I could roll onto the platform as quickly as possible and escape the croc, which was still right there with me. I gave the croc the eye then *whoosh*, I'm out of the water and onto the platform. I watched the croc just cruise between the two hulls towards the bow then come to the surface about 20 metres in front of the boat, where everyone got a good look at it. The old dude was ashen with shock and just stared in disbelief when he saw I was alive.

As bad as that was, my worst encounter with a croc came when I was diving in what we call soup – really murky water – at Olive River, which is just south of Margaret Bay. There is a lot of tannin flowing into the sea from the shore, so that's why the water is always dark. Olive River is renowned for its big lizards and there's a sandbank there that we call

Crocodile Strip because there are so many of them. The area is also full of crayfish, and that's what we go diving for. It's where you make your money: you can pull anything up to 10 grand a day out of there, so in a sense you don't really care about the crocodiles. Each diver goes into the bank in one of the trawler's dories with another guy driving. His job is to look after you. But he won't ever tell you about seeing crocodiles because he doesn't want you getting scared – because you are also making money for him as the driver; he's on a percentage. If a croc or shark comes at you he has a chance of saving you by getting the boat between you and them. This particular time my mate Macca, who'd saved me a few times, was my driver, and he saw this lizard moving into the water from the beach and heading towards me, but it was a long way away, so he didn't think much of it.

Macca had seen heaps of them do the same thing over the years. Normally they wouldn't come anywhere near the boat because they are scared of the outboard, but this one turned out to be inquisitive and cagey. I didn't see him because he came up from behind and I was too interested in plucking crays. I'd just been up to the boat with a load and was diving back down when I felt something pulling on my flipper. I thought it was another diver tugging at me just to give me the 'willies', trying to put the wind up me, as we often do to each other just for the fun of it. Then I felt this really good tug on my flipper, so strong that it almost pulled it clean off my foot. I looked around expecting to see a mate there but instead it was this big lizard. Well, I cut for it — Macca was only about 10 metres away and I almost walked across the water to get to him, leaping into the boat as I got there. Macca saw it coming after me and all he could say was 'Shit!' I took off a flipper and there were perfect puncture marks from its teeth all the way down one side of it.

There's always something entertaining going on when you are diving for crays. If it's not lizards or sharks it can be a giant groper. I've had some pretty hairy experiences with them too, from having my arm just about pulled out of my shoulder socket to being grabbed on the arse by one of them.

These things are monsters. They're not as big as a Mini Minor, but they are close — 200 to 300kgs and more, better than three metres long, and with a mouth roughly the diameter of a 44-gallon drum. They can be more than 200 years old – they've been there since Captain Cook came past – and they are highly intelligent. Crayfish is their favourite food: they know every rock and where every crayfish lives, so when one finds you in his territory he will come at you and flare up his gills in a show of aggression, as if to say, 'You're in my territory. You're taking my crays.'

If you let go of a cray, he'll come and grab it, so once he clues on to the fact that you're feeding him he'll actually take you to the next rock where he knows there are crays. You give him one out of there while you take the rest, then he'll take you to the next spot. While you keep doing this he'll keep taking you to the best spots. In the end you get a relationship going with this critter, and everyone is happy. They're that smart, even to the degree where they will recognise the sound of your outboard motor and follow only you and no one else. There's one at Margaret Bay that's made me a fortune over the years. He's a winner. When I first worked out what to do with these groper – establish a relationship – I was smashing all the other divers up there when it came to the size of the catch. I cleaned them up — 100-plus kilos a day, every day, while they would only get 30 or 40kg. No one could figure it out and I wasn't letting on what I was doing. They were bouncing from rock to rock while I was just following my old mate who was taking me to all the best spots. It was only when one of the guys I confided in spilled the beans that the others caught on.

This one particular time I was diving for crays at a place called Old People's, which is near Princess Charlotte Bay. It gets its name from the fact that every crayfish there is between three and five kilos, making them the biggest crayfish in Queensland. They're crackers. When you grab the first one you put it between your legs, tail first and with its legs towards you so they wrap their legs around. The tail is sticking out of your bum between your wetsuit; that way you can lock your crutch together and hold him there while you grab the next one, which you put under your arm, then another one which goes under your other arm, and so on, then you go and put all three in your catch bag.

Well, this time I grabbed a big fella out of a small cave and I shoved him in between my legs. So there I am half bent over and holding him in my crutch while I leaned in to grab the next one, only to suddenly have this huge groper weighing near 300 kilos come up from behind and bite me on the arse. He had me folded over in his mouth from my knees to near halfway up my back. I was squashed up in his mouth and all I could feel was him going *suck*, *suck*, *suck* like a giant vacuum, trying with all his might to suck the crayfish out of my crutch. I can tell you, these things have some serious suction power. There's so much suction you think he's going to suck your stomach out through your arse. It's quite amazing. This fish was so big he just lifted me up off the bottom and took off with me, just like when a fish picks up a bait and runs with it.

You can imagine what it was like for the bloke driving the boat. One second everything is all calm and relaxed and the next thing he sees the hooker hose that's curled up at his feet rocketing out over the side like a fishing line coming off a reel after a big strike. That's what happened. There was nothing he could do, and the only thing I could do was let go of that cray, and as soon as I did he spat me out so hard that I finished up about three metres in front of him. The force was amazing.

There's one other experience I have had a few times with big groper. It's when you lean in to a crevasse or small cave and grab a cray in your hand then lean in with your other arm and grab another one. While you're doing that you suddenly find that your arm holding the cray is jammed down the throat of a big groper; your arm is engulfed up to your shoulder and they start twisting around just to get the cray out of your hand. If you let the cray go he'll let your arm go, but then, when he goes to swim away, you have to swim forward and fold your arm in otherwise he will pull it out of the socket. I've had all the tendons in my arm busted because I didn't do that properly.

When it comes to sharks I've got plenty of stories, like coming up from 25 metres with a bag full of crays on my way to the surface and having a 14 foot hammerhead hit me in the ribs at full noise and knock the wind out of me. You don't see them coming; they just come in and hit you – they don't bite. A hammerhead will hit you first then wheel around and have another look, then they'll have a bite. Tiger sharks will always come in when you're not looking but you'll feel the turbulence he creates; then you'll turn around and sure enough, he's there. Tigers are submissive creatures – being overpowering is not in their nature and they're not really that quick underwater. Most times when a tiger shark is coming at you he opens his jaws and rolls his eyes back, and that's when you can put your hand on the end of his nose and get pushed along. If you rub his nose nice and gently as he's pushing you along he'll just roll over. Then you can push him away and he'll wheel off to one side of you. After that he'll swim off five metres or so and come round again and you can do the same thing again. You can push him away as long as you like; he's not a problem.

A lot of times when sharks are around you're instinctively aware of them being there; you've been in the water so long that you can sense their presence. There's just something about the situation – you see that little shadow move across the bottom some distance away and you know he's there.

Aggression will turn most sharks away. You don't have to move quickly but you have to have him convinced that you only plan to kill him if he comes near you. They are remarkably sensitive creatures; they can sense everything, especially aggression and fear. They have a heap of sensors on the tip of their nose and down the side of their eyes. They are always looking for the vulnerable prey. That's why the shark takes the fish that fears him out of the pack, or the one that's wounded, or the one that's pissing itself because it's scared: it's easy prey. So, while with a crocodile you are submissive, with a shark you must be aggressive towards him. You must honestly believe and be saying to him, 'You come near me and you're fuckin' dead.' Do that and he won't come near you; he'll turn away – unless he's a white pointer; they just keep coming.

Most people would think you need to have big balls to do this but that is not the case when you've grown up with them and know what you're doing. It's not really that hard. I've had run-ins with probably 30 or 40 big tiger sharks over the years and am still here to tell the tale.

I can understand why some people see my life as being full of death-defying experiences. Some of them come courtesy of nature while others come from what some people might see as sheer stupidity – like the time I jumped out of a helicopter and tackled a live feral pig so that we could take him back to a mate's place and put him on the spit for a barbecue. We were out in the chopper pig shooting when we found a big mob in a swamp, so we swooped in with the chopper and I jumped out onto the back of one and tackled him. I killed him then we took him home, salted him and had a great time eating him. That's something you don't do every day! However, most of my experiences just come with the job – crocodiles and sharks are all part of it. The truth is that it's the fishing that I really love, both as the skipper of a trawler and as a guide for well-heeled guests aboard superyachts. The reality is that boats have been the focus of my life since I first stepped onto that crab boat in Brisbane when I was 11 years old. But, just as there has been plenty of action for me in the water, there have been many memorable experiences on the water, like surviving cyclones and the time I had a boat explode into flames off Port Douglas one night and sink under me.

That time we were in the middle of the trawl grounds about nine miles off Port Douglas when the unthinkable happened. It was one of Michael Wicks' boats, *Brave Laurie*, and it had been in Daintree for an extensive refit after a faulty starter motor caused the batteries to explode and trash the interior. When the structural work was finished a young fella, Nick, and I had to take the boat to Cairns for a repaint.

We headed down the Daintree River and crossed the bar around sunset then turned south. At around nine o'clock we were off Port Douglas and making good progress. The young fella was down below having a sleep and I was on the wheel, steering the boat with my head up through the hatch in the top of the cabin so I could get a good view of everything around us and spot any trawlers that might be crossing our track. What I didn't know was that the whole time the starter motor hadn't released itself from the ring gear: it was jammed in and causing the batteries to be overcharged in a big way. The wiring was burning and the batteries were blowing up like balloons, but I couldn't smell anything because I had my head stuck up in the fresh air. Next minute, BOOM! The batteries had exploded like hydrogen bombs, but I still didn't realise what had happened. I hadn't been looking behind us so my immediate reaction was 'Shit – we've been hit by a boat from behind', but there was nothing there. I jumped down into the wheelhouse and suddenly realised that I had battery acid all over me from the waist down. It was fortunate that I didn't have a full crew on board because they would have been sitting at the table in the wheelhouse and would almost certainly have been killed because the batteries were under the bench seats, which were no longer there. The young fella, who had been sleeping in the bunk up in the bow, came scrambling out and grabbed an extinguisher in an effort to put out the fire that had erupted, but it took only a couple of minutes for us to realise that there was no way we were going to beat it.

Now, this beautiful timber boat had been my home for eight years and among other things I had thousands of rounds of ammunition on board, five 100lb gas bottles for cooking crays plus 1300 litres of outboard fuel in a tank on the roof, other jerry tanks full of fuel and the boat's own tanks were full. So, it was a huge bomb and already an inferno. We were in major trouble.

I pulled the boat out of gear but it was still moving ahead, so I could only assume that the wiring from the gear shift had burnt through. I also sent out a frantic May Day call but didn't know if it was heard by anyone else because I couldn't hang around. Young Nick dived over the side and I followed him. We wanted to get to the dinghy, which I had managed to untie before jumping over the side, but we couldn't get to it because the boat had done a u-turn and was cutting a course straight back to it. Next minute all hell broke loose: bullets started going off in every direction, punching holes in the dinghy and hitting the water all around us. Every time I heard another packet start to go off, I'd grab Nick's head and push him underwater then I'd go down myself. Worse still, the water all around us was on fire because of the fuel that had come from the boat. All we could do was dive underwater and swim as far away from the boat and the flames as we could. Next thing there was one almighty explosion as the fuel tank on the roof exploded and gas bottles were launching into the sky like rockets while bullets were still spraying across the water. We wanted to stay near the boat because we knew we were in trawler grounds and if anyone saw the fire or heard the May Day, they would come looking for us. However, an hour after the first explosion, when things started to subside, there was no sign of help coming from anywhere and the boat, which had moved about a mile away from us, was still burning and not far from sinking. I didn't know at that stage that I had burns all over me but I did know that we were swimming through shark territory. But there was nothing we could do about it. The fact that we were nine miles offshore didn't worry me either. We were both cray divers; we can swim 20 or 30 miles in a day no worries. So we were treading water, just talking, and young Nick was showing a little bit of fear. I just said to him, 'Whatever you do don't start panicking – we're cool, man. We're cray divers. Nothing will come near us if we're not panicking. When the sun comes up in a few more hours, we'll cut for shore. We'll be right, man. The wind will push us towards the shore. We might end up a fair way north of where we'd like to be but we'll get to land, mate. We'll be right.'

If we'd made one mistake it was to try to save the boat instead of ourselves. By the time we realised that we weren't going to stop the fire there was no way we could get to life jackets or anything else. I learned that day — and will never forget it — that you never save the boat first. You make preparations to save yourself then you worry about the boat.

There was no moon so the night was as black as you can imagine, but our hopes that we might be rescued went up when we saw a trawler heading for the fire. They got to what was left of our boat and when they realised there was no one on board or in the water around it they started searching, going around the boat in ever increasing circles. After a while their spotlight hit us, and as it did we shoved our hands as high as we could into the air. Incredibly, even though there were two-and-a-half metre seas running, the deckie spotted us. They came over, picked us up and stayed there while we watched the boat sink and waited for the Coast Guard to come and take us ashore. We had been in the water for more than three hours.

I had lost everything – all the cash I'd ever saved, all my clothes, spear guns, rifles, fishing rods, photos and videos. But worse still, I had to tell my mate that we'd lost his boat.

A fire onboard is probably the worst thing anyone can deal with, and I'm sure they are the reason for so many small boats disappearing off the face of the planet without trace, taking their occupants with them. However, in my business, which is centred in the tropics, there is another equally terrifying experience – a cyclone – and I've had to deal with plenty of them over the years. The problem that comes with a cyclone is that it quite often develops very quickly and heads on a somewhat unpredictable path. This means that if you are fishing and are a long way offshore you could well be trapped.

In all I've faced seven cyclones, and by far the scariest one – the one where we were really lucky to survive – came when we were at a place called Eastern Fields. It was the closest thing you can imagine to *The Perfect Storm*.

Back then, you'd leave home and head out of Daintree even in the cyclone season, and as you left you'd say to the missus, 'We're off.' She'd ask, 'When will you be back?' and you'd say, 'Well, we should be home in about three months' time.' So, we'd steam up the coast in this 45 foot timber trawler towards Cape York and out into the Bay of New Guinea where you have no radio contact or weather forecasts. Eastern Fields is a massive reef and lagoon way out in the middle, miles from anywhere. We went there because the fishing was so good and we used to tow four or five dories in a daisy chain behind us, each one between 14 and 16 feet long and powered by a 50hp outboard. Once we'd put four or five tons of fish fillets in the hold out at the reef we'd head for a place in Torres Strait and unload them before heading back out again.

This particular time we were out we could just sense that something bad was happening; you could feel it in the air. We soon knew a cyclone was coming because all the birds began to land on the boat, from pretty little coloured pigeons and seabirds through to other flying creatures, like dragonflies and huge moths by the thousands. This usually happens about six to 10 hours before a cyclone hits. They're all resting, knowing they have to go through it. At the same time you see that your barometer is starting to tick down. I said to the guys, 'Right, there's a low coming. It's time for us to cut for Cape York.' It was about 100 miles to where we could anchor with some level of safety and we had no alternative but to go for it. It was no use staying out there because there were only two little reefs you could anchor behind and there was no way they would protect you from cyclonic seas.

We started steaming towards Cape York and all the time the seas were building and the wind was climbing; 25 knots to 50 knots, 60 knots then up to 80 knots.

The worst thing for us was that the following and very confused seas were getting bigger and bigger. Before long it got to the stage where the waves were breaking and playing havoc with the dinghies, which we were still towing because we couldn't afford to cast them adrift. The waves were picking them up and surfing them past us.

They'd then flip arse over head and get pulled underwater, and when one went under the others would just crash into it. *Boom, boom, boom, boom, boom.* So, you've got all these dinghies under the water while these massive curlers were breaking over the roof of the boat. We had to keep running with the swells because there was no other option. The only thing I could do was drive ahead at near-idle speed whenever possible then go into reverse as the wave picked us up from behind and broke all around us. That was the only way we could minimise our chance of being driven down the face of the wave like a surfboat and pitch-poled. When we were at full noise in reverse the whole boat would be shuddering as the wave lifted it up then broke right over the top. At that stage it was actually a benefit to have the submerged dories still there behind us because they acted like a sea brake. By then everything had been washed out of them; the sterns were ripped out and the outboards were gone. They only stayed attached because we had the one towline threaded through the lot of them, but we were going to be lucky to have just a few hull frames left by the time we got to Cape York.

So, here I am, 20 years old and skippering this trawler and I've got grown men around twice my age crewing for me and they are crying and literally pissing themselves with fear. They were sure we were all going to die and I was too. I have to admit I was shitting myself but I just couldn't show it. The waves were by then as big as they can get out there, more than 15 metres high, and I can't tell you how many times we came close to losing it. The waves were so big they were breaking right over us. We were actually embedded in the wave, in the green water, and every time that happened our ears hurt from the increase in pressure inside the cabin. It was just like when your ears hurt while diving deep into water. The pressure was unbelievable.

By then it was dark so we had no real idea how bad things were outside. I just knew that I had to do everything I could to keep the boat on course and safe. There was nothing else we could do if we were going to survive. We couldn't head into it and out to sea because we wouldn't have had enough fuel to get us back to shore after the cyclone had passed. As it was, we were going to be close to empty by the time we got to Cape York.

As if all this drama wasn't enough, the next thing I

knew was that the boat was starting to feel heavy, and I realised that the engine noise had all of a sudden changed. It was as if it was gargling. Unbeknown to us the engine hatch, which was mounted on the deck aft of the wheelhouse, had come off and the boat was filling with water faster than you want to know. It was actually beginning to wallow in the water, that's how fast we were filling up. The only thing to do was to get myself outside, put the hatch back into place and pin it, then go below and start the bilge pumps. The older guys couldn't do anything to help − they were too scared − so the only thing I could do was grab the 16-year-old young fella and have him drive the boat. I tied a rope around myself as a safety line then went outside into a mass of white water that was washing across the deck. Once I got the hatch in place I climbed below and kicked the pumps into gear. They run off the engine and fortunately the water level in the engine room hadn't got high enough to stop it running.

When we got things back to normal we continued on our course towards Cape York, through what was still a pitch-black night. After a while we sensed that the wind and seas were beginning to abate, a sure enough sign that the cyclone was moving away from us. But our situation was far from safe. It was still dark when we arrived at the Cape and our only way to shelter was to weave a path through a reef, but there was no way I was going to do that at night. It was a case of us idling around just off the reef in horrendous conditions until daylight came.

Finally the light we needed arrived and we reached safety. All I know is that I never want to go through something like that ever again. It was fucking hair-raising, especially for someone who was only 20 years old and had never seen anything like it.

The other seriously bad cyclone I've experienced was off the coast of Western Australia back in the '90s. We were aboard *The Wicked*, heading north from Geraldton when we found ourselves about six hours behind the cyclone that took out Exmouth. Now it's an open paddock from that coast all the way across to Africa, and suddenly we were trapped. The seas built up faster than you can imagine, and we had nowhere to go, so we had to press on. We went past Ningaloo, about 70 miles south of Exmouth, when it was blowing at around 80 knots, and the waves were cracking: no bullshit, the swells were about 100 foot high. They looked like mountains, and the peaks were breaking. *The Wicked* is a bloody big and powerful catamaran, but even so we were in real strife. All we could do was run to the nor'east, down the front of these massive waves at 17 knots with both motors in reverse just trying to slow her down. We went so fast down one wave we snapped one of the rudders clean off, and had another mammoth wave break right over us with such force that the boat was completely submerged in the white water. We were so far into the swell, so far underwater, that the two liferafts we had stowed on the cabin roof burst open and inflated, and they're not designed to do that until they're three metres under. Next thing we've got these two fuckin' big red things in the piss and dragging along behind us on their towlines, and we're in full reverse trying to stop the boat from nose-diving down the wave. The only thing to do was cut the liferafts free because if we didn't they'd get sucked under the boat and finish up around the props. Then you're really stuffed. It was a case of, 'Stuff saving the liferafts; we have to save the boat.'

It seems that no matter what you do when you have a lifestyle like mine, there's always something lurking that can hold fatal consequences. It's a bit like Russian roulette, but even so I wouldn't swap it. Incredibly, things as large as crocodiles and as small as cone shells can end your days. I can't count how many stonefish have hit me – so many that I'm now immune to their venom – and while I haven't been bitten by sea snakes I've had hundreds wrapped around me. They always put the willies up me because for some reason they like licking the back of your neck. At other times, through my own stupid fault, I've had several run-ins with Irukandji jellyfish. They are attracted to the deck lights at night and just hang around, so when you get up in the morning and dive over the side to clear your head, you dive straight into one. Bang! It's an incredible sensation because no matter where it touches you it feels like a bit of tingling on your neck. Then the tingling travels around your neck and the pain starts. Then it hits your spine and that's when you know you're in trouble; you start doubling up and go into convulsions that are so severe you feel like you'll break your back from the inside out.

Obviously I survived the jellyfish, but the one thing I thought was really going to get me was a little cone shell. I didn't know what it was that had hit me when it happened. I was in about 18 metres of water looking for crays at a place called Dead Man's Peanut, which is off Cape York. Why is it called Dead Man's Peanut? Because there are two reefs and a dead man was found years ago washed up on one of them, and the second reef is shaped like a peanut. How original! It's a great place for crays and I was swimming around a rock that was about the size of a dining table, looking for crays under a ledge which was about a foot off the bottom. There were a fair few nice ones there and I leaned in to pull one out when I felt a little flick on my hand. It went through my Kevlar glove and from that very moment I knew from the sensations I experienced it was the worst thing that had ever touched me in my life. Every hair follicle, every pore, each fingernail, my teeth, tastebuds, every sense in my body reacted, but it was bizarre because there was no pain.

When I surfaced I told my dory driver, Macca, what had happened. 'Mate, you had too many Sudafeds this morning. You're half tripping!' We used to take Sudafeds so we could dive more often; most of the guys lived on them like junkies. They keep the mucus out of your head and stop your eyes from popping out.

I saw I had a little black dot on my hand – the mark is still there today, jet-black and about the size of a one cent piece. I picked at it and found a little barb which I pulled out. I thought it might have been part of a barb from a stingray that had been lying under the rocks, but then Macca said, 'I think it looks like a cone shell barb. You'd better go back down again to see if there are any around.' I wasn't hurting and I wasn't tripping out so I decided I'd go back down for more crays while I had a look around that rock to see what was there. I found a few crays around one side, put them in my bag then moved around to where I had been and started dusting away the sand. Sure enough, there was a deep purple cone shell, and I realised straight away that's what had hit me. I just accepted that and because I wasn't feeling any pain I moved on to another rock that was absolutely chockers with crays. I started plucking them off the rock one after another, then all of a sudden I couldn't squeeze my hand to grab one. It was swollen and tight. 'Shit!' I said to myself because I knew straight away I couldn't even get my glove off. I headed for the surface and when I got to within about 10 metres of the top the pain was unbearable, absolutely excruciating. I got to the surface, jumped in the boat and cut my glove off only to find my hand was black and continuing to swell. I was watching my fingers grow at a rate you couldn't imagine skin could swell at. Macca rushed me back to the boat. We were 80 miles from anywhere so the only thing we could do was get straight onto the radio and call the Flying Doctor Service. We explained to the Flying Doctor what I was experiencing and that we thought it might be a barb from a cone shell. The Flying Doctor said, 'Right, a cone shell?'

'Definitely.'

'Okay. A few stings in Queensland. One survivor. Two deaths.'

'Oh beauty,' I said.

'How fit are you?'

'Superman-fit. I swim 11 hours a day. Eat well. Eat fish. All the good things. Don't do drugs. Don't do alcohol very often. Fit. Fit.'

'Have you put a pressure bandage on your arm?'

'Yes, that's already done.'

'Well, you might be okay, but this is what's going to happen to you. You're going to take a stroke, have a mini heart attack and be paralysed down one side of your body. You must stay standing if you can. You won't be able to – you're going to lose consciousness – so make sure the guys with you keep you upright and keep you going. If you can survive for the next five or six hours, you'll be right.'

I was already starting to lose consciousness while I was talking to him on the radio, so young Mick, a 16-year-old, had to take over the boat and also look after me. Fortunately we had performed medical safety drills on the boat for an emergency like this, so everyone had a pretty good idea of what needed to be done.

The boat was heading back to shore and I was then rapidly losing consciousness, so two of the guys held me up, and when they got tired of doing that another two would take over. They knew they had to keep me vertical to keep my heart pumping so as I lapsed into unconsciousness they'd start slapping me around: 'Stay with us, Damo. Stay with us, Damo.'

They were actually watching me take a stroke, and occasionally I'd stop breathing, and they'd have to resuscitate me — give me the kiss of life. None of them were really impressed about having to do it; they reckoned I was a shit of a kisser, and obviously afterwards the jokes would do the rounds: 'I slipped the tongue into you, Damo, and you didn't even notice, did you!'

We were heading for Thursday Island which was the nearest point of land where we could get medical help. About 20 miles offshore the boys decided that the conditions were smooth enough for them to put me in the dinghy as that would get me ashore faster than the trawler could. What the doctor didn't tell me on the radio was that my legs would swell to such a degree that the skin would actually split, and it would stay that way for at least two weeks. You can't imagine the swelling and the blackness; it was beyond belief.

Anyway, the guys got me in the dinghy and started heading for shore as fast as they could but then the wind kicked in, the seas rose, and we were punching into it, *bang*, *bang*, *bang*. All that was doing was pumping the poison through my system even more rapidly; I was getting another boot. The guy driving the dinghy was freaking out but there was nothing he could do about it. I said to him, 'Don't worry about it, man. Go as fast as you can because no matter how slow you go it's going to still pump poison through me. Just give it to it. If I make it, I make it. If I don't, tell Kimmy I love her with all my heart.' And I was serious. He just looked at me and said, 'I hope I don't have to, man.'

So we are cutting for Thursday Island and the boys have radioed ahead through the Flying Doctor Service to make sure there was an ambulance on the dock waiting for us. But, wouldn't you know it, while the ambulance was at the dock when we got there the nurse was a native girl who couldn't speak English. All she wanted to know was if I had ambulance cover, and she wasn't going to take me to hospital until she knew the answer.

When we finally got to the hospital there was only one ward open and it was full of old ladies who were just lying around in their beds. Everyone on the island calls the hospital 'The House That Jack Built' because they didn't need a hospital there until everyone started getting 'the Jack', so it became The House That Jack Built! When I arrived, there was a going-away party happening for a few nurses and the doctors, and they were all on the piss. There was one young Chinese acupuncturist there and he was trying to tell me I hadn't been hit by a cone shell; I had only sprained my wrist while underwater and the consequences I was experiencing were because of the bends.

'Bullshit, man,' I told him in no uncertain fashion. 'You haven't seen what I've just been through the last six fuckin' hours!' He decided that while he wanted to help me he couldn't, so the bloke who had come ashore with me in the dinghy started screaming at him: 'You're a fuckwit. Get the fuck out of here. Give him something to take the pain away.' So this nurse who's half-cut came up to me to give me a jab in the arse, but she just pricked me. As I leaned forward she missed the target and squirted most of it onto my back. She didn't know how much she'd got into me so all she could do was hit me with what was left in the needle; there was no way she could give me another needle. She jabbed it into me and I thought it was going to break through my bone. Your body is so sensitive at this stage that the tiniest little pin prick feels like you've been hit by a bullet.

That was enough for us. We knew that there was no future for me if we stayed there, and because I was still alive six hours after being hit by the barb, we decided to steam 60 miles south to Hicks Island where we knew a mate had a good medical kit at his house. When we got there I gave myself a shot and the pain began to ease. I did that every day until it was gone completely.

It's a situation like this that makes you realise the respect you have for the guys you are with on a trawler. The bond between you is unique because at any second one of you could be at death's door and so far offshore that it's impossible to get immediate medical help.

It took me a year to completely recover from this cone shell experience. I lost the use of one side of my body: I was dragging one foot behind me, my face collapsed and one eye sagged. I couldn't even lift my arm on that side of my body. I had to clamp my mouth to one side just so I could drink, otherwise it would run down my shoulder, and just about every time I did this I either bit my tongue or my cheek. There were times where I thought I'd never recover. The best thing I did was go swimming as often as possible and force myself into trying to use that side of my body. Initially I was swimming around in circles, but with time I literally straightened things out and got back to being 100 per cent Damo.

CHAPTER 9

TORPEDOED INTO THE HISTORY BOOKS

Poon Lim was little more than a skeleton with skin and near death when he was dragged from a disintegrating raft in the Atlantic, but his mind was still strong enough for him to know he held an unenviable record, one he hoped no one would ever break.

The 25-year-old seaman from Hainan Island, in China, had survived an incredible 133 days aboard the raft after *SS Benlomond*, on which he was a steward, was blasted out of the water by a torpedo fired from a Nazi U-boat. It was 23 November 1942 and World War II was at its height. *Benlomond*, with 55 crew aboard, was at the time some 750 miles to the east of the Amazon en route from Cape Town to Dutch

Guyana when it came into the sights of the prowling U-boat.

The ship was a sitting duck as it was not under naval escort on this passage. The German crew lined it up, fired a torpedo, and just seconds later a direct hit decided *Benlomond*'s fate. The massive explosion that tore the hull apart was so severe that the ship sank in no time, giving the few crew who survived the blast little opportunity to escape.

Poon Lim managed to grab a life jacket and tie it around himself before leaping overboard. He knew he had to swim fast and as far away from the ship as possible because once the boilers in the engine room came into contact with the cool waters of the Atlantic the ensuing blast would bring another volcano-like eruption. As he swam away he could hear the desperate cries from shipmates who were trapped amid the wreckage. At one stage he saw five others clinging to a Carley float, which was the only form of liferaft in that era, but it drifted away so rapidly he was unable to reach it. He came to realise those five sailors were the only other survivors, but they were never to be seen again.

Immediately after *Benlomond* disappeared below the sea surface in a burst of massive bubbles, Poon Lim began swimming among the flotsam in the desperate hope he could find something that had broken free from the ship and was large enough to give him support. As he rose over the crest of each wave he would frantically scan the area around him, but it wasn't until almost two hours later that his prayers were answered in the best possible way. He spotted a Carley float only 30 metres away, swam to it and dragged himself aboard.

Carley floats were constructed from a length of copper or steel tubing between 30 and 50 centimetres in diameter which was formed into an airtight oval ring. This ring was sheathed, usually using cork, and then covered with a layer of canvas which was made waterproof using paint or a doping liquid. The floor of the raft comprised a grating made from either wooden slats or webbing.

For Poon Lim this float was truly heaven-sent as he immediately discovered the emergency rations which were stowed aboard had not been destroyed by the blast. The supplies comprised a few tins of biscuits, a container of water, flares and a torch. Even so he knew immediately that the odds were very much stacked against him when it came to surviving long enough to either be rescued or reach land: the world was gripped by an intense war and he was a near inconspicuous dot in the middle of the Atlantic Ocean. To give himself the best chance of being found he had to apply a high level of self-discipline from the outset, so he immediately imposed rations upon himself. By doing this his calculations told him he probably would be able to last for one month.

Regardless, there were other life-threatening challenges beyond the miserly amount of food he had: there was no shelter on the raft, so he was completely exposed to the elements – the blazing sun, dehydrating temperatures and storms – but incredibly not even this could outweigh his determination to survive.

Twice during the first month he became convinced he was destined to be rescued, the first time when a freighter came within hailing distance, then later when an American Navy patrol plane buzzed overhead. There was another time when he was spotted by a German U-boat, but instead of taking him aboard the crew of the sub decided they would leave him to his own fate. This convinced him even more that his destiny lay in his own hands, something confirmed by the fact that he was then out of flares.

He also knew that he had to retain a level of fitness, so whenever conditions permitted he would swim around the raft, despite the chance of being attacked by sharks. It was a regime that worked because he was able to maintain a surprisingly high level of strength, even though he was losing a considerable amount of weight.

Self-preservation remained his sole objective – it was his own version of 'every man for himself'. When his supply of rations dwindled and there was still no sign of rescue, he turned to fishing in a bid to get much-needed food. Somehow, using the water container as a hammer, he managed to form a crude fish hook from some of the metal and wire he had pulled from inside the torch. It took him days to bend and beat the metal into an effective shape then form a fishing line using the hemp rope that had been used to tie the rations into the raft.

When everything was ready he put a small piece of biscuit on the tip of the hook for bait then gently lowered it into the water – and much to his delight it wasn't long before he had secured his first fish. Then, using the sharp edge of a biscuit tin as a knife, he managed to fillet the fish. He quickly devoured some of the flesh in its raw state, savouring every morsel, and then put some aside so he could 'bake' it in the heat of the sun. It would be a change of flavour in his paltry diet. The innards of each fish he caught became valuable bait.

This was a repetitive cycle that kept him alive for more than a month, until the time when seabirds began appearing on the scene. By taking some of the seaweed which had by then attached itself to the bottom of the raft, Poon Lim was able to devise an amazing method for catching these birds. The weed was formed into the shape of a nest and beside this he placed some rotting fish, then while lying deathly still in the bottom of the raft he would wait for one of the birds to land. When the moment arrived Poon Lim would strike out in a flash and grab the bird by the neck, only to then be subjected to severe scratches and bites from his quarry until it was subdued and killed.

As is always the case in desperate situations, necessity was the mother of invention. He managed to extract a loose nail from the wooden planking in the base of the raft and, using one of his shoes as a hammer, he then hacked from a metal ration tin what would become a more effective knife – a tool which would be ideal for carving the bird into edible portions.

All along he had managed to replenish his limited water supply by tearing off the canvas covering from a life jacket and using it to catch the precious liquid each time it rained.

Not surprisingly, whenever Poon Lim saw sharks he cancelled his plans to exercise in the water. Instead, he set about trying to catch them using the carcass of a bird as bait. Fortunately the makeshift fishing equipment he had so cleverly created proved strong enough for him to haul a shark into the raft, but he hadn't considered the consequences. The moment the shark realised its days were done it set about attacking Poon Lim – it was like a fight to the death inside a tiny 10 square metre ring – and it was only a couple of hefty blows with the metal water container to the shark's head that gave Poon Lim what would prove to be a crucial victory.

It had not rained for some time and he was becoming extremely dehydrated. The blood that he sucked from the shark's liver quenched his massive thirst and helped keep him going until the next time it rained. This same fish provided him with a delicacy that he had enjoyed so often in his homeland – sun-dried shark fin.

For week in, week out, his lifestyle remained both monotonous and repetitious: catch fish and water, try to survive – and all the time enjoy the waxing and waning that came with each cycle of the moon. He could only live with hope, but it was a hope that was dwindling like a waning moon, especially when he realised that the marks which he had etched into a piece of timber in the raft revealed he had been drifting for more than four months.

It was on the day that he carved the 131st mark into the timber that he noticed a change in his environment – the colour of the ocean had transformed from the darkest of blue-black to a soft shade of sea-green. There was also a considerably greater number of birds overhead, and seaweed was drifting by. These were encouraging signs: land could well be just over the horizon.

What was nothing short of a miracle came on the 133rd day when Poon Lim spotted a tiny sail in the distance and set about waving frantically in a desperate bid to attract attention. His focus remained locked on the sail until the glorious moment when he saw the small vessel change course and head towards him. It was 5 April 1943 when three almost disbelieving Brazilian fishermen guided that boat alongside the raft and set about returning the gaunt but still strong Poon Lim to civilisation. The incredible drift had taken him to a point that was just off the immense mouth of the Amazon River: he had drifted about halfway across the Atlantic!

The fishermen took him to Belém, a city just inside the entrance to the Amazon, and there his amazing story began to unfold. No one had ever managed to go close to surviving for so long in such extreme circumstances.

Poon Lim's determined efforts to remain strong saw him able to walk unaided when he reached shore, even though he had lost 20 pounds in weight. He was admitted to hospital in Brazil and stayed there for four weeks while the impact of his exposure to the elements was erased.

News of this remarkable feat of endurance spread rapidly across the world and before long this humble ship steward, the sole survivor from *SS Benlomond*, was being feted by royalty and politicians. He went to New York and Washington where the US Senate and House of Representatives passed a special bill which allowed him to become a permanent resident of the United States. In England, King George VI personally presented him with the highest of civilian awards, the British Empire Medal. The British navy printed booklets describing Poon Lim's survival techniques, and these were placed in all liferafts.

Poon Lim took up residence in Brooklyn, just across the river from New York City. He died there in January 1991 aged 72.

CHAPTER 10

HALF-SAFE IN A HURRICANE

It started with a casual comment in March 1946 when Australian Ben Carlin was at Kalaikunda airfield in India. There were hundreds of vehicles on the field that the United States Air Force had abandoned for the Indian Government's benefit following the end of World War II. These vehicles were of no particular interest for Carlin – his involvement with the war meant he'd seen them all before; at least that is what he thought until a small and battered amphibious Ford jeep came into view. It stopped him in his tracks: there was an immediate connection – a fascination fuelled by his love of the sea and small boats, and unusual vehicles. For the next 15 minutes he clambered all over, around and under this battered little boat on wheels. He imagined where it might have been and what it might have achieved during the war. He then mused to his mate, 'Y'know, Mac, with a bit of titivation you could go round the world in one of these things.'

'Nuts!' was Mac's singular response, but it didn't register with Carlin. It was already too late; from that very moment his mind was locked onto an adventure that would snowball into what would become one of the most remarkable feats of endurance and courage seen last century! This was the start of an arduous adventure of gargantuan proportions that a war-weary world would devour: an adventure that went completely against the odds.

Carlin was born in Northam, Western Australia, in 1912 and educated at Perth's Guildford Grammar School before studying at university to be a mining engineer. His career path led to China in 1939 and there he began work at a coal mine near Peking (now Beijing). It was a career brought to an abrupt halt by World War II; he enlisted in the Indian Army's Royal Indian Engineers and served in the Middle East and Italy.

After the war ended one of Carlin's last military assignments was to inspect the ground installations the Americans had left as a legacy for the Indian Government, and that's how he came to be at the airfield on that fateful day – the day a floating jeep leapt into his life.

Until this love–at–first–sight moment Carlin's overwhelming desire had been to get out of the Indian Army and back to Australia asap. Now things had changed: he was obsessed by the amphibious jeep and the spirit of adventure it manifested. And while others might see his rapidly evolving dream of literally driving round the world via land and sea as being pure fantasy, far-fetched and hare-brained, he saw it as something that would be 'quite reasonably possible. It would be difficult enough to be interesting, a nice exercise in technology, masochism and chance, and a form of sport. It might even earn a few bob.'

Suddenly Carlin's life was consumed by the project/adventure. He was convinced it would take only 12 months to complete and be 'a last flutter before the inevitable relapse into domesticity'. Within two weeks he had written to his military superiors requesting they cancel his passage back to Australia and instead send him to the United States, where he expected to find the key element, a suitable World War II surplus amphibious jeep. This request was granted, and soon after he was aboard a ship bound for San Francisco via Hong Kong.

It was during the Hong Kong stopover that he received a much desired and very pleasant surprise: Elinore, an attractive American Red Cross nurse from Boston, whom he had met in India, was there to welcome him.

Carlin was desperate not to explain to Elinore why his plans had changed ... that he was on his way to America because he had fallen in love with an amphibious jeep; that he was planning an adventure that was almost beyond comprehension. But as is so often the way with women, Elinore sensed she was being sheltered from a secret, and she had to know. Eventually the pressure to tell all became too much for Carlin; he crumbled and the words spilled from his lips ... and much to his amazement there wasn't a reaction suggesting he should be committed to a mental institution. Incredibly, Elinore was as excited about this plan as its creator, and she wanted to be involved! But Carlin wanted no part of that suggestion, so much so that right down to the moment his ship was easing away from the dock in Hong Kong, he was still shouting to her, 'No' – this was no adventure for a woman.

Once American soil was under his feet, Carlin set about realising his bold ambition to see the world like no one before him. It was now an insatiable desire that could not be stopped: a runaway locomotive laden with determination, even though there was total frustration and adverse reactions at every corner he turned. Potential sponsors and supporters either couldn't comprehend or weren't remotely interested in his plans, and he was struggling to find a jeep.

At that moment he had only $10,000 and a dilapidated Plymouth motor vehicle to his name, and he wasn't quite sure which way to turn. He decided his first target would be Toledo, in Ohio, where the manufacturer of the Willys-Overland jeep was located. There he actually got to talk to the head man in the company's Sales Promotion department, but he did nothing to help, as Carlin explained: 'He was a Middle

Westerner; a smart cookie, and no sucker — he told me so. Yes, this chap had heard of the Atlantic but obviously didn't believe in it. The fact that he had it confused with Atlantis didn't help. He asked what experience had I with amphibious jeeps in or out of the water. None! I had only seen one. Had one ever crossed a large body of water, like Lake Erie? No. Had I ever crossed the Atlantic? No.'

The man from Willys–Overland then said 'No' to Carlin's request for assistance, as did every other major vehicle manufacturer where he sought support. There was only one solution: if this project was to get off the ground he would have to back it himself. With that decided he fired up the old Plymouth, threw his few possessions into it 'and headed for Washington DC to pick up the scent of a real, purchasable jeep and trail it to a kill'.

Bingo! Once in Washington he soon discovered two war-surplus amphibious jeeps were being auctioned in nearby Aberdeen. It was January 1947, and after orchestrating a bidding scam with a mate he managed to secure one of them for $901. Even so, this move would prove to be literally a stuttering start towards his goal: the engine in the tired old girl hadn't been run in years. Carlin's mechanical expertise was put to the test from the outset, and even when he completed what was a major effort just to get it started it remained barely alive. And even with it running roughly there was still the challenge of getting it sufficiently roadworthy for the 70-mile trip to Annapolis, the magnificently majestic old town on the shores of Chesapeake Bay which would be his home base. This was where the preparation for Stage One of his incredible dream – the crossing of the Atlantic – would be incubated.

On the road trip to Annapolis Carlin became increasingly excited by his purchase. The further he pushed on down the highway the more the sticking valves in the engine freed themselves, and soon the ailing machinery had coughed its way to where it was firing on all four cylinders. And the speed: it was quite amazing – 50mph at full flight!

However, soon after arriving in Annapolis, Carlin's excitement was quickly tempered by the dawning of a new awareness. As soon as he commenced his planned modifications there came a massive reality check. This was the first time since that moment at the airfield in India when he actually realised the magnitude of his undertaking with his chosen form of transport, along the route he proposed to take. He now realised this might be a misguided adventure. For example, while the jeep was amphibious by design, its crude underwater shape gave it a maximum speed of just four knots, and this would only be achieved through disturbingly high fuel consumption: three gallons per hour! On top of that, the weight associated with the modifications needed to make what was already an unseaworthy craft capable of crossing open expanses of ocean was becoming frightening: the jeep's overall weight would climb from 2400 pounds (1100kg) to 3650 pounds (1660kg). It had also to be accepted that this vehicle was a mere 18 feet 3 inches (5.56m) long and a skinny 5 feet 3 inches (1.6m) wide. It was an overgrown toy!

Carlin explained his dilemmas: 'In military service the vehicles had proved almost useless. Without loading, the open cockpit had no more than 15 inches of freeboard; except in calm inland waters, it was easily swamped. Because of its relatively great weight and ungodly shape, the jeep's reflexes were too slow to roll it away from waves as a normal small boat; it simply took them as it lay — straight over the sides. Scores, probably hundreds, never survived their first launchings.

'The way I saw it, my problems were simply retention of sufficient imbalance between the amounts of water inside and outside the hull, and cannage of enough fuel to keep the engine running for 2000 miles in the right direction at sea without destruction of the vehicle's mobility over land. Almost no one perceives or even believes that comparable problems are met ashore. It is dead-easy to build a small boat stout enough to withstand any pounding sea; it is no trouble to contrive a vehicle able to propel itself over desert. But it is quite a trick to make that very stout boat light enough to carry itself over continents on a pair of jeep axles. Whatever I did or added to the jeep I had to be conscious of weight.

'The whole vehicle had to be made so watertight as to withstand complete submersion for short periods. The cockpit and engine compartment I could enclose with a weatherproof superstructure. The radiator hatch could never be open at sea, so I should have to provide alternative cooling for the engine. My estimated fuel mileage at sea was about four miles per gallon, so I would need to carry 500 gallons: the only available space inside the hull was in front of the radiator and would hold a 25-gallon tank; the rest of the extra fuel, oil and fresh water must be contained outside the hull and carry themselves by their displacement.

'The original prow was broad and shallow; in a short sea it would pound heavily. It was strongly constructed and would stand attachment of a false nose in the form of a fuel tank of around 100-gallon capacity. The stern was square and stubby; across the transom I could strap a 25-gallon fresh water tank. I would rebuild the original 12-gallon gasoline tank and tow the balance of the fuel in a free tank.'

To ensure that the pressed steel panels which were spot-welded together to form the body of the jeep didn't work loose and leak, Carlin covered the entire outside of his vessel/vehicle with neoprene that he brushed on like paint. By late October all necessary work on the then nameless contraption had been completed, so it was launched for preliminary sea trials, which it passed 'in a sort of a way'.

With his car then sold and all bills paid Carlin was down to his last $300. That meant only one thing – he had no option but to start his round-the-world odyssey there and then; he couldn't afford to stay ashore any longer. It also meant he would have to brave the inhospitable Atlantic Ocean in winter, but that didn't cause him great concern. He continued on with his plans, deciding immediately that the leap-off point for his venture onto the often wild and wide open expanses of the Atlantic would be New York. A few days later he was piloting his ungainly and cumbersome vessel across the waters of Chesapeake Bay and setting course for New York via the inland waterway.

Fate, however, would soon intervene. It was as if he was not meant to throw himself to the mercy of the Atlantic at that time of the year. The jeep was plagued by a myriad of problems on the passage to New York and by the time these were resolved, winter had passed.

All along Carlin had hoped he might find a shipmate silly enough to accompany him on the

Atlantic crossing – someone who would share the physical and mental load associated with operating the vessel, and who would contribute to breaking the tedium. He knew, though, if that person wasn't forthcoming he would be prepared to go it alone.

At the same time Elinore, who was back home in America and spending time with Carlin, was still in a state of limbo about her part in the adventure and where she was headed in life, so Carlin decided to change all that: 'Elinore had been "Yes, I'm coming", "No, I'm not" all winter. The eighth of June happened to be a "yes" day so, not yet having bought an alarm clock [to wake himself on a regular basis should he undertake the passage solo], I waltzed her down to City Hall during the lunch hour; the man said "... pronounce-thee-man-and-wife-kiss-the-bride-and-send-the-next-parties-in".'

He had his crew!

There was no way this floating jeep could ever be described as remotely close to being seaworthy. Fully laden it boasted barely 30cm of freeboard! But that did nothing to deter the would-be adventurers. Just eight days after they took their vows they crawled aboard, started the engine, left the dock and cruised slowly down East River, past the Statue of Liberty and out to the open sea. By the time they reached the river mouth the newlyweds had already had plenty of time for contemplation, so much time in fact that both husband and wife were accepting that maybe their undertaking wasn't such a good idea after all. Carlin described the claustrophobic environment that confronted them: 'You are sitting in the left-hand driving position before a normal set of vehicle controls except that there are four extra gear levers which engage the propeller, bilge pump, four-wheel drive, and high-low wheel-drive ratios. Twenty inches away on your right is another bucket seat and beneath it a toilet: mounted beside it on the floor is a manual bilge-pump. In the floor between the seats are two flaps giving access to the bilge and transmission. Immediately behind the seats a bunk stretches the full five-foot width of the car; a shelf bearing a radio transceiver projects forward over the far end of the bunk. Directly behind you where a rear window should be is a 20-inch-square Perspex door.

'There is no upholstery and the interior is wholly austere, resembling a workshop rather than a car. All out-of-the-way space is occupied by shelves, racks, bags and boxes containing food, tools, spare parts, cans and clothing. The windscreen extends along both sides back to where you are sitting, but outside all is black. When you switch off the overhead lights, the windshield remains black because it is covered outside by a canvas dodger, but inches away through the side windows you can see occasional flickers and flashes of light on water which is sometimes below your waist, sometimes above your shoulder. Inside nothing is visible save a small compass glowing dimly two feet ahead of your eyes.

'You feel no road shocks but the car is wallowing drunkenly every which way. There is no whine from a differential, but from the same direction the booming rumble of a propeller occasionally swells above the steady snarl of the engine. The air is pleasantly warm and spiced with the fragrance of gasoline and oil.

'Already nauseated by movement and smell, you are going to sit or lie in this crazy cage for perhaps four weeks on end. You can imagine the trend of Elinore's thoughts as she lay helplessly sick this night, her first time in the jeep since the inaugural launching in Annapolis.'

What Carlin did not disclose in his description of the cell-like environment they now called home was that both he and Elinore were heavy smokers, a habit that would make the already fume-laden air in the cabin even more nauseating.

With the chilled 25 knot headwind and rolling seas playing havoc with their progress Carlin was beginning to accept he was aboard an unseaworthy dream: one that was under threat of foundering. They faced too many mechanical and structural problems, so they turned back and headed for shore.

This, it would turn out, was a change of plan that went very much in their favour. Their proposed voyage to Europe had been 'discovered' by *Life* magazine, and for an impressive fee of $500 Carlin agreed to return to New York so that the magazine could photograph their departure in grand style.

As impressive as it was, the $500 fee was quickly absorbed by the essential repairs he had to make before their 'official' departure on 3 July. With camera flashlights exploding and a small crowd waving farewell, Carlin guided his floating brick out onto the river and headed down the same track they had previously travelled. But it would prove to be yet another false start. There were many more problems, ones that would have convinced most other people it was time to end the dream: but not Carlin. Once more he turned back to port, this time unannounced, so he could try to get things right and give it another shot.

Their likely surrender came in mid-August. Carlin and wife had then returned to sea and navigated to a point 300 miles out into the Atlantic. For the first time things looked promising, but any thoughts they held about really being on their way were soon dashed: foul weather and a mechanical problem with the propeller shaft proved so serious that they prepared to abandon their vessel and leave it to the elements. There was no option but to be rescued.

'Steamers were frequently within reach but we didn't rush to call them,' said Carlin. 'But after a few days I persuaded myself that it would be unnecessarily foolish to delay the parting any longer; it was the hurricane season and we lay on a common track [to commercial shipping]. Still choosy, we turned down many prospects [for rescue] because they were southbound, too large and shiny, or too small and rusty.

'Finally, on the evening of 26 August we hooked an American tanker making, I thought, for Boston. When she stopped we had our valuables ready so we could abandon ship, and a hammer handy to tap a hole in the jeep's skin [to ensure it sank]. I shinned up a ladder and asked Captain Hans Brown – an old Norwegian and a gem – if we might come aboard. He said, "Hell – you not going to leave dat goddammed yeep lying around?"'

With that the crew winched the jeep aboard and the tanker got underway – bound for Montreal! It wasn't exactly where Carlin and wife wanted to go, but at least they were safe, and during the time they were aboard the tanker crew insisted that the barely amphibious jeep be given a name: it was to be *Half-Safe*.

Once in Montreal, and with *Half-Safe* still part of their life, the vision the Carlins held of circumnavigating the world re-emerged, and they set about rectifying the problems their 'sea trials' had exposed.

One year later a much modified *Half-Safe*, complete with a 280-gallon torpedo-shaped fuel tank that would be towed behind, was ready for another shot at Stage One of its journey: crossing the Atlantic. Montreal would be their official point of departure and Halifax, Nova Scotia, was where they would hit the water.

'I cannot imagine a finer departure point than Halifax: I'd gladly leave it any time for anywhere in anything,' said Carlin. And while they waited for the right weather the Royal Canadian Mounted Police, who perform the role of coastguards, paid them a visit: 'Notebook in hand, a Mountie corporal solemnly and courteously asked our intentions,' said Carlin. 'Equally solemnly I replied, "Corporal, we are going fishing." Stifling a grin he wrote the libretto and departed. No one was fooled, but nothing could be done to prevent our suicide.'

On 19 July 1950, *Half-Safe* tasted the Atlantic once more: destination, the Azores, approximately 1800 miles (2900 kilometres) away. The vessel was burdened with 735 gallons of gasoline, 30 gallons of water, 8 gallons of oil and enough food for a six-week passage. Incredibly, there was no stove on board, so meals usually came from cans.

Elinore's note in the log on that first day read: 'Left the Neanderthal pastures at 11.45 … The new tank tows like a dream. Now passing McNab's Island (he can keep it) … The feeling of great relief at seeing the last of Nova Scotia tempered only by the fact that we may yet just have to come back for some little thing.'

Their planned departure in smooth weather was perfectly calculated and after three days of motoring, the first navigation sun sights that Carlin was able to take with his sextant revealed that they had covered 125 miles at an average of 3.1 knots, a speed that would frustrate most mariners. But their progress was slowed even more on the fourth day when the wind strengthened from the northeast. Elinore became so violently seasick she could not take her turn at the wheel, so Carlin, who was totally exhausted from having been in the driver's seat for an inordinate number of hours, had no option but to shut down the engine and get some sleep. It was night, and just before he collapsed into a comatose state, his mind had been playing tricks on him. He was hallucinating. The drone of the engine had lured him into believing that *Half-Safe* was tearing through the water at 30 mph – her road speed at that engine speed – but instead it was a meagre 2.5 knots. Two days later, with Elinore still struggling with seasickness, the fatigue Carlin faced when driving at night brought more mind-bending experiences: 'Now that's a funny thing; acres of flower-patterned linoleum all around. The colours have changed; there's a red rose springing from the centre of each pattern; they were roses but now they're pink tulips. Interesting ... "Look out!" I jerked the wheel hard left just in time to clear a mob of sheep ahead; a close thing! Now all is black ...'

Suddenly he was jolted back to reality. The real world had returned: 'Black, nothing! There was no road-shoulder to jar me awake; it must have been the change of motion. I re-focused to see the compass reading 350 degrees – we were heading for Newfoundland. "Damnation!" I swing her about to 160 degrees, slowly to avoid the towline [attached to the fuel tank being towed astern].'

On the 11th day at sea, when they were a quarter of the way to the Azores, unusual noises emanating from the engine began to cause concern. A possible source was sticking engine valves, so Carlin shut down and became the ship's engineer, pulling the engine apart to remove carbon deposits in the hope that it would solve the problem. While it proved to be a successful operation *Half-Safe* was then forced to hove-to for almost 48 hours due to bad weather. Then, once underway, *Half-Safe* ventured into a trans–Atlantic shipping lane: 'To our relief none of several passing steamers – two within 100 yards – had seen *Half-Safe*,' Carlin said. 'Experience had taught us that shipmasters tended to panic at the sight of the tiny and "hopelessly unseaworthy" jeep and inevitably wanted to save us.'

After 25 days at sea they were still on track, albeit slowly. They had survived a wide gambit of weather, from glassy calms through to winds of 35 knots and big seas. This particular day was exceptionally calm so Carlin grabbed the opportunity to cast a line in the hope of catching a fish, not for food but for amusement: he wanted to break the humdrum. Bang! Within seconds he had hooked a dolphinfish: 'Instead of fighting he swam in with the hook like a dog retrieving a stick and climbed aboard almost unaided; I felt sure that until the end he thought it was all a game or at worst a practical joke. I felt like hell – as though I had caught my granny in a rabbit trap – but we had to have a colour photo. Elinore cut the engine and we hurried the photography so we could get the dolphin into the water in time; no go – he died in my arms and I just about wept in shame.'

With there being no stove, Carlin devised a novel cooking method: 'I dressed half the corpse, split it and wired it round the exhaust pipe. The results varied: the outside was raw and the inside burnt to a frazzle; but the core was delicious, and Elinore gorged and gorged.'

Half-Safe had to be stopped on a regular basis so Carlin could again pull the engine apart and breathe life into its aging body via minor repairs. At the same time it became apparent that *Half-Safe* was leaking. By the 30th day the voyage was taking its toll on Elinore. Her note in the log read: 'Leak somewhere – much water in bilge and engine ready to give out anytime … today settles it – the Azores are the end of the road for me.'

The next day, with *Half-Safe* stopped yet again for repairs, there was, for the first time since setting out from Canada, cause for celebration: the islands of Flores and Corvo could be seen in the distance! Incredibly, *Half-Safe* had remained safe – just – but there was more trouble to come. The engine was soon restarted and as the slow progress continued the islands became more clearly defined in the distance. *Half-Safe*'s engine was still stuttering and spluttering, then there was silence once more. Another breakdown. There was water in the carburettor. Again Carlin's mechanical talents saved the day. This would be another temporary stop of just 30 minutes duration before they headed into what they hoped would be their last night at sea before landfall. *Half-Safe* chugged on through the night, but it wasn't until daylight, when the bold red lava cliffs of the island were towering overhead, that the Carlins began to relax: 'The release of tension after 31 days times 24 hours of exhaustion and worry was sufficient to induce a surge of elation,' said Carlin. 'We were not yet round the world but, after three years of slogging, had already demonstrated the feasibility of what all the experts had deemed wildly impossible.'

As *Half-Safe* was guided towards a tiny cove an open launch appeared on the scene with the intention of giving them a tow. Carlin politely declined the offer, then when asked, he explained in fractured Portuguese that they had come from Canada. The gibbering among those on the launch left no doubt they were in a state of disbelief. When *Half-Safe* arrived in the cove the 200 islanders who were there to welcome them were also struggling to comprehend how something that resembled a half-submerged coffin had made it all the way from Canada. Carlin recalled what it was like stepping ashore: 'Our first few minutes ashore were physically delirious: we weaved, wobbled and staggered to the amusement of all. For a month we had never stood upright without arm support. Both of us had lost weight: Elinore from alimentary abstinence and I from loss of sleep. But we were both very healthy and muscularly fit.'

Once on land Elinore's declared desire mid-passage to abandon the adventure and head home to America quickly faded into obscurity. The pain and the misery she had endured days earlier no longer clouded her mind: she was ready for the onward journey. Within a few weeks though, she would be wishing she had stood by her original plan: *Half-Safe* would then be heading into a hurricane.

A few days after arriving Carlin set about eliminating the mechanical problems which so often threatened their very survival on the first stage. With those solved it was time to head to sea once more, this time leap-frogging from island to island in the Azores. At each port of call they endeavoured to put *Half-Safe* on display – at a price. This was their way of raising the money needed to pay their bills and top up the remaining $US200 they had to their name. Their stopover at this group of islands was Ponta Delgada, the capital of San Miguel. From there they would take another big step on their voyage across the Atlantic – 520 miles (836km) to Madeira.

But again things didn't go as planned: they made three false starts, each time being forced back through mechanical failure. It was incredibly frustrating, especially on the third occasion when they returned to Ponta after being 107 miles offshore and cruising along in superb weather.

The Carlins finally farewelled the Azores on 17

November – a Friday, a bad day to set sail, according to superstitious sailors.

By 22 November rough seas had slowed *Half-Safe*'s average speed on the passage to just 2.25 knots, and there were some ominous signs brewing with the weather as both the wind and sea began to rise. That night the wind reached gale force and the hammering the beam-on seas were delivering to *Half-Safe*'s superstructure and side panels left Carlin no option but to adopt a safety-first policy. He brought her to a halt then deployed the sea anchor (a drogue) from the stern, and the fuel tank that was being towed behind was then streamed from the bow.

'The wind rose to beyond 40mph during the day,' Carlin reported. 'The sea and sky were a sullen grey – cold, mean and menacing. *Half-Safe* rode much better by the stern: her flanks were not exposed to the breakers, but the aft end of the superstructure took a pounding.' As an added precaution he set an oil bag at the stern. The oil in the bag seeps from it slowly and spreads a light slick over the surface of the ocean. This to some degree quells the seas and decreases the damaging impact of approaching waves.

At best, sleep was intermittent in those conditions as checks for water in the bilge and the jeep in general were called for on a regular basis. At around midnight Carlin decided to poke his head through the hatch in the roof of the cabin to check the outside world – and spotted a 'bobbing bunch of objects about 20 yards away in the wan moonlight'.

'As I scratched my head my innards froze: it was our emergency gear, including the rubber raft! In a flash I dived overboard and had the stuff aboard before Elinore could respond to my yell. For a rapid bail-out [from *Half-Safe*] the gear had to be carried topside and lashed not so securely that it couldn't be yanked free.'

After spending 57 horrendous hours at the mercy of the conditions Carlin was becoming increasingly concerned about *Half-Safe*'s ability to survive in such hellish weather. Massive breaking waves, some well above 10 metres high, loomed above and ceaselessly threatened to entomb the cumbersome craft and its occupants. They were in survival mode, so he decided to try a new tactic: start the engine and turn downwind, then keep the power on to see if the ride became any safer. It took only minutes to realise that this manoeuvre was even more dangerous – they were exposed to even greater threat from the raging seas – so the sea anchor was deployed from the stern once more, the engine stopped, and a slow drift to who-knows-where resumed.

By then they had been at sea 10 days, the time they expected to take to cover the entire distance to Madeira, but they were only halfway! Fuel was already running low, so Carlin decided it was time to play safe: common sense would prevail over a compelling urge to make progress. They would only move when conditions were favourable, even though life onboard, at best, was miserable.

Using Morse code and a radio that offered only intermittent communication with Ponta and Madeira, Carlin was able to glean from weather forecasts that an intense low had formed to the northwest of their position. What he didn't know was that it was a hurricane! Their predicament could only get worse.

Over the next five days, conditions went from bad to extreme as comments from both husband and wife revealed:

'… Elinore and I wallowed in a damp coma; our breaths condensed directly overhead and the drips were inescapable.'

'This is serious. Pitching very badly … We almost go over with some smacks [from the massive seas]. It's rather cold in the jeep – getting colder all the time … Moreover, the bed-roll is so wet that the blanket is too.'

'Wonder how we'll keep warm when the brandy goes – only four swallows left.'

'I used to think it was an exaggeration when people talked of seas 30, 40 and 50ft high. I've now seen them … bloody huge waves, and the wind is blowing like hell.'

Carlin wanted to believe that there was no chance of *Half-Safe* capsizing, but as the hurricane continued to close on their position he was becoming less certain: 'When the jeep rolls from the blow of a breaking wave on the side panels its movement is really quite small, but the shocking violence makes it seem enormously greater.'

By late afternoon on the 15th day the seas were

'especially dangerous'. Outside the vessel the mounting fury was alarming as the wind increased to more than 50 knots. More drama was added to the mix when the sea anchor disintegrated through the sheer pressure being placed on it.

'I discarded the sea anchor and kept the motor idling to keep the jeep's head into the wind. On one such burst I felt the towline attached to the fuel tank foul the propeller.

'For half a minute I hesitated. On the one hand, after such a buffeting it was difficult to imagine any change but for the better. There was something eerie in the air, in the inexorable steadiness of the crescendo without – a wild madness. I stripped, grabbed a knife, looped it to my wrist, and went over [the side].

'First I cut the [fuel] tank free and hitched it to the stern; then I tackled the prop. An unnatural darkness had descended; underwater all was black. I cannot remember the details of what followed, how long I clung, clawed, and sawed, but I do remember vividly that delicious moment when I was able to turn the screw by hand. Back aboard, I didn't wait to dress before pressing the starter and getting under way.

'Within seconds we heard or felt a "ping". Instinctively I knew what it meant and swung the jeep about, yelling to Elinore to spot the lost tank. When she signalled that she could see nothing I yanked her down to the wheel and peered myself; too late – I got one glimpse of the tank veiled in spindrift and then it was gone. Initially I jogged *Half-Safe* into the storm to conserve ground, but an especially big wave that crashed on the windshield rattled us rigid and changed my mind; I turned about and ran. I can judge wind speed at sea up to 60 knots within a few miles, mainly by the height and behaviour of the wind riffles, but from there on the riffles dissolve into spindrift. It was now blowing well over 60 and still rising in a way I had never experienced. From each breaker the jeep's after-end was taking a frightful pounding. Now there was a full hurricane outside.'

Elinore was continually concerned that the safety equipment lashed to the roof might again be ripped away by the force of a wave breaking over the top of *Half-Safe*, so after each one of these impacts she would open the hatch and fumble around with her hand for the reassuring feel that it was still there. Carlin remembered that each time she did this she would 'glance at me self-consciously; I would grin; she would pout and snarl an inaudible "I don't care a damn what you say. I'm going to make sure!"'

Now, more than ever before, *Half-Safe* was on the absolute edge of being overwhelmed by the enormity of the breaking seas, yet fear was never going to save them: 'Our personal reactions were interesting,' said Carlin. 'Elinore and I are rather nervous by nature. Early on, the mounting onslaught raised many a hackle. Perhaps we went through fear and beyond, for when the show was really on there was no sense of fear – only a drum-taut tension, alertness, expectancy. Only one thing was certain: sooner or later the superstructure would cave in and we'd have to bail out in one large hurry. A couple of times I had Elinore recite the escape drill aloud – she yelled it into my ear as the symphony outside drowned even the sound of the motor: "You shout 'OUT': I get out and wait. You follow and grab the gear; I follow you. KEEP IN CONTACT!"

'There was no question of inflating the raft in that sea – inflated, it would have scudded away like a panama hat — but, provided the equipment wasn't wrenched from our grip before the wind moderated, there was no reason why we shouldn't go on living. I had no doubts concerning our ability to survive in the water, but the matter of getting out and away quickly was very much on my mind; once holed, *Half-Safe* would sink in a twinkle. And so we sat hour after hour waiting for the moment; feeling neither wet nor cold, neither tired nor hungry. I guess we shouldn't have felt cold; in readiness we had donned every scrap of warm clothing.'

At 3 am the next day *Half-Safe* was still being pummelled by the abominable seas and hurled every which way when another crisis arrived — the jeep's motor coughed a couple of times then expired. Immediately a powerful smell of petrol fumes filled the cabin. Carlin ripped the engine hatch open and in an instant saw the problem. A fuel pump gasket had failed and petrol was spilling over parts of the hot engine. They were now aboard a floating bomb, and at the same time, with *Half-Safe* drifting aimlessly, she was more exposed than ever before to also being bombed from the outside — by a raging sea. The only thing he could do was tear into making a replacement gasket and solve the problem.

Working in the dim cabin light Carlin had a makeshift gasket made and fitted in record time. The fuel leak was stopped, but now he faced one of the greatest dilemmas imaginable. The bilge was full of explosive fumes and the spark that would come when he pushed the starter button could blow them and their world to high heaven. Equally, though, the malevolent seas that were running wild outside could deliver their own death blow. A decision – to press the starter button or not – had to be made: 'Deeming the sea more dangerous, I pressed the button. WHAM! – a flash of orange-red flame [but no huge explosion]. No fire followed – don't ask me why.'

With no sea anchor to provide at least some form of a safety net *Half-Safe* was being driven slowly downwind by the bullying force of the hurricane and the life-threatening waves it was generating. The conditions were so demanding that neither crewmember could stay at the wheel for more than an hour at a time, yet amazingly, while having had no sleep, they were not experiencing mental or physical fatigue. Adrenalin was proving to have an amazing influence on them.

Carlin continued to describe the onslaught the hurricane was handing out, and their desperate bid to counter it: 'In such winds there is no defined cleavage between air and water; the aqueous concentration simply diminishes with increase in altitude. *Half-Safe* was shrouded constantly by a horizontal hail storm that blasted her panels with a solid roar. In daylight the sea around smoked like the aftermath of a bushfire in a high wind.

'At times the jeep was smashed and submerged by two or three breakers within five minutes, but it might be half an hour before the next one. Sometimes there was a warning; sometimes none. When the break was far astern the express-train roar of the thundering white wall drowned even the constant blast of the spindrift while we cowered tense and braced for the coming shock – *WHAM! WHSSH!* – and it was gone. When close behind, there was no warning before the stunning crash. Several times crests breaking close behind – virtually over her – hammered the jeep down with such violence that we were left sitting in mid-air. A moment later our seats were regained with a bone-rattling thump.

'There, separated from that howling wet wilderness by three-sixteenths of an inch of transparent plastic, we sat warm, relatively dry and comfortable, breathing as freely as chain smoking permitted, controlling with ease the power of many horses emanating from a complex metal mechanism fashioned in Detroit and making 3400 electrically fired explosions per minute, and we were there voluntarily. Most people would prefer jail for life.

'Even after a day of survival I could never believe that the next breaker wouldn't smash the superstructure. I don't fully understand how the structure stood. Partially it was design and materials: a nice combination of strength and resilience – a steel fist in a plastic glove. Partially it was her lack of freeboard. The velocity of flying white water is more to be feared than the weight of green; and the closer to the solid surface the slower the white water flies. (I see excess freeboard as a chin stuck out to be hit.) Partially it was *Half-Safe*'s weight and stability: she behaved like a waterlogged balk of timber, while an orthodox small vessel is much more "live" and throws herself about violently.'

By this stage they were convinced they would die. It was highly unlikely they could live through another night like the last, and as there was no sign of an improvement in the weather it was definitely time to consider every conceivable option for survival. First, though, Carlin owed it to Elinore to ask if she was ready to go 'safety first' and abandon the jeep, or stay on and take the chance. She chose the latter.

Carlin's efforts to communicate with the outside world were continually frustrated, primarily because everything aboard *Half-Safe*, including the radio and Morse code equipment, was damp – and those things hate water. At one stage he was so determined to succeed he grabbed a belt and strapped the Morse key to his thigh then kept hammering out a message. But it was all to no avail. As a consequence, he and Elinore were convinced that their inability to make contact with a shore base, plus knowledge in the outside world of the magnitude of the hurricane, and the fact that they were so far behind schedule, would convince family and friends they had perished.

The jeep was about 260 miles from Madeira when the hurricane struck, and still had enough fuel to cover at least 300 miles. But now the conditions were forcing them on a course to the southwest – at right angles to their desired track. Carlin's calculations that day confirmed his worst fears. They had been driven a lot further away from their destination and had only enough fuel to cover 180 miles. He was beginning to think that the time would soon come when their only escape route from this drama would be for them to motor towards an inter-island shipping lane, and hope that a ship would find them and give them fuel.

'There was nothing but hope in my head,' Carlin said. 'The wind had faded to 50 but the sea remained immense.'

While the storm continued to rage outside, a ray of sunshine entered their otherwise gloomy lives that day. Carlin finally managed to make radio contact with shore, meaning word would soon be out that they were alive. Even so, there were still no guarantees that they were safe. They remained in survival mode.

All storms must end sometime, and eventually the wind had eased to a relatively comfortable 35mph. Twenty-four hours later it was all but gone.

Carlin and wife could not believe their good fortune: 'Elinore and I grinned at each other like monkeys in a tree,' he said. 'Equally suddenly a yearning for food and sleep submerged us (I hadn't slept for 72 hours; Elinore for 60) and keeping awake until 1600 [when the next radio communication was scheduled] was hell. From this point onward, our only concerns were radio-fuel and food-sleep.'

At a previously agreed time Carlin was again able to communicate with shore, and this enabled him to arrange for a Portuguese naval vessel to bring 50 gallons of gasoline to them. That would put Madeira within range.

While they waited for confirmation of where they would rendezvous, Elinore's diary note on their 20th day at sea reflected their improving circumstances: '1700. Had HOT ravioli (warmed on the exhaust manifold) and DEVOURED same – hungry for first time in weeks. Going along very well ... feel most cheerful. Just finished 2¼ hour watch, which is good for me.'

Carlin's firm belief that the worst was behind them was shattered when, after taking sun sights with his sextant to fix their position, he realised for the first time in days that their compass had an error reading of 16 degrees. In simple terms, they had been heading on a course that was nothing like what they believed they were on. However, this frustration was short-lived: later in the day he achieved strong radio communications with their saviour, the navy ship *Flores*. The radio signal was so strong that Carlin had no hesitation in throwing open the hatch in the top of the cabin and leaping out to look for the ship – and there it was, just two miles away!

A short time later the storm-battered *Half-Safe* was hitched onto the stern of *Flores* like a bedraggled rat on a rope, and its crew were aboard being feted and fed. The ship's commander, Henrique Pessoa, told them that the storm had been so fierce it had actually damaged his ship. They had recorded wind gusts of up to 90mph.

After bringing new life to his tired body with a reinvigorating shower, and then being fed to the stage where he felt 'stuffed like a Christmas turkey', Carlin transferred the desperately needed fuel to *Half-Safe*, then he and Elinore clambered back aboard and cast off. They were then 115 miles from Madeira.

It was 23 days after they departed San Miguel that a sight they often believed they would never see beckoned on the horizon. Elinore wrote in her diary: '0800. We can see Madeira – spotted the light during the night. Still a headwind and another grey day. On last loaf of bread – everything else gone – such appetites!

'1600 … Ben fighting the wheel all day … the last 30 miles will be the longest …

'… Still haven't reached the western point of the island which we could see early this morning. Horrible day in all respects – I shall henceforth hie me to a nunnery. Punching into the headwind *Half-Safe* was making little more than two knots. I know of no nunnery that might tolerate my shocker.'

At 2300 hours on that 23rd day at sea the Carlins reached safe sanctuary, and there was no welcome as such. Carlin recalled: 'At 0630 [the next day] *Half-Safe* rounded the breakwater and groped for a buoy in the sleeping harbour. I remember the surface of that buoy every time I walk bare-footed; it was patronised by over-fed seabirds.

'That was Tuesday, 12 December 1950. Instead of an easy nine- or 10-day downhill run, it had been a hellish 23 compounded by bad weather, bad luck and bad judgement.'

With this monstrous achievement behind them, the Carlins were ready to literally take on the world. *Half-Safe* had survived everything the Atlantic Ocean could muster and hurl in their direction. Surely this would, with time, prove to be the most arduous and dangerous part of the circumnavigation they were now determined to complete.

The reality was that what would become one of the more remarkable adventures the world would come to know had only just begun. There was much, much more ahead, and England was their next goal.

From Madeira they cruised almost incident-free to the Canary Islands and the coast of Africa. At Cape Juby, on the southern coast of Morocco, *Half-Safe* returned to being a motor vehicle and headed off on the trek north to the entrance to the Mediterranean where it would sail across the Straits of Gibraltar.

On reaching the southern tip of Europe the Carlins meandered north through Spain and then across the border into France. By their standards it had been a relatively uneventful drive but as they headed towards Paris mechanical problems began to emerge, problems which reminded Carlin that he was beginning to ask too much of his 'ugly duckling': 'At Annapolis I had built the jeep to last 12 months which I reckoned ample for the circumnavigation. Now, four years later, she was showing signs of decay, mainly from internal corrosion. Before tackling Eastern Europe and the long, rough stages of Asia she would require a major overhaul, and Britain was not only the obvious workshop but also the most promising potential source of funds from exhibition, even if that meant a donkeys-on-the-sands sort of thing. London as soon as possible was our programme.'

Carlin's intention was to head directly from France to England but that changed when the *Daily Express* newspaper in London confirmed the hire of the jeep for a one-month exhibition in London for a £500 fee – money that would cover the cost of the much-needed rebuild of *Half-Safe*. However, the newspaper didn't want the jeep in London for another two months, so that meant the Carlins had time to kill. They decided this would give them the opportunity to continue exploring so headed north through Europe to Belgium and then Holland and Germany before crossing 14 miles of water to Denmark: 'This perfect evening *Half-Safe* steamed so well that by 1930hrs she was weaving through a tangle of canoes, rowboats and small buoys to be mobbed by a delighted Danish crowd on Korsor's Beach. Rescued by Commander Hertz and bathed and nourished in the sanctuary of the naval station, we were quite well groomed and chipper when Copenhagen press photographers descended. After a night in a hotel the 68-mile triumphal procession to Copenhagen was a new experience.

'All along the road people waved and waved and half a dozen times we were flagged to stop. One old Dane followed us for miles, waving, smiling and cheering. Finally we stopped, whereupon he grasped our hands and shook them wildly, saying that in his estimation Columbus was a piker by comparison and wasn't there something, anything at all, he could do for us.'

On 13 August 1951 *Half-Safe* bid farewell to Copenhagen and was set on a sea and land course back to France and then England. Mechanical problems continued to plague its progress, including a broken suspension spring. It was an all too solid reminder for Carlin that his amphibious jeep was close to giving up on him.

On reaching London one would have expected Carlin to be filled with elation and a great sense of achievement, but incredibly, just as *Half-Safe* was ready to give up the ghost, so was he. He'd had enough. His long-held dream of circumnavigating the world was being eroded by physical and mental fatigue.

'Without trying I could assemble a sound case for its ending forthwith,' he said on reaching the coast of England. 'Her Montreal–London achievement was prodigious. It had convinced my friend Mac and the rest of the world of the circumnavigation's feasibility. She was one-eighth the size of any other vessel that had crossed the Atlantic under power – and she was not even a boat. She was the only amphibian to have mastered an ocean. The jeep had carved her tiny notch on the Pillar of History.

'Five years after conception she remained only one-fifth of the way around the world and the rest of the trip would be more hazardous. Now aged 39 I had lived from a suitcase or kitbag for 13 years; the travel urge was long satisfied and I yearned for a permanent hat-peg, a lawn mower, the pit-a-pat of "footsies". If beforehand I had been persuaded that the trip would take longer than a year I would have dropped it; now five years later I was barely started.

'Nor could the law of Chance be ignored: anything can and will happen sooner or later. The "obvious" dangers didn't scare me: although the sea is always menacing, always ready to slash at any chink in the wall. It has no magic; a great foolish beast of unlimited power and patience, capable in time of breaching the citadel by blind pounding yet lacking the wit to slip the simplest latch. Trans-ocean jeeping resembles bullfighting: outmatched physically one may survive only by guile. But, whereas the bull can be killed, one can hope only to fool the sea and live to fight again.'

Half-Safe's achievement made headlines throughout England and in many other parts of the world. Accolades poured in, one of the most noteworthy being from pioneer aviator, America's Cup challenger, and one of the century's great sportsmen, Sir Thomas Sopwith. He wrote: 'I am full of admiration for your Atlantic crossing, but don't do it too often!'

While the reasons to abandon his dream were near overwhelming, Carlin knew he could not walk away until there was 100 per cent conviction that it was the right thing to do. There was still a small percentage of desire saying 'don't quit', and before long that percentage was on the increase.

'It was a psycho-factor that counter-tipped the imbalance,' he said. 'Of my past imbecilities the omissions rankled longer and stronger than the commissions: "if only I had grabbed that opportunity … taken a chance that time in … given that par-boiled redhead one more break!" Those are the pangs that gnaw in the night. Such an opportunity could never recur and I would kick holes in my coffin if I passed it up.'

By New Year's Day 1952, Carlin and wife had completely surrendered to a greater force. They drove their jeep into a mechanic's workshop in Birmingham and there *Half-Safe* would be taken apart bit by bit and completely rebuilt.

Their odyssey would continue.

More than two years after arriving in England, Carlin resumed the story: 'The 30th of May 1954 was a big day for Clan Carlin: friends obscured the river's bank as I nosed down through the willows at Bray-on-Thames. Amid cheers the jeep was afloat for the first time in three years ... and seconds later the rudder and propeller were stuck fast in a mud bank. Otherwise her performance was fine; and not a flaw showed. Elinore and I were jubilant.'

It was a much different looking *Half-Safe*. It was more streamlined in appearance, much more modern-looking than the amphibious jeep that had been wheeled into the garage in Birmingham for surgery.

As keen as they were to get rolling once again, media commitments, including a book and possible film about this arduous adventure – projects which promised much-needed cash to finance the ongoing journey – meant the Carlins could not put England behind them until April 1955. This next stage of the odyssey would start with another crossing of the

English Channel, from Dover to a beach in Calais, where *Half-Safe* came ashore somewhat ingloriously. When the jeep's wheels reached French soil *Half-Safe* immediately became bogged, and it wasn't until some hours later, with assistance from locals, that it was exhumed through much shovelling, grunting, pushing and dragging, and put on the road.

France, Switzerland and Italy made up the next stage of this incredible 'passage' before *Half-Safe* turned east to Venice, Istanbul, Ankara, Damascus, Baghdad and Teheran on roads that were little more than rugged tracks comprising rock, rubble and suffocating dust.

It was 86 days and 8550 miles after departing London when *Half-Safe* trundled into Calcutta. Remarkably, the jeep was in fine shape; however, Carlin and wife had taken a beating. The plan he had devised in England involved *Half-Safe* crossing land and sea south through Asia and on to Australia, with his home port of Fremantle being a particular goal. However, it was becoming obvious through circumstances beyond his control that this was an impossible dream. His only option was to ship *Half-Safe* from Calcutta to Fremantle, drive across much of

Australia, then ship it back to Calcutta before resuming the journey east towards China, Japan, Alaska and the finishing line in Montreal.

Calcutta also represented an emotional milestone for the Carlins, as Ben explained: 'Elinore's constant seasickness across the Atlantic had imposed a great strain on her … each time at sea she swore she was getting off at the next stop; each time ashore she quickly forgot and gaily shipped out again. It was with infinite reluctance we decided that beyond Calcutta, Elinore would be replaced by a male. After her courage in tackling the Atlantic, in braving its repeated trials and in suffering (me and) the Middle East and India in summer, it was a crying shame that she couldn't be in at the kill but … she would accompany me to Australia before taking a ship back to New York.'

Half-Safe was loaded onto a ship bound for Fremantle where, after almost 17 years of absence, Carlin returned home in October 1955 with his wife and their well-travelled jeep.

After more than two weeks of reunions and celebrations the Carlins then clambered aboard once more to begin their journey across the continent. This included putting *Half-Safe* onto a train for part of the way — across the Nullarbor Plain, an often impassable desert track in those days that made up much of the distance between Perth and Adelaide. Melbourne followed, then it was north to Sydney. Carlin noted with interest that on this latter leg of their journey Elinore was far from impressed by the rough country pubs they visited, and both he and his wife agreed that Canberra, where sheep were grazing within sight of Parliament House, was 'the deadest and most uninteresting town in the world'.

Once in Sydney, Carlin exposed Elinore to a way of life she struggled to comprehend. This led her to note: 'Australians seem to live in the past, evoking old memories ... they will sit up all night talking, talking, and drinking — beer ... completely lacking in manners/finesse; if you want a drink you pour it yourself; when you enter a home you are not asked to remove your coat ... how they love to go over the past.' Carlin was quick to explain: 'Australian reasoning (and mine) differs from Elinore's: a non-obnoxious guest is treated as one of the family: "help your bloody self, mate!"'

In December *Half-Safe* was driven back to Melbourne where it was put aboard a ship for the voyage back to Calcutta.

No matter where *Half-Safe* and its owner went on the journey to the east from Calcutta there were extreme levels of disbelief relating to where they had come from and where they were headed. Having survived an Atlantic hurricane and some of the world's most treacherous roads, Carlin quite understandably hoped the worst was behind him, but Burma would throw down a challenge that came from hell. At this stage he had been joined on the trip by a chap named Barry Hanley, and it was on the so-called roads in the dense jungle in Burma that the adventure went close to being brought undone: 'Things got worse and worse until all sense of comparison was gone,' said Carlin. 'Beyond "hellish" and "superhellish" one's power of description breaks down. Soon came an incomparably worse stretch – and then another – and another. Mentally I was out of touch with the rest of the world. I was in a state resembling drunkenness – a trance – induced by dread and determination: certain senses and skills are tremendously heightened. A drunken superman on wheels, I was running a miles-long gauntlet paved like Hell with evil intentions of devils thrusting and bashing with an endless armoury of gigantic clubs and spears. I ducked, dived, backed, bobbed, weaved, and crashed forward, knuckles whitened by defiant gripping of wheel. Now our predicament was irrevocable. Regrets? Yes — enormous — but there was no more thought of turning back.'

Hanley had to act as an escort on this horrendous stretch, doing his best to guide Carlin, who was at the wheel of *Half-Safe*, over a road strewn with jagged boulders up to 75 centimetres high.

'For miles Barry conned me foot by foot. Many times he and I squatted to plan an attack: "Eighteen inches forward on full right lock. Straighten. Back six inches. Half-left. Forward nine inches ..." This track would have strained a snake.

'I felt no heat, although once I noticed a reading of 146 degrees Fahrenheit [63 degrees Celsius] inside. I am prouder of nothing than that day's driving. Although I had done nothing but drive a jeep for 25

miles it had been the most exhausting day of my life –
mental exhaustion. The first seven miles had taken
no more than 40 minutes as had the last eight miles;
thus the 10 miles of mountain had taken 10 hours.'

Eventually *Half-Safe* moved on through Bangkok
to Danang before crossing the South China Sea to
Hong Kong. The Formosa Strait, Taiwan and the East
China Sea leading to Japan formed the next
undertaking.

From Japan this remarkable journey would
continue with a crossing of the North Pacific to the
Aleutian Islands and the Bering Sea until finally the
wheels found North American soil. Carlin was then
on the home stretch, one that would include a loop
through mainland USA. The road ahead took *Half-
Safe* down to Vancouver then Los Angeles and
through Texas to Buffalo, New York, and finally
Montreal. It was April 1958, when he was passing
through Fort Worth, Texas, that Carlin experienced
for the first time a hint of the disbelief that people
would hold when it came to them hearing what *Half-
Safe* and he had achieved; it was deemed to be
impossible in the eyes of most people: 'City Texans

were subdued and seemingly uneasy, as though waiting for something to happen. The only question ever asked of me by a Texan came as I drove out of Dallas: at a stop light a cop in a patrol car drew alongside to ask, "You hit any water with it yet?"'

Similarly, in Buffalo, New York, only 400 miles from the end of this amazing journey, a service station attendant showed exceptional interest in *Half-Safe* and the maps drawn on the side of the superstructure showing the route it had taken around the world. After 10 minutes of contemplation the young man turned to Carlin and inquired: 'You bin any dem places, or did somebody just paint dem on?'

On 12 May 1958, this courageous and almost incomprehensible journey, one that demanded a level of endurance few men could muster, came to an end when *Half-Safe* arrived in Montreal and completed its lap of the world – a staggering 62,000 miles by road and 16,000 miles by sea.

When looking back over every mile, and every one of the most challenging and death-defying experiences that had confronted him, Carlin said there was one highlight that stood tall above the rest, and it wasn't the Atlantic hurricane: 'Without doubt that hideous 10 miles in Burma between Kawkareik and Myawaddee, was the apex; quite literally I would rather face two Atlantic hurricanes.'

Special thanks is extended to Guildford Grammar School, Guildford, Western Australia, for granting permission to use text and photographs from the book, The Other Half of Half-Safe, *which the school first published in 1989.* Half-Safe *is on display in the school grounds.*

CHAPTER 11

THE BAILEYS – A WHALE TALE

It's the ocean's hidden dangers that can all too often destroy the dreams of cruising sailors.

Threats come in many forms. In a severe storm there is always a sense of fear and foreboding; and great anxiety can manifest when navigating a poorly charted area of ocean. But nothing can compare with the horrendous element of shock that comes with an overwhelming element of surprise – like when a fire suddenly erupts on board, or the yacht smashes into a semi-submerged and unsighted object. This is when your world of sheer bliss transforms into one of sheer terror. No longer are you cruising, you are fighting for your life.

In 1973 English couple Maurice and Maralyn Bailey were cocooned in their very own idyllic world aboard their 31-foot plywood cruising yacht, *Auralyn*. They were migrating to New Zealand, and after departing England the previous year and crossing the Atlantic they had transited the Panama Canal. From Panama their initial course into the Pacific was set for the Galápagos Islands, where, after some cruising, they planned to enjoy the islands of the South Pacific before sailing to their ultimate destination.

It was 4 March and they were making good speed on the planned 10-day passage out of Panama. *Auralyn* was then about 250 miles from the Galápagos Islands, and the Baileys were all the time sampling the pleasures and serenity only cruising sailors know. This was a day when a refreshing tradewind was propelling them under full sail across a relatively smooth sea directly towards their destination.

Soon after 7 am, when Maurice was responding to having been roused by his wife to go on deck and stand his watch at the helm, there was a near-silent but incredibly preponderant impact with a then unknown object – an impact so forceful that the yacht was heaved up out of the water. Until that moment *Auralyn* had been ambling along with the auto-pilot doing the steering while Maralyn went to the galley to prepare breakfast.

The shock of the collision sent the Baileys rushing to the cockpit. Maralyn was there first and after taking a few seconds to absorb the scene she shouted to her husband that they had hit a whale and it was badly injured – the sea was turning red. Their immediate fear was that the wildly thrashing tail of this huge, 12 metre long mammal, which was then right at the stern of the yacht, would come crashing down and create imponderable carnage. But that thought was incredibly brief: what of the yacht? Had it been damaged by the impact? Was it taking water?

Maurice charged below like a man possessed, and as his feet hit the flooded cabin floor his worst fears were confirmed. He bullocked his way forward to the area of impact, and there it was – a hole below the waterline near the galley on the port side that was so large he could almost climb through it. Water was pouring into the boat so rapidly through this gaping breach that he knew straight away their chance of keeping *Auralyn* afloat was already remote.

After 40 minutes of a panic-infused effort to slow the ingress of water and pump out what was already inside the hull, the Baileys accepted they would be surrendering their yacht to the sea: there was no hope of keeping it afloat. From that moment their attention turned from saving their yacht to saving themselves.

Both the liferaft and *Auralyn*'s inflatable rubber dinghy were launched, and then every possible item of food and equipment they had time to grab was thrown into the dinghy. It was a purposeful procedure, and while anxiety and urgency prevailed, both held a deep-seated belief that it would be only a very short time before they would be rescued, primarily because they were cruising in close proximity to a shipping route.

Less than one hour from the moment of impact the Baileys were aboard their dinghy with the liferaft in tow, all the time watching what was their life's dream disappear agonisingly slowly below the ocean's surface. It was like watching the sun setting: the hull began to submerge then disappeared in a burst of bubbles and turbulent water, then the mast and sails literally slipped out of sight. When the very tip of the mast vanished beneath the sea surface the only evidence of what had been were a few small pieces of equipment which had floated free. Maurice then rowed the dinghy into the debris field so the two of them could recover any additional items they thought might be needed. This included pencils, a container of margarine, and plastic water containers. Even so, they were surprised how few things had actually appeared on the surface.

With the yacht gone, the Baileys entered a world of total isolation, one which was then overburdened by shock and disbelief. Maralyn was weeping while Maurice struggled desperately to come to terms with what had happened.

They slowly gathered their senses, and soon they were calculating how many days their supplies would last: probably one month, at a stretch. Their thoughts also turned to when it might be that someone would realise they were missing. They didn't want to acknowledge the obvious answer to this question because since leaving England they had been living in a transient world of indefinite destinations and with no real timeframe. On top of that, even if a search was initiated there would be no certainty as to where it should be concentrated. Such was the ensuing despondency that even at this early stage Maurice was contemplating what it would be like to experience death.

There was also the question of how they would retain their sanity and keep themselves occupied. The reading material they had grabbed and thrown into the dinghy only reflected their hasty departure from the yacht. There were two books, one titled *Richard III* and the other *Voyaging*, written by a cruising legend of that era, Eric Hiscock. Worse still, there were two dictionaries.

Fortunately some vital pieces of navigation equipment, including a sextant, had been thrown aboard the dinghy, but in reality these items were of little use because the dinghy and raft were on no fixed heading: instead of being on a course towards the Galápagos Islands they were destined for points unknown, and there was no need to navigate. And with there now being so much uncertainty in their lives, especially when it came to how long they would be on this aimless drift, they quite wisely rationed food from the outset.

Initially the Baileys took to rowing towards the Galápagos, doing this at night because the heat of the day made conditions too exhausting for them. They would take it in turns to row for two hours: one person being in the dinghy and the other towed along in the liferaft. They continued with that procedure until 8 March, the day a navigation calculation plotted on a chart by Maurice revealed that the wind and current were having a greater influence on their trajectory than the rowing: they were being carried on a course to the west that would take them well to the north of the Galápagos Islands. Not even ditching the liferaft so they could cover a greater distance by dinghy alone was considered viable.

While they accepted there was then no chance of reaching the islands they consoled themselves with the knowledge that they were drifting along in a shipping lane, and this promised the best chance of rescue. They also had to accept that they were extremely vulnerable. Their survival now relied on

two inflatable craft – a small circular liferaft and an inflatable dinghy about 2.7 metres long. Should both end up being punctured, the Baileys' chance of survival would deflate with them. They were made all too aware of this within a week of *Auralyn* sinking: the liferaft in which they had stored the bulkiest of their supplies, and which had become their sleeping quarters, began to lose pressure.

Because they were in the vicinity of a shipping lane it was decided they should establish a three hour on/three hour off watch system with one person sleeping while the other kept a lookout for passing vessels. At the same time, the person who was awake had the task of pumping air into the raft on a regular basis to counter the continual loss of pressure.

The exhaustion that came with their rowing had seen them deplete their water supply faster than they had hoped, but at the time they felt there was no alternative. At that stage dehydration was their greatest enemy, and because there was no sign of rain it became their greatest fear. The reality was that a passing ship was now their only hope for rescue, but they also had to accept that their liferaft and dinghy represented only the smallest of dots on a massive expanse of ocean. Their chances of being spotted were remote, to say the least.

After eight days of mind- and body-draining exposure to the elements the Baileys were suddenly sure that their day of rescue had arrived. They saw a small ship two miles away and it was heading in their general direction. Maurice's calculation was that it would pass about one mile from them.

As it drew near its closest point to their position Maurice went to fire off a flare, but it was a fizzer. He grabbed another one and it worked, as did the next, but much to the Baileys' horror the vessel held its course. Those on board remained oblivious to the plight of the stranded sailors who could only watch the ship continue on its way towards the horizon.

This was the first time both felt the despair that came from being so isolated, and there was an added emotional burden: their food and water supplies were dwindling.

They knew they could do nothing about the absence of rain, but food they could. It was by then imperative that they accepted it was quite possible they may not be rescued for some considerable time, if ever, so they had to adapt to the world they were then forced to endure. This change of attitude saw them decide to set about catching their first meal since they abandoned *Auralyn* – and it would be one of the many turtles that were now attracted to the dinghy and liferaft. These turtles had become so familiar with the raft in particular that they would swim beneath it and rub their rough shells against the rubber floor so hard that the Baileys often feared it would be punctured.

The thought of killing one of these turtles didn't sit well with the marooned couple, but they knew they had to adopt a survival mentality if they were to give themselves any chance of going on. The first slaughter was a tortuous affair. It was, quite understandably, amateurish as it was conducted by people who had never been exposed to anything like this in their real world.

As if the divine hand of providence was with them, they discovered once they had completed the grisly task there were additional benefits to be had. When they threw the unwanted parts of the turtle into the sea there was an immediate feeding frenzy by schools of fish that had congregated beneath the dinghy and raft but which until then gone relatively unnoticed. Instantly they realised they had an additional food source on their doorstep, if only they could find a way to catch them.

A quick search of the raft located metal safety pins, and after some clever improvisation they had their fish hooks. Minutes later they were pulling their first fish aboard using meat from the turtle as bait and a light cord for a fishing line. But as exciting as this was, both struggled to come to grips with chewing, then swallowing, their uncooked catch. It was only their diminishing stomachs and an increasingly desperate desire for food that overruled this mental aversion to such a primitive way of life.

While the turtles continued to bother them by rubbing against the bottom of the raft, it was a frightening encounter with a whale just 10 days after their odyssey began that almost brought them undone. A huge sperm whale of similar proportions to the one that sank *Auralyn* cruised up to the raft and literally stopped within arm's reach of it. Maralyn, a non-swimmer, was petrified while Maurice accepted that there was absolutely nothing they could do about their predicament. They could only sit like ducks in a shooting gallery and await their fate. If the whale took a liking to the raft and flipped it over, or decided to 'crash dive' and smash it with its tail, then so be it. This denizen of the deep sat motionless on the sea surface alongside the raft for some 10 minutes, the only activity being its regular and loud breathing, from which a foul-smelling and fine mist of spray blasted into the air. The Baileys' hearts were pounding while they spoke in a near whisper about what might happen. Eventually the whale decided the raft was of no interest, and with that it lifted its massive tail above the surface of the water, descended and went on its way.

About two weeks into this meander across the ocean it was becoming apparent that the elements were taking a toll on both the raft and dinghy. Some rubber and fabrics parts had already chafed through, including the supposed strong-point to which the sea anchor, or drogue, was attached. With that gone – and it being essential that their drift be slowed if they were going to be able to fish for food – the always innovative Maralyn very cleverly created a new drogue using a pair of plastic wet weather trousers which, when held open at the waist, filled with water and created the desired resistance. Maralyn also set an oar like a mast atop the liferaft and attached a pair of orange oilskins to it, the intention being to make the raft more conspicuous should a potential rescuer appear on the scene.

While their food supply was by then becoming somewhat plentiful it wasn't until their 17th day of drifting that the heavens opened and delivered the rain they so desperately needed for drinking water.

It took three weeks for them to get into the mindset where they accepted that they had no influence whatsoever over where they were heading or what might happen to them, so they then settled into a routine aimed at maximising their chance of surviving. Turtles and fish remained their staple diet and they replenished their drinking water supply every time it rained.

Monotony was one of the greatest mental challenges they would face, so they decided to create a set of playing cards and dominoes, all cut from sheets of paper they had with them. The entertaining games that followed whiled away countless hours and provided the much-needed stimulation of their minds.

The 25th day brought more torment. In the early hours of the morning, when it was still dark, Maralyn sighted another ship, a tanker, coming towards them. It got so close they could clearly define the inner glow of lights inside the ship shining out through the portholes. Here was their chance! Confident that the ship was close enough for someone to see a flare, Maurice grabbed the first of the two that remained and went to fire it off – but it failed. There was just one flare left. What should they do, they asked themselves. Their lives were hanging in the balance, and the chance of rescue was right there, just a short distance away. There was no other option but to launch the one remaining flare. This one worked. It filled the night sky with an extremely bright light, but it was to no avail. The tanker remained on course and the Baileys could only watch the glow of lights fade and the bright white stern light disappear into the darkness. They had to fight on.

A most amazing experience came five weeks after the sinking when a large male turtle swam up to the raft. They grabbed it and hitched a rope around its rear flippers to retain it, the plan being to kill it a while later. Incredibly, the moment the turtle was released into the water it began swimming in the direction of the Galápagos Islands, towing the raft and dinghy behind it. Their imagination ran wild: they had a vision of being towed all the way to port – arriving at the islands under tow from a turtle. They did this again when they captured another turtle a few days later, but it shattered their dream when it decided to swim in the opposite direction. Both turtles became food.

Bad luck again dogged them on day 37 when yet another ship cruised past in broad daylight just half a mile away, yet no one on board saw them frantically waving brightly coloured clothing. Just two days later the Baileys were better prepared when another ship came by. Maurice created what they hoped would be a smoke flare – a wad of clothing soaked in kerosene and methylated spirits that he placed inside a cake tin. Hopes soared when the contents of the tin ignited, but luck proved to be absent yet again. The smoke was nothing like what they hoped for and what little there was quickly became a wisp because of the windy conditions. Then suddenly they realised it might have worked. The ship actually stopped and circled back towards them and they began to rejoice; at last rescue was at hand. But minutes later their elation turned into a tight knot of agony when the ship stopped and rolled gently in the ocean swell some distance from them. The Baileys clung to the hope that those onboard were searching the ocean, trying to find the source of the smoke someone had spotted: it would only be a matter of time before they were found. Instead, after an agonisingly long period of holding station, the white-hulled ship turned away and headed on its course. Despondent as they were they could only assume that the smoke had been sighted, then when the ship turned around the raft and dinghy were hidden in the troughs of the waves and by the glare of the sun reflecting off the surface of the sea.

Incredibly, while the Baileys continually suffered the anguish that came with being so near to but yet so far from rescue, they continued to do everything possible to keep their spirits high. They became fatalistic about their predicament. Maralyn actually shocked Maurice by suggesting that once they were rescued they should return to England and build a new yacht to a design based around what they had learned from owning *Auralyn*. They then spent many hours boosting their morale by sketching ideas for their new dream yacht in a book they had with them. Maralyn in particular was certain they would be found out there – one day.

As time rolled on fatigue and the wasting of their bodies took a toll on their emotions, something quite understandable in those circumstances. Their appearance reflected how their extremely limited diet was ravaging their bodies: they looked emaciated and their ribs protruded because the skin dipped in deep hollows between the bones. Their lack of strength greatly impacted their ability and desire to remain ever-vigilant for passing ships. If there was a plus side to all this, it was that they experienced only short bursts of energy-sapping rough weather.

About seven weeks after they lost their yacht the Baileys felt great despair. Such was their frustration that they agreed they didn't want to see another ship unless there was a 100 per cent chance it would stop and find them. They accepted they were on a conveyor-belt-like ride in an east flowing current that was taking them into no-man's land in the middle of the Pacific. Their despair was reinforced by the knowledge that they were drifting at up to 25 miles a day and at that rate it was possible they could reach America's west coast within a month – but by then they might not be alive.

On 24 April, Maralyn's birthday, there came a

surprise that neither wanted when Maurice caught an all-too-large fish on one of the hooks they had improvised from a safety pin. As he dragged it to the surface the fish confirmed it had no desire to be landed and it suddenly made a desperate bid to free itself from the barbless hook. It succeeded, but as the spring-like hook ripped from its mouth it flew through the air and punctured the dinghy. Fortunately the dinghy repair kit was still with them, so they took great pride in patching the problem. But this self-adulation quickly turned to extreme disappointment when they realised that when they rolled the dinghy over to get at the hole they had somehow lost one of their large water containers – four days' supply.

It seemed their desperate efforts to remain alive were forever being ambushed. First the patch that they so purposefully attached to the dinghy came adrift, and after that they had to inflate the dinghy twice every day. Then the lower ring of the liferaft deflated. It was apparently punctured by the thorn-like spines on the back of a spinefoot fish which decided the raft was a mid-ocean refuge and had accordingly taken an all-too-affectionate liking to it. The puncture was so bad that the Baileys failed in their effort to patch it. So from their 55th day at sea the liferaft, which until then had comprised two circular inflated rings, was down to just one. It had lost half its freeboard. They could then only pray that the remaining ring would stay inflated, because as well as being their 'home', the canopy that covered the raft provided desperately needed shelter from the scorching sun.

Going into the third month the heat and ultraviolet rays from the sun continued to wreak havoc on the liferaft. At this time the Baileys' health began to fail, due mainly to their diet and the environment they were forced to live in, which could easily have been described as water torture. The canopy over the raft had become little more than a mesh: it was no longer waterproof, so whenever it rained there was no protection. There were two levels of misery – wet and wetter. Also, the webbing holding the two inflatable rings together was beginning to fail, so water was then seeping into the raft through the gaps. On top of that, because one ring was deflated and the raft had less than only 50 centimetres freeboard, waves would continually slop into the raft any time there was bad weather. For the Baileys it was like living in a kiddies' wading pool 24/7. The heat was also contributing to their ill-health: their fresh water supplies in the plastic containers were becoming contaminated and it was also causing any fresh fish they caught and stored to spoil in a very short time. Regardless, they had to eat and drink if they were to survive; they were left with no option but to take some form of nourishment and water. This necessity brought with it severe bouts of dysentery.

Despite having to face these challenges they were becoming increasingly fatalistic about their destiny. They certainly had plenty of time to contemplate their situation. Maralyn, in particular, remained convinced that a greater power was controlling their experience. At one stage, when she was going through the depths of depression, she convinced herself that she would rather be serving a prison term which offered a definite date of release than endure this living hell.

Come the 62nd day and nature provided a significant reprieve. A massive thunderstorm allowed them to refresh their water supplies while a 250lb turtle, which had casually cruised up to the dinghy, became their largest catch. By this time they were consummate experts at butchering a turtle: they knew where to find the best meat and what made the best bait. In particular, they had grown to enjoy the heart and liver.

Two days later there was more frustration as a cargo ship cruised silently by in the early evening. This was the stage when they accepted that their mental and physical state would see them last only another 14 days: there were just two weeks for a ship to come along and find them.

Ten days later the seventh ship they had sighted came and went.

On the 75th day it was obvious that the assumption they held at that depressing period of their drift – that they would soon be dead – was a far cry from fact. Somehow they had dragged themselves over that hurdle of apathy and moved on. They were actually feeling better both physically and mentally.

Still, for the next six weeks their life remained in a primitive form; they were little more than hunters and gatherers, desperate to survive. They held a matter-of-fact attitude towards the realisation that they had not sighted a ship during the period. They could only assume they had drifted away from shipping lanes, so they had to accept that their fate had been preconceived. But preconceived or not, neither was prepared for the severe and lingering illness that struck Maurice towards the end of May. He became almost paralysed by the pain that was racking his body, a pain he compared to a bout of pleurisy he had suffered many years earlier. This ailment, coupled with coughing fits so acute that he spat up blood, led to him accepting he was probably close to dying. Maralyn took command of the entire situation: as well as being Maurice's nurse she had also become the sole provider.

Good fortune came in an interesting form on the last day of May when, while carving up a turtle she had captured, Maralyn discovered it contained hundreds of eggs. It was a find that added much-needed nutrients to their otherwise mundane diet.

This same day also brought high drama: for the first time since *Auralyn* sank, their inflated islands became the centre of attention for sharks. Day and night these sharks buffeted the liferaft, scooting underneath and thumping the floor of the raft as they did. Understandably, the Baileys were wondering if this was an effort to get at them, or maybe they were out to feed on the fish which had gathered there. This assault by the sharks, which went on for days, was so powerful that the Baileys' bodies were actually bruised from the encounter.

Maurice continued to struggle with his debilitating ailment, his recovery being slowed by seemingly endless days of heavy rain and cold breezes. By now their lifestyle was completely primeval and free of all inhibition, including when it came to the call of nature. If there was a bonus to come from the rain – apart from providing more drinking water – it was that they could cleanse their bodies and long, straggly hair and, for Maurice, his wiry beard.

Problem followed problem. The last improvised sea anchor had broken away and this meant they were again drifting too fast to be able to fish. Their existence became even more deplorable when on the 93rd day they were subjected to a severe storm that generated huge and threatening seas, the likes of which they had not previously experienced. But even in those conditions it was imperative that they continued to fish for food – and this desperation went close to killing Maurice.

He had been fishing from the dinghy for some time and was not overly concerned by the rough seas; however, while he was preparing to move from the dinghy back into the liferaft a huge wave charged onto the scene and almost claimed him. It was so big and powerful that it capsized the dinghy and hurled him into the churning sea. Maralyn watched in horror as her husband disappeared into the turbulence, then there was relief when, a few seconds later, his head appeared above the boiling white water. As weak as he was, he somehow mustered the energy to get himself to the liferaft and clamber aboard. Unfortunately though, this proved to be an extremely expensive incident because everything that wasn't tied into the dinghy was lost, including all their fishing gear and bait.

The suffering they faced during the night that followed would never be forgotten. The violent motion that came from the liferaft being buffeted by the large breaking seas pummelled them. They were battered and bruised, but worse still they had to contend with excruciating pain as their bodies, which were covered in ulcer-like sores, were bashed against the side of the raft. It was as if their soft and wet skin was being rubbed by sandpaper.

This storm lasted for four days and in that time the only food they could consume came from their small and all too valuable supply of tinned stores, which they were keeping as an absolute last resort.

When the storm cleared and the sun reappeared they set about creating new fishing equipment. They discovered they still had some safety pins which could be bent to form fish hooks, just like they had done many weeks earlier. Better still, while they were going about this task, an inquisitive turtle came too close to the liferaft, and within a matter of minutes it was destined to become their next meal. Maralyn's creative skills saw her also devise a novel way to make a fish trap. She took a large plastic fuel container and cut away the end that was opposite to the pouring spout. She then tied a small piece of bait onto a string, took the container by its handle and submerged it just below the surface of the water, then dangled the bait down the open pouring spout. Within minutes small and inquisitive fish decided the meal they could see was too good to resist, and as they darted into the container to grab the bait they were scooped up into the dinghy.

On the 98th day they received, in a unique way, a pleasant change of diet. A booby bird landed on the dinghy and promptly deposited the contents of its bowel all over the water containers. In a bid to make it fly away, Maurice took a swing at it with a paddle – and connected. The stunned and wildly flapping booby crashed into the water in an ungainly fashion and immediately regurgitated four whole flying fish. More food for the Baileys. They grabbed them so they could enjoy a special side dish of flying fish with their meal that evening.

Over the next few days an increasing number of boobies decided that the raft and dinghy provided ideal lodging, presenting the Baileys with the opportunity to further supplement their diet, this time with some poultry from the high seas. It was a welcome alternative to fish, and it brought an added benefit. After breaking off the bird's wings, the

Baileys dipped the bloodied and meaty end into the water to clean it, and as they did it was attacked by voracious small fish, so greedy that they wouldn't let go when the wing was lifted out of the water. They did it again and sure enough the fish came again, so this time they just flipped them into the dinghy and kept them for food. This technique and their ability to catch fish using a safety pin for a hook meant they were then able to catch everything they wanted, but that wouldn't always be the way. However, apart from ensuring an ample supply of food, the warmer water also provided entertainment in the form of many and varied species of fish, plus dolphins and a wide variety of birds. If there was a downside to this environment it was that this zone also delivered thunderstorms with greater frequency, and this brought far greater misery for the stranded and soggy sailors.

It must be remembered that in these conditions the Baileys' energy was being drained faster than they would have liked because they had to regularly pump air into the remaining tube of the liferaft and bail out water. Such was their plight at times like this that their minds would ask if death was far away. Their condition would further deteriorate in rough weather when their diet rarely involved more than a can of tinned food a day shared between them. Their level of exhaustion in these extreme conditions was also accelerated by the number of occasions the dinghy had to be righted after it was capsized by the force of a large wave. Fortunately for them these same waves weren't powerful enough to upend the liferaft they called home.

After 109 days the clock was continuing to tick for the Baileys and by this time they were asking themselves more than ever just how much longer they could last. This was because they had been struggling to catch fish and replenish their water supplies, but on this particular day things really looked up. Amazingly, they managed to capture by hand three small sharks, each about three-quarters of a metre long. Apart from providing plenty of meat, these sharks brought a change of flavour to their meals. And birds were back on the menu because they once again came to rest unwittingly on the side of the dinghy.

The extensive salt water sores that had again developed over much of Maurice's body were bringing even more agony, especially when they rubbed on the bottom or side of the always moving liferaft. For relief, both he and Maralyn spent as much time as possible in the dinghy because it provided a far more stable situation.

By this time their winding course had taken them from a position near the Galápagos Islands to a point well to the west of Costa Rica – from the equator through to 10 degrees north – but they didn't know that.

Dawn on 30 June signalled they were ending their 117th day adrift. It was for them a normal day. They did everything possible to add to their food larder and rested when the heat of the sun forced them to retreat into the shade of the liferaft canopy. After a lunch of raw fish they fell asleep, then sometime around mid-afternoon, when Maurice was struggling with the fitful form of sleep they both had learned to live with, he realised Maralyn was shaking him, desperate to wake him and tell him that a ship was approaching. It was enough to spur Maurice into immediate action. He clambered into the dinghy as quickly as he could, stood up and frantically waved a jacket in the air. He could tell that the white and rust-streaked vessel he could see in the distance was a Korean fishing boat.

At the same time Maralyn was waving from the raft with equal vigour. This was their moment for real excitement. The day they thought might never come had arrived.

The ship sailed to within half a mile of them then, incredibly, did not stop. For Maurice it was déjà vu: yet another 'near but so far' situation. Once again they had not been seen. His elation was shattered: there would be no rescue. He stopped waving and slumped into the dinghy, totally depressed. But Maralyn, who was shouting in desperation for the ship to come back, kept waving. Suddenly she felt a moment of disbelief. Was the ship actually stopping and turning back towards them? She stared at it. Yes, it was!

There was no doubt about it. Their rescue was only moments away. Then, equally quickly, they realised they were both stark naked, and their rescuers were on approach. They scurried to find what few clothes they had left to cover their nakedness and prepare for guests.

As *Weolmi 306* moved close to them, the heaving line tossed by the crew to the Baileys became an umbilical cord – survival was guaranteed.

With the dinghy and raft then secured alongside the ship, a ladder was lowered to them. They somehow managed to scale it, but the moment they set foot on the deck they collapsed, they could not stand up. Four months of sitting in such cramped conditions had taken its toll.

The crew, still struggling to come to grips with the sight of the bedraggled and skeletal humans before them, helped them onto a blanket on the deck so they could rest.

Once there, the Baileys had to convince each other that their incredible ordeal had come to an end. With that came an awareness – they could now keep a promise made to each other: *Auralyn II* would become a reality.

Maurice and Maralyn Bailey chronicled their epic story of survival in the book 117 Days Adrift.

CHAPTER 12

THE HORROR HOBART RACE

It was 27 December 1998, the height of the Christmas festive season in Australia and across the world, but there was nothing festive about what was confronting the 115 yachts that had set sail the previous day in what is arguably the world's most acclaimed ocean yacht race, the Sydney–Hobart classic.

By this time the bulk of the fleet was crossing the most dangerous part of the 627 nautical mile course, an area off the southeast corner of the Australian mainland. To the west of the track were the shallow waters of Bass Strait; to the east lay the Tasman Sea – an often brutal wilderness of ocean that holds too many memories of lives lost. Confounding this environment on many occasions – and in particular this one – was a fast flowing current that streamed south down the coast of the mainland.

That combination could be considered bad enough, but this time there was an additional killer element lurking above: two severe weather systems had combined with little notice, and in doing so they became the detonator for a weather bomb, the scale of which was unprecedented in the 58-year history of the race. Before long the wind gusted to between 80 and 100 knots while the seas grew to gargantuan proportions, many taking on the stature of a 10-level building, around 30 metres in height. In a matter of hours a maritime holocaust was unfolding, and by the time nature dealt its deadly hand six sailors had perished, five yachts had sunk, and in what was Australia's largest peacetime search and rescue operation, 55 of the more than 1300 sailors had been winched to safety by heroic helicopter crews. The fleet of 115 was decimated – scattered like shrapnel across an unforgiving stretch of ocean. Only 44 yachts were able to battle through and reach Hobart – many because turning back was not an option.

Panic-stricken calls for assistance crackled inexorably across the radio airwaves as the storm, which in any other language could have been called a hurricane or cyclone, corralled the fleet into a colosseum where few had the chance to escape its full fury. Too many times crews did not have the opportunity to declare their dire predicament to the outside world before their yacht was overwhelmed.

Michael 'Zapper' Bell was a crewmember aboard Stephen Ainsworth's 44 foot yacht, *Loki*. They were about 70 miles offshore and battling south under a tiny storm jib when the yacht's wind instrument registered a staggering 74 knot squall. Simultaneously, a rogue wave of titanic dimensions loomed out of nowhere and towered over the yacht – a cliff face of ugly grey ocean. The crew did the only thing they could if they were to minimise its full force – they turned *Loki* bow-on into the wave. But as they did they looked up and saw it was breaking – a mass of white water was cascading down its vertical face. In an instant it had completely engulfed *Loki* before cartwheeling her bow-over-stern back down the wave into the trough, where she landed upside down.

'What followed was the most amazing experience I've ever had at sea,' said Bell, a well-seasoned offshore sailor who was with two others on deck at the time and could only watch helplessly as the drama unfolded. 'There I was underneath this upturned yacht in the most incredibly serene situation. I could have been swimming in the fishpond at home. In fact, it was like swimming in the Caribbean – clear and warm. Everything was still and beautiful. I saw my glasses get washed off my face and had time to simply reach out and grab them. I remember all the coloured halyard tails and lines just wafting through the water like sea snakes. I was amazed that I felt no panic. I knew I had to release my safety harness at my chest to get out. There was no gasping for breath or panic, just deliberate movements to escape. Then, all of a sudden, the yacht righted itself with the rig and everything intact, and all hell broke loose again. We were back into the real world.'

Not surprisingly, the *Loki* crew decided they'd had enough: they could no longer try to sail in those conditions, so they set a sea anchor and ran under bare poles – still doing seven knots in what was survival mode for them.

Bell recalled that some of the crew wanted the yacht to sail towards Eden, a port on the New South Wales–Victorian border – but it was 70 miles upwind.

'Bugger that,' Bell announced emphatically. 'We're heading east for New Zealand. It might be 1200 miles away but I know I can catch a jet back to Australia from there. We are not going upwind in this.'

So many others on the same stretch of ocean were nowhere near as fortunate, if you could call the *Loki* experience fortunate. Yachts were literally being smashed apart by the crushing power of the waves, or capsized. It seemed that every wave had the intention of taking sailors to the edge of the precipice that separated life from death, and sadly, some were going over that edge.

In the initial stages of this developing disaster the ABC News helicopter piloted by Gary Ticehurst took on the role of a sentinel over the area where the worst carnage was occurring: where yachts were sinking and crews were in desperate need of being rescued. His chopper did not carry rescue equipment, so Ticehurst did the next best thing – he monitored the position of yachts that were in serious trouble and relayed information to the Australian Maritime Safety Authority in Canberra.

Soon though, when confronted by 65 to 70 knot headwinds and with fuel running low, Ticehurst knew he had to abandon the scene if he was to get back to the coast safely. But just as he turned his chopper towards land yet another spine-chilling May Day call penetrated his radio headphones: 'May Day, May Day, May Day. Here is *Winston Churchill, Winston Churchill!*'

Ticehurst responded in an instant: '*Winston Churchill, Winston Churchill*, ABC chopper, go ahead with your position. Over.'

'We are 20 miles southeast of Twofold Bay. Over.'

'Nature of your May Day? Over.'

'Affirmative. We are getting the liferafts on deck. ABC chopper, we are holed. We are taking water rapidly. We cannot get the motor started to start the pumps. Over.'

Ticehurst reassured the nine *Winston Churchill* crewmen that their May Day was covered and that he would relay the message to the race radio relay vessel, *Young Endeavour*, and to shore. There was nothing more he could do in what was an extremely burdensome dilemma. He could not initiate his own search even though the yacht was probably within 10 miles of the chopper – perhaps five to 10 minutes away. All he could do was relay the May Day back to Canberra and then make the slow return trip to Mallacoota to refuel.

If there was a classic yacht in the Hobart race that year then *Winston Churchill* was it. Built in 1942, this stout 55 foot long timber cutter contested the first Sydney to Hobart in 1945. In 1997, after being purchased by Sydney yachtsman Richard Winning, every part of her traditionally planked hull was restored to pristine condition. One of the team working on the restoration was John 'Steamer' Stanley, a 51-year-old highly regarded boatbuilder who had covered more sailing miles over the years than most people in the race. Not surprisingly, Winning had no hesitation in making Stanley the leader of his crew for the Hobart race that year, and after they walked down the dock at the finish feeling proud of their result they decided there and then the 1998 race was to be next on the yacht's agenda. At the same time they made a pact: 'I entered again just for the fun of doing it,' Winning said. 'We planned to do it every year until we got too old.'

Winning had assembled an experienced and well-balanced crew which, apart from 'Steamer' Stanley, included other highly experienced sailors, Bruce Gould and Jim Lawler. Gould's impressive credentials included 32 Sydney to Hobarts, while Stanley had notched up 16.

But not even men of such calibre in the world of offshore sailing, or anyone else for that matter, could have imagined the magnitude of the storm that Mother Nature would unleash on the fleet that year.

Like all the other yachts continuing in the race, *Winston Churchill* was down to minimum sail by early afternoon on the 27th. By then clouds of spume were starting to burst from the tops of the waves as 50 to 55 knot winds whipped them into a frenzy. Occasionally the alarm on the wind speed instrument would activate – a signal that a wind gust had topped 60 knots.

As rough as it was, Winning, Stanley and Gould were more than pleased with the way the 'old girl' was handling the conditions. However, when it came to steering, each of them could only manage 30 minutes at a time at the wheel. It was impossible to continue much longer because the heavy rain and spray propelled by the savage winds ripped at their eyes and face. Gould was on the helm for half an hour in the early afternoon. They were sailing under a storm jib and doing about five knots at an angle of between 50 and 60 degrees to the face of the waves. They debated what their next mode would be should conditions deteriorate and at that time decided it would be unsafe to turn back to Eden. Stanley also voiced some reservations about whether or not it would be safe to heave-to in such huge seas as they would then be unable to guide the yacht over them.

At around 3.30 pm Winning was on the helm with crewman John Dean sitting nearby, seeking what little shelter he could from the coach-house, a box-like cabin near the stern. Stanley was in his bunk inside the coach-house while Gould was trying to sleep on the cabin floor of the main saloon – the most comfortable spot available despite drips from some annoying leaks coming through the deck. All the time

Winston Churchill continued to power impressively through the big seas – 25 tonnes and five knots seemed a great combination.

Suddenly, and very dramatically, that all changed.

'We had a massive sea that just came out of nowhere and towered above us,' said Stanley. 'I could feel it from where I was in the coach-house. It just picked the boat up and rolled it down its face – 25 tonne of boat – into the trough at a 45 degree angle. It was like hitting a brick wall when we got to the bottom.'

The power of the wave dealt a merciless blow to *Winston Churchill*; it was as if a giant hand had picked up a rock and smashed it on the ground. The yacht was now lying on her side and buried under tonnes of white water, all the time struggling desperately to come upright, like a downed and dazed boxer trying to climb off the canvas.

Stanley found himself pinned to the windward side of the coach-house, which had three windows on one side smashed in. He heard crewmembers on deck calling for help, so he struggled free and rushed up to find Winning and Dean hanging like puppets in the backstay rigging and around the boom with their feet well off the deck. Stanley quickly started to untangle their harnesses so he could get them down.

Below deck, crewmember John Gibson was rummaging around in the main saloon, tidying up and stowing sails that had been brought down, when the wave hit. Suddenly, as the yacht rolled, he was catapulted almost three metres across the saloon before slamming into the side of the cabin. He was stunned by the force of the impact. When he regained his senses a few seconds later he realised he'd done a complete somersault because he was sprawled upside down. He was also covered in blood – the result of a nasty gash to his head.

When *Winston Churchill* did come upright Gibson regained his feet and saw that all the cabin floorboards had exploded away from their locations. On looking into the bilge he immediately felt dread. He could see the boat was taking water, but it was impossible to pinpoint where it was coming from or how serious the damage was. Simultaneously, he and Gould rushed up to the deck and saw Stanley still trying to untangle their dangling crewmates.

'There was no one on the helm so I grabbed the wheel,' said Gould. 'I could feel straight away there was a lot of water in the boat. I stayed on the helm because the others knew the boat better than me. Steamer was then going around trying to sort out the shit-fight, on deck and below. He told Richard to try to start the motor so we could operate the bilge pumps.'

Winning turned the ignition key and the engine started. It ran for just five seconds and then spluttered to a halt. By now Gould was in no doubt the yacht was going to sink, so he suggested they send out a May Day. The main radio had been 'drowned' by the water that had found its way below, so Winning went to his only source of communication, the short-range VHF radio. It was vitally important to give an accurate position, but the wave that had wrecked the HF radio had also taken out the yacht's charts and GPS unit. Winning could then only guess the yacht's position and give a DR (dead reckoning) position.

When Stanley went to go below into the main cabin he noticed that two metres of the heavy timber bulwark amidships were completely smashed.

Planking had been ripped away and the ribs were exposed. Little wonder *Winston Churchill* was foundering.

Once he'd descended below he saw an even worse scene: already there was 50 centimetres of water over the floor, and debris was everywhere. He shouted to the rest of the crew to get on deck and take the two liferafts with them. They did just that – quickly!

'We decided that we wouldn't put the liferafts in the water until the deck was awash,' he recalls. 'I had heard of people launching rafts too early and the boats going one way and the rafts going the other. Also, you should always step up into a liferaft, not down.'

In the middle of all this drama Stanley shouted dryly to the crew, 'Well, fellas, this looks like the end of our Hobart.'

While the team prepared to abandon ship Gould turned *Winston Churchill* onto a course that had her heading directly downwind. The storm jib was lowered, but as it came down its sheets were flailing perilously through the air like lethal steel bars. Still, Mike Bannister worked on lowering it while the remainder of the crew showed no signs of panic, all working tirelessly and methodically towards saving themselves and their mates. The question was raised as to whether the EPIRB had been activated and there was a reply to the affirmative.

Some 20 minutes after impact it was time to abandon ship: 'We were running in these huge seas with the wind over our quarter, getting lower and lower in the water,' Gould said. 'Next thing a massive wave, 40 feet plus, came over us and swamped us. It filled the boat. I said to Richard, "Well mate, this is it. You'd better tell the boys we're abandoning ship."'

Gibson, who was one of the last to leave, followed Lawler into a raft: 'As the rafts were being launched I was just thinking to myself that I'd like to go in the same raft as Jimmy Lawler. That was my confidence in him, and that's exactly what I did. It just happened that there was a spot available anyway. I would have got into either raft but I just consciously felt very comfortable out there because I regarded Jim as my mate. We were from the same club, and also John Stanley was in the same raft.'

Winston Churchill was sinking quickly but the line securing the raft was still attached. There was a loud bang and the lanyard to the raft parted. Gould recalls being hit by another enormous wave before he finally abandoned the helm. He ran forward, did a swan dive towards the open tent flap of the nearest raft and was dragged inside.

All nine crewmembers had managed to escape successfully into the liferafts, and once there they looked back and watched in awe as the once mighty *Winston Churchill* disappeared below the surface. They knew even before they entered the rafts they were far from being safe, and now the liferafts were their only hope for surviving in such heinous conditions. They were then facing a new battle: to see through what would be a traumatic and horrendously challenging night.

In the four-man raft with Richard Winning and Bruce Gould were 19-year-old Hobart race novice Michael Rynan and Paul Lumtin. In the other raft with Stanley, Lawler and Gibson were Mike Bannister and John Dean. They felt it important that the two rafts remained tied together by a short lanyard, especially considering that Winning's raft carried the one EPIRB the yacht was required to have for the race. However, the lanyard soon proved no match for the shock loads it was subjected to by the waves forcing the rafts apart. It snapped, and from that moment the two teams were heading their separate ways.

Stanley's raft carried a drogue which they then set to slow the rate of drift, but as it was let out it became tangled. John Gibson tried valiantly to hang on to the thin line, and was going okay until the surge from a wave put so much pressure on the line that it tore through his fingers, cutting the flesh to the bone. Before long he was wishing he hadn't even tried to hang on to the line because the drogue couldn't cope with the load anyway and broke free.

Then far greater drama: 'Suddenly a big wave hit us and lifted my side of the raft,' recalled Stanley. 'The problem was that my body went up but my feet were still pinned under the other guys' legs. That was when I broke my ankle. I could do nothing more than say, "Oh my God, my ankle's broken. That's not very good." That meant both Gibbo and I were out of play.'

Unknown to Stanley right then, he had also torn tendons around both his artificial hips.

As with the other raft, the drogue attached to Winning's raft parted within an hour of them having abandoned *Winston Churchill*. Once settled as best they could the four crewmembers decided to rummage through the raft's ration pack. It was like going through a show bag at a fair: it contained a small amount of very basic food, water, medical supplies and other rescue and survival equipment, an emergency pump for the raft, a knife, flares and a reflector mirror to attract attention.

The Royal Australian Navy sail training vessel *Young Endeavour*, a 44 metre long brigantine, had been shadowing the fleet as radio relay vessel. The race organisers from the Cruising Yacht Club of Australia who were onboard were immediately aware of the May Day call from *Winston Churchill* when it was received by the ABC helicopter, so had *Young Endeavour* change course to what was considered to be the search area.

It quickly became a nightmarish passage dead downwind for those on board. On no less than three occasions the massive steel-hulled ship had skipped uncontrollably like a dinghy down the waves that peaked more than halfway up her 52 metre high masts. She was surging forward at around her maximum speed of 14 knots, the decks were awash, and at one stage the pressure of water coming across the port side of the vessel cracked the 25mm thick plate glass in a steel-encased porthole. Visibility was down to a measly 100 metres in conditions so rough that most of the crew were incapacitated through seasickness.

Once they arrived in the vicinity of where they believed *Winston Churchill* was when the May Day was issued they reported back to AMSA in Canberra that there was no sign of the yacht. What they didn't know was that they needed to be looking for liferafts.

The charge from the massive breaking waves continued for those in the rafts, but they somehow remained safe until around dusk when Richard Winning's raft was hammered so hard by a breaking wave that it was flipped upside down. The four, then trapped in a small air pocket inside the upturned raft, tried to undo the tent flap but couldn't because it was tied together with nylon rope. The only choice was to cut their way out with a knife, and when this was done Winning took off his life jacket, dived through the hole and swam to the surface – an incredibly heroic feat as he did this without a tether line, simply because there was no suitable line in the raft. He grabbed the edge of the wildly bobbing raft and eventually found the righting line, and with the help of the wind he used his body weight to roll the raft upright. The three in the raft then pulled him back inside. They then realised there was more bad news: at some stage during the incident the aerial on the EPIRB had broken in half, making it next to useless.

Around midnight yet another prowling and monstrous wave broke around the raft, capsizing it once more, and yet again it was righted.

Towards dawn things got worse: the lower chamber of the two making up the liferaft began to deflate. The four became worried that should this chamber deflate completely the canopy would start to collapse as well. They consulted the instructions on how to inflate the raft manually but then discovered the adaptor they needed for the job had been lost during one of the roll-overs. They had to improvise and pulled a nylon piece out of the end of the pump hose and managed to jam that into the valve and tape it up. It worked, and while the raft continued to be hurled, tossed and tumbled, the four tightly packed occupants in it remained upright. Soon after, as if they hadn't been through enough already, a 5cm slit appeared in the floor of the raft and soon they were sitting in something akin to a toddler's wading pool.

'We don't know what caused the hole,' said Gould. 'It might have been the gas inflation bottle that was hanging off the raft or the broken aerial of the EPIRB. We couldn't find a bailer so we decided it was best to jam a sponge in the hole. We ended up having between six inches [15cm] and two feet [60cm] of water in with us for the rest of the time. The level depended on how big the wave was that broke over us. After a while someone said, "Hey, here's the bloody raft repair kit." We ripped it open and read the instructions – *rough the rubber surface; make sure it's clean and dry and apply the patch*. We chucked the repair kit out of the raft.'

Through a process of elimination they soon concluded the best bailing method involved using their seaboots and a plastic bag which had been the wrapper for a *Winston Churchill* T-shirt that one of the guys had grabbed when they were abandoning ship. The presence of the T-shirt brought another form of relief for the survivors – a hint of humour. All four debated whether the shirt from a yacht that was now sunk was bringing them good luck or bad. It was decided, in a bid to appease the weather gods, that the shirt should be consigned to the deep. It too was thrown from the raft.

An unknown distance away the five crewmembers in the other raft faced a far more serious predicament. They were forced to lie across the floor of the square raft in sardine-like formation, all the time being hurled about by the hugely menacing seas. 'No one seemed worried,' said Gibson. 'The spirit in the raft was excellent. We were very concerned about John's obvious distress, not that he was complaining. Every now and then, when we were thrown around, there were significant exclamations, totally involuntary moans from him like "Oh Christ". We were trying to make him as comfortable as we could and keep away from his legs. We went through the bag of goodies we found and discussed some of the stuff that was in there. We found some fishing hooks and I recall there were jokes about what we were going to use for bait. Deanie and I were also saying how nice it would be to have some Scotch to mix with the water that was in the little plastic vials.'

By nightfall they had accepted that rescue was highly unlikely before the next day. The waves continued to be the major threat to their safekeeping; sets of 12 to 20 metre high waves were continuing to roll through, and with each one came the high chance that the raft would be flipped upside down in the cascade of broken water. Then what they believed to be inevitable, happened: a near vertical wave that was on the verge of breaking flipped the raft over. Before they knew it, all five were standing on the inflated arch that was built into the raft to support the canopy: what was previously the raft floor was now the roof. Still there was no great fear.

'We felt surprisingly comfortable but we knew we were going to run out of oxygen,' said Stanley. 'You could just feel the air starting to get a bit tighter. Jim Lawler was next to the opening. He wanted to take off his vest and get out so he could do something about getting us upright. But it was just raging out there. We all decided it was too dangerous to get out one by one to turn the thing up. It would have taken just one bad sea when someone was getting out for us to lose them.'

'It was a very calm discussion for about 20 minutes,' Gibson recollected. 'Certainly the comment was "Well, the damn thing's a lot more stable this way up than it is the other way." It was certainly a lot quieter. Michael said words to the effect, "We've got to get out and right this thing otherwise we're going to be in terrible trouble." I recall saying to him, and my words are indelibly etched in my mind, "Michael, it's death out there." When I said it I thought to myself, "Christ, that's a very dramatic thing to say; that's overstating the issue a bit." But I really was very concerned about it because it was pitch black and there were very, very large waves coming through. Anyone outside would struggle to hang on to anything.'

The five were then standing in waist-deep water in pitch blackness. Torches were produced and an inspection of their inverted environment began.

'It was definitely safer being the way we were so we

decided to cut a small hole in the raft floor – which was now our roof – so we could breathe,' explained Stanley. 'There was a handle on the floor that had reinforcing either side of it. We slit it longitudinally, 4 inches [10cm]. To do it the other way would have been better, but it would have been only two inches, and that wouldn't have let in enough air. When we made the cut the raft submerged about another inch in the water. That didn't matter. At least we had enough air to breathe.'

They were 'comfortable and quite happy' being upside down while their new 'roof' was pushed up and down like a giant rubber bellow in a bid to circulate fresh air into the raft. They drifted along for what they believed were a few hours until another rogue wave could be heard roaring towards them. It was like being trapped in a dark railway tunnel with a locomotive coming at you without a light on it.

The wave thundered in, picked up the raft like a beach ball and threw it back upright. Bodies spilled everywhere and crashed on top of each other, and then the wave was gone. A headcount was done immediately. Everyone was present.

It signalled the start of a night of implausible terror. Conditions deteriorated to the degree where the raft was rolled, tumbled and turned some 30 times by the marauding waves. This caused the floor to start splitting open where the cut had been made, and it was widening as they watched. The canopy was also ripping apart.

Soon, with the canopy fully shredded and the floor split wide open, the five could only hang on to webbing and rope handles on the inside and outside of the raft, which now resembled a square inflated tube – nothing else. Gibson had been in full sailing gear when he left the yacht, including his seaboots and complete harness, so he quite wisely attached his safety harness to the inflated roof arch, which remained. Most others were wearing cumbersome life vests around their necks. Seasickness had thus far spared all five.

Sometime in the very early hours of 28 December the mother of all waves arrived.

'Normally we had some warning, we could hear them coming like breaking surf,' Stanley remembered. 'But this almighty wave gave no warning. Suddenly the five of us were just crashing. The raft was hurled from the crest of the wave and was tumbling down its foaming face, 40, 50, 60 feet. I could only think about hanging on. I wrapped my arms around the roof frame and just hung on and held my breath until the wave went away. I knew if I didn't hang on I was going to die. God knows how long it went on for, but it was for some time. When we finally stopped and I came up for air I was still hanging on to the roof frame but was on the outside of the raft. I yelled out "Who's here?" The only reply came from Gibbo.'

Stanley looked back to see a wide white veil of water stretching for 350 metres into the night. Amid the turbulence, a considerable distance away, he could see two people.

'I'm not sure who they were,' he said, his voice loaded with emotion. 'All I could do then was dive underneath the raft and get back up inside so I could grab the roof frame again and hang on. I said to Gibbo, "Mate, we're by ourselves here. We can't do anything for those boys. The wind is going to blow us faster than they can swim, and we can't go back. We can only hope they can hang on till daybreak and be spotted by a search plane."'

John Gibson holds vivid memories of that night: 'What talk there had been during the night was very positive but at that stage everybody was semi snoozing. We were just floating around and hanging on. My next recollection was my harness being taken up sharply, and then all hell broke loose. I went on what I can only describe as the most extraordinary ride of my life. I was obviously in white water and travelling at great speed with a huge sensation of sound. I was just being dragged by my harness at terrific speed through white water and being hurled all over the place. Whatever hand hold I had had gone and my body was being spun in all directions. I don't recall that I was scared. I just recall thinking, "This is the most extraordinary experience." I don't recall having a problem with breathing. I don't recall panicking. I just recall this experience went on, and on, and on, and on, and on, and I couldn't believe it.

'I just went with it. I didn't fight it. It went for a long time, a remarkably long time. There was also a sense of falling, I knew I was falling. I knew I was in fast water: I knew I was in white water yet I didn't feel I was going to drown. I just didn't know what was going to happen. I was trying to somehow or other go with it, not fight it and at the same time try to work out what the hell was going to happen next. But at no stage did I have the thought that I was going to die. Then it all stopped. It just stopped, and it was dark. There was white water all around me and the raft was still. There wasn't a sound. I looked around and there was no one there. I heard a voice. It was from outside the raft. It was John. He said, "Who's here?" I said, "It's Gibbo." He popped up inside the raft. He'd obviously been flicked outside the raft but had hung on. How he did it I don't know.

'We turned around and tried to see what was happening. I thought I'd lost both my contact lenses as my vision was restricted. I was aware of white water but on recollection I still must have had my right lens in because I was able to see a strobe light come on. I knew exactly who it was – Jim Lawler – because he was the only person who had one. I had one as well so I activated mine and held it up. I thought, "Well, he can see that I'm still alive," but he was a long way back. Then I heard voices. I couldn't tell you what they were saying but I assume

I might have heard words to the effect of "Where are you?" or "Who's there?" ... something like that. I'm sure I heard "Who's there?" or "Where are you, Mike?" I don't recall exactly. They were human voices in the dark, in the white water further back.'

Through a miracle, divine intervention, or sheer guts and determination, Stanley and Gibson somehow continued to defy the odds that night and hang on. Stanley said they were rolled at least five more times before daybreak.

By mid-morning on 28 December the conditions remained horrifying for the survivors of both rafts. The four in Richard Winning's raft had somehow managed to get through the night of meteorological malevolence relatively unscathed, but there were still no guarantees they would survive.

It wasn't until later in the day that conditions began to abate. Bruce Gould remembers the wind easing to around 30 knots and changing direction to the southwest, and while the waves were still huge and breaking regularly, they had decreased in size.

Inflating the raft and bailing out the water kept those in Winning's raft amused during what remained a fairly uneventful day. Most of the time it was Winning who was sitting at the small entrance to the raft canopy scouring the skies for any sign of a search aircraft: 'I kept seeing ships and submarines and hearing aircraft all day. I wasn't hallucinating. I think it was just wishful thinking.'

At around 3 pm they heard, then spotted, a plane, but by the time a flare was found, unwrapped and ignited, the raft occupants could only watch as the plane disappeared towards the horizon. Then, about 20 minutes later, the plane reappeared. It was obviously flying a planned search grid. The red phosphorescent flare – Gould and Winning's last – rocketed into the grey sky. Anxious, tormenting seconds passed as four sets of eyes desperately watched for any sign that it had been seen. Hopes lifted: the twin-engine plane, a civilian search aircraft, began a gentle turn that gradually became more and more pronounced. It was turning back! But no – it didn't come to them. It kept circling, going around their position twice.

Unbeknown to the four in the raft the plane spotters were frantically trying to locate the source of the flare. The reality was they were trying to see a small black spot with a tinge of orange on it somewhere on the surface of the wild, storm-tossed and grey ocean a few hundred feet below.

Eyes strained in the aircraft: there it was! A liferaft! Thumbs went up and the aircraft was turned for an approach. AusSAR search and rescue headquarters in Canberra was immediately sent a message that wives, families, fellow sailors, and the media across Australia had hoped to hear for nearly 24 hours but were beginning to think might never come. A liferaft with occupants had been sighted 80 miles off the coast.

About 20 minutes later the four survivors heard 'the sweetest sound you could ever want to hear – a bloody big helicopter coming at us'.

If successful search and rescue missions equalled a good day at the office, paramedic Cam Robertson and the rest of the team aboard the *Helimed 1* helicopter out of La Trobe, in Victoria, were going gangbusters. They had already found *Solo Globe Challenger* that morning and successfully completed that mission. Since then they had been assigned to searching and identifying some of the many EPIRBs which were still transmitting distress calls. By mid-afternoon it seemed things were quietening down, until AusSAR contacted them and asked them to investigate a flare that had come from a one-man liferaft which had been sighted by an aircraft about 80 miles offshore. Pilot Stef Sincich acknowledged the request and turned the powerful red and white chopper towards the target.

'We located it without a problem,' said Robertson. 'We looked at the raft and discussed the fact that it wasn't a one-man raft, it was bigger, but we still didn't know where it had come from or who might be aboard. The guys winched me down and I finned over to the raft then stuck my head in. I couldn't believe my eyes. There were four blokes inside, and they were very pleased to see me. The noise of the chopper was so loud I had to yell out and ask if there were any injuries. They all seemed okay. I told the guy closest to the door – it turned out to be Richard Winning – that I'd take him out first. I asked him if he was happy to get in the water so I could get the strop around him and he said he was. I told the other guys to collapse the canopy and get on top of it so the raft would be more stable if it got into the downwash from the chopper.

'Everything went really smoothly. Just as we got clear of the water I yelled across to my first guy, asking if he was okay. He was. I also asked what yacht they were from and he said *Winston Churchill*. I couldn't believe it. I was shocked. It was a very special moment for me because a lot of people involved in the search were thinking *Winston Churchill* was lost and it was very doubtful that we would find any survivors. In no time at all we had all four in the chopper. It was a great feeling to know that we had got those guys. Sometimes you think it's a privilege to rescue people, and that time it really was.'

Gould recalls: 'It wasn't until we were up in the helicopter and could look down at the sea that we really appreciated what we'd been through. It was just a white mass of waves. It was an absolute shemozzle. We also realised how hard it had been for the poor guys in the search aircraft to find us.'

The four survivors inquired as to the safety of their five other crewmates. They were told they hadn't been found – news that concerned them. At the same time, the fact that they had survived would hopefully mean the others were safe in their raft and somewhere nearby.

That wasn't to be the case. By then the rafts had been separated by some considerable distance.

With almost a day having passed since *Winston Churchill* sank, the search area was now huge. And making a tough task even more difficult for searchers was the fact that the cloud base was so low the visibility was little more than a few kilometres at the very best.

'Steamer' Stanley and John Gibson had hoped they would see search aircraft during the morning of the 28th. Their raft had disintegrated to a stage where it was little more than a black ring drifting on a savage ocean – near impossible to see from the air or sea. Also, during their numerous capsizes, flares and other emergency equipment had been lost. In their estimation, they must have been at least 50 miles from where the yacht had gone down.

As the day dragged on they began to realise it was almost impossible for the other three crewmembers to have survived. They were still hopeful they themselves would be rescued as they knew there was an EPIRB in the other raft, and it would have been alerting the searchers. But with the aerial broken the device hadn't transmitted properly since not long after all nine had abandoned *Winston Churchill*.

'We were at the stage where we had to do something about securing ourselves to the raft because all we were left with was an inflated ring,' said Gibson. 'If you leaned on any one section of the ring it would submerge and the whole thing would flip over. We always had to be very careful about what we were doing. We had to work out a system whereby we could control what was happening, bearing in mind that John had very restricted mobility. The raft had lost all its shape. It seemed to take whatever shape it wanted.

'We worked out that if we positioned ourselves opposite each other, and John put his good foot in my crutch and pushed against me, we could then move our shoulders sort of above the wall of the raft and lock ourselves in. We were parallel to the arch so we could also hang on to it for support. Our bodies also gave us some buoyancy with our backs pushed against the rubber. We took that position in the early hours of the morning and held it until we were pulled out at 11 o'clock that night.

'All I can say about that arrangement is that John now owes me a few beers because he got the good end of the deal. His foot was wedged hard against my balls and I can tell you that when it was all over, the whole of my crutch was black. My balls were up underneath my eyes.

'We were hallucinating all the time. I remember thinking there was definitely a section of the raft that had a soft floor and I could walk round and put my feet on it. Then I hallucinated about a solid floor. There was a corridor I went down and I could simply just stand there. It was the most blissful feeling. We both saw bucket-loads of ships and sailing boats; cutters and schooners. I went past millions of them.

'John told me exactly the same. There were vessels with lights on that went past us. I also spent lots of time with some of the lovely things in my life, particularly on the romantic side. I revisited all the beautiful people of the opposite sex I've known. I spent hours with them. It was a lot of fun and certainly helped pass the time. I won't elaborate except to say it was much better than counting sheep. I also thought about Jane, my wife of three years –

they were beautiful, lovely thoughts. There was some conversation with John, and although he's a great talker, there were long hours of silence. I felt it was very important to have some sort of dialogue. I knew John was in pain and I was quite concerned about him.'

Sometime during the afternoon a beautiful albatross landed in the water near the raft and looked sadly at the two forlorn sailors. It then flew over and sat right beside Gibson. Both agreed it was a good luck sign.

'We just lay there for a long time in silence. I remember thinking to myself, "Jesus, I'd better try and liven this up a bit," so I said to John, "Do you reckon we're on a steamer path, a ship's path here?" He said, "No, Gibbo." Then we just lay there in the water with the raft going splish, splosh, splash, splat.

'After a while I asked: "Steamer, do you think any of the Hobart boats would come out here?"

'"No, mate."

'"Steamer, where do you think we are?"

'"I reckon we're about 90 miles east of Eden."

'"Well, Steamer, there are no boats."

'"No, Gibbo."

'"No yachts."

'"No, Gibbo."

'"We're 90 miles off."

'"That's right, Gibbo."

'"Mate, who gets to eat whom first?"

'There was no answer. Not even a grunt.

'We continued to drift along and I started looking at my hands. They were both oozing blood. Steamer also looked at them and then we looked at each other. We didn't say anything, but we were both thinking the same thing: old "Jaws" sniffing along behind the blood trail towards us. It was an additional part of the equation that we weren't ready for. We just dismissed that one altogether. The cold started to move through my body; muscle contractions, shudders and shakes. I distinctly remember as I attempted to shuffle my shoulders back up – to try and keep as much of my upper body out of the water as I could – that the effort needed to push against John for leverage was growing all the time. It was getting harder to do.'

All the time the pair were also listening and looking for search aircraft.

'Gibbo was trying to have a chat all the time — probably because he's a barrister,' Stanley recalls. 'But he never complained about his hands, not once. I suppose I didn't complain about my ankle either. Gibbo had lost his contact lenses and couldn't see, so I was his spotter for planes.'

At around four or five o'clock in the afternoon Stanley and Gibson were convinced they had seen a fishing vessel, a big commercial trawler. They were also hearing aircraft. Then, finally, more than 24 hours after *Winston Churchill* was lost, came their first real hope of salvation. Stanley first heard, then spotted, a plane to the north of the raft. He waved frantically but was not seen. About 20 minutes later the plane returned but once again missed the raft. It confirmed how difficult the remnants of their raft were to see on such an evil ocean.

However, Stanley's efforts were rewarded sometime later. He saw a large aircraft at a low altitude coming straight at them and he shouted to Gibson to pass him his yellow life vest. Stanley grabbed it and waved it in large, sweeping arcs over his head. He was desperately hoping that the vest would give a better contrast against the sea than the black raft. He kept on waving furiously as the plane approached, then was overjoyed to see the wing lights flash – but then it flew on!

They remained little more than two small dots on a vast expanse of storm-ravaged ocean, but about an hour later their hopes rocketed once more: the plane returned, this time accompanied by a helicopter – and both flew straight past them. Stanley and Gibson had not been spotted. The chopper was on its way to rescue the four others!

With their emotions absolutely shattered, Stanley and Gibson watched darkness close in on them for a second night. They had no food or water yet were still, somehow, managing to hang on.

Suddenly, new hope burst from the night sky. The pair were roused from their near comatose state by the noise of a search plane. Next they saw it emerge from the blackness, its navigation lights flashing brightly. Gibson had a strobe light and Stanley had a Mag light which were both working. They aimed them at the plane and much to their joy it began circling. It did this for about 10 minutes, leaving the pair in no doubt they had been spotted, but as comforting as this was, they still had no idea how or when they would be rescued.

A short while later that answer came. Above the roar of the storm they began to hear the deep-throated engines of a large helicopter that was on approach. It became louder and louder – then a lumbering Navy Seahawk chopper emerged from the clouds with its searchlights blazing.

The fact that the Royal Australian Navy frigate, HMAS Newcastle, manned by a skeleton crew, was in the area proved to be a springboard back to civilisation for Stanley and Gibson. It provided an offshore refuelling point for the Seahawk helicopter piloted by Lieutenant Nick Trimmer. He and his crew had been searching offshore almost all day for disabled yachts and missing sailors.

'It was dark and we were heading back to Merimbula,' helicopter crewman Leading Seaman Shane Pashley remembers. 'We heard an Air Force PC-3 Orion on the air – he was obviously searching using infra-red stuff – advise AusSAR in Canberra that they had seen a light, a strobe in the water, and someone was shining a torch at them. Obviously it wasn't just an abandoned liferaft but someone alive and in the water, but he couldn't get a good enough ID on it with his infra-red. He had also dropped a couple of flares in the water near the target, which we judged was abeam of our track into Merimbula, probably about 20 miles to the south. We waited to hear if any other aircraft were around and when it was obvious that there was nothing available we advised the PC-3 we'd come down and have a look. When we got closer to the search area the PC-3 dropped a couple of flares in the water for us, close to the liferaft. Through the murk we started seeing the torch. It was still a few hundred yards away and hard to see, but it was there.'

The crew aboard the Seahawk now had to work out the most effective rescue strategy. They knew the two stranded sailors had been in the water for some time, possibly were injured and most definitely were fatigued. This ruled out dropping the strop into the water and letting them fend for themselves. The only option was to winch Pashley down on what was his first ever night-time sea rescue in conditions that he didn't want to know about. He was also concerned about the threat of a shark attack. He landed with a splash in the water and went straight under before popping up and flipping into the raft – and going straight under again! He hadn't realised there was no bottom in it.

'He was an agile bloke and jumped over the top of the raft – straight into the water,' said Stanley. 'I had to shout to him, "Watch out, mate. We haven't got a floor. Be careful." I told him to take Gibbo first because of his hands, and away they went. All of a sudden I saw the pair of them take off sideways, really hard and fast. I thought the pilot must have wanted to move them that way before he started lifting them. Regardless, I have to say the guy who grabbed Gibbo, and the pilot, did a magnificent job.'

Pashley explained: 'Just as I got the strop over the first man the aircraft had an auto-hover failure and slid away a bit. The wire just went tight and literally tore us sideways and out of the raft. It felt like you'd tied a rope around yourself, attached it to a car, and then the car took off at high speed. You just go. Gibbo went sort of backwards and sideways while I went forward and over the top of him. That's when my knife in the leg of my wetsuit caught on the side of the raft and carved into my knee, so much so that it subsequently needed surgery. At that time though, I could have lost my whole leg and probably not realised it. I also knew then that if either of us had any of the wire wrapped around us at that very moment we would have lost a body part. It's fine wire. It would have ripped a limb off pretty quickly.'

With the chopper now on manual hover Gibson and Pashley were winched out of the water. Gibson was placed on the floor of the machine, covered in a space blanket, given some water and a quick check-over. It was then John Stanley's turn to be rescued, but as Pashley prepared to go down he was advised the plan had changed. The chopper crew felt it would be too dangerous lowering Pashley again and thought that two men on the winch would work better. Pashley drove the winch while another crewman guided the aircraft into position using a thumb control beside the door.

'I was surprised to see that the guy didn't come back down on the cable to get me,' Stanley said. 'They just lowered a ring to me, so I thought they must have assumed I was okay. They landed the ring right beside me and I started putting it on. I got my arms and shoulders through it but while I did that I must have tangled a rope from the liferaft into the ring with me.

'He started lifting and all of a sudden I looked down and said to myself, "The liferaft's coming with me. I must have a rope tangled." I got to about 25 feet and thought, "Oh no, this is going to be dangerous," so I just put my hands in the air and bailed out, straight back into the water. The next thing the guy just landed the ring about two feet away from me, so I climbed back into it. I remembered having watched rescue procedures before; you don't put your hand onto the wire but lock your hands underneath the strop.'

Stanley and Gibson were in remarkably good condition considering their 30-hour ordeal. They told the Navy crew everything they could about what had happened with their three mates during the previous night, all in the desperate hope they might still be found alive. Pashley and fellow Seahawk crewman Lieutenant Aaron 'Wal' Abbott talked to the two incessantly, knowing it was vital to keep them awake and alert to minimise any shock that might set in before they were in the hands of doctors back on shore.

Winning and his three co-survivors from that liferaft had already been choppered into Mallacoota, a tiny town on the south side of the New South Wales–Victorian border, and once there they quickly discovered this was a place of exceptional community spirit. From the moment they were helped from the rescue chopper, still wet and bedraggled, they were made to feel safe and comfortable. A local resident was allocated to each survivor, their role being to comfort and care for them. The Red Cross and local Volunteer Coastguard group were also on hand to help.

'They were just unbelievable,' said Gould. 'The hospitality, the way that community pulled together was just fantastic. They took our names and telephone numbers so they could call our families and reassure them we were okay while we were checked over by a doctor and then taken to the showers. Dry clothes arrived for each of us. Nothing was a problem.'

The joy of speaking with loved ones on the telephone was followed later that evening with the news that the second raft had been found.

'We assumed, obviously optimistic after our rescue, that all five of them would be on board,' said Gould. 'We didn't know how or when they would be picked up or where they would be taken, so we had a beer in celebration. Then, because we could hardly keep our eyes open, we went to bed. The sweetest thing on earth that night – after being jammed into a liferaft with three others for so long – was to be able to stretch out my full six-foot-three-inch body in a bloody big bed.'

Next morning Richard Winning rose early to do a national television interview, still unaware that three of his crew had been lost – until it was mentioned unwittingly by the interviewer. Mike Bannister and John Dean, two of his closest friends since they sailed dinghies as 10-year-olds on Sydney Harbour, were gone. Jim Lawler, a friend in more recent times, was also gone.

Winning bowed his head, then, deeply shocked and choked with emotion, he walked away from the interview.

ABOUT THE AUTHOR

Rob Mundle OAM is a bestselling author, journalist and competitive sailor whose family heritage is with the sea, dating back to his great-great-grandfather, who was a master of square-riggers.

Rob has spent a lifetime combining his passions for sailing and writing. He has written fifteen books – including the international bestseller *Fatal Storm* – reported on more than forty Sydney-to-Hobart yacht races (and competed in three), and covered seven America's Cups, four Olympics and numerous international events. He is the winner of many sailing championships, has been a competitor in local and international contests, and has sailed everything from sailboards and 18-foot skiffs through to supermaxi yachts and offshore multihulls.

Rob was awarded an Order of Australia Medal in the Queen's Birthday Honours List 2013 for services to sailing and journalism. He is the only Australian member of the America's Cup Hall of Fame Selection Committee, an ambassador for the Cure Cancer Australia Foundation, a director of the Australian National Maritime Museum's Maritime Foundation and a past commodore of Southport Yacht Club. His most recent book was *Great South Land*.